ARBUCKLE AND KEATON

Buster Keaton and Roscoe "Fatty" Arbuckle.

ARBUCKLE AND KEATON

Their 14 Film Collaborations

James L. Neibaur

McFarland & Company, Inc., Publishers
Jefferson, North Carolina, and London

ALSO BY JAMES L. NEIBAUR
AND FROM MCFARLAND

The Bob Hope Films (2005)

The RKO Features: A Complete Filmography of the Feature Films Released or Produced by RKO Radio Pictures, 1929–1960 (1994; paperback 2004)

Tough Guy: The American Movie Macho (1989)

Movie Comedians: The Complete Guide (1986)

BY JAMES L. NEIBAUR AND TED OKUDA
AND FROM MCFARLAND

The Jerry Lewis Films: An Analytical Filmography of the Innovative Comic (1995)

LIBRARY OF CONGRESS CATALOGUING-IN-PUBLICATION DATA

Neibaur, James L., 1958–
Arbuckle and Keaton : their 14
film collaborations / James L. Neibaur.
p. cm.
Includes bibliographical references and index.
ISBN-13: 978-0-7864-2831-1
(softcover : 50# alkaline paper) ∞

1. Arbuckle, Roscoe, 1887–1933.
2. Keaton, Buster, 1895–1966.
I. Title.
PN2287.A68N45   2007
791.4302'80922—dc22 [B]   2006033182

British Library cataloguing data are available

©2007 James L. Neibaur. All rights reserved

No part of this book may be reproduced or transmitted in any form or by any means, electronic or mechanical, including photocopying or recording, or by any information storage and retrieval system, without permission in writing from the publisher.

On the cover: Arbuckle and Keaton on the set of *The Bell Boy*, 1918.

Manufactured in the United States of America

McFarland & Company, Inc., Publishers
Box 611, Jefferson, North Carolina 28640
www.mcfarlandpub.com

For
Ted Okuda,

Gail Trottier
and her husband, Bruce,

Kai Kazarian
and his wife, Gay,

and Nishan Akgulian:

Old friends are the best friends.

Acknowledgments

Many fine people kindly offered their valuable assistance during the research and writing of this book:

Rob Farr, David Pearson, Paul E. Gierucki, Bruce Lawton, Tommie Hicks, Jr., Richard Roberts, Eric Grayson, Steve Massa, Ted Okuda, David Sheperd, Gary Crowdus, Dennis Doros, Cole Johnson, Bret Wood, Joan Myers, Andy Edmonds, Simon Louvish, Phil Hall, Brent Walker, Frank Reighter, Adrian Booth Brian (Lorna Gray), Bill Cappello, Jeffrey Vance, Jim Beaver, Paul Dellinger, Richard Corliss, Doug Sulpy, Cineaste, Image Entertainment, Kino on Video, Milestone Film and Video, Blackhawk Films, *Time* Magazine, the Wisconsin Center for Film and Theater Research, the Racine Public Library, and the late Jules White, Edward Bernds, Emil Sitka, Buster Crabbe, and Al "Lash" LaRue.

All quotations are from interviews with the author unless cited otherwise.

All photographs are from the author's collection unless otherwise credited.

Table of Contents

Acknowledgments vii

Introduction 1

1. Roscoe "Fatty" Arbuckle — 9
2. Joseph Francis "Buster" Keaton — 20
3. The Butcher Boy — 24
4. The Rough House — 34
5. His Wedding Night — 46
6. Oh Doctor! — 55
7. Coney Island — 61
8. A Country Hero — 70
9. Out West — 76
10. The Bell Boy — 85
11. Moonshine — 92
12. Good Night Nurse — 102
13. The Cook — 112
14. Roscoe Without Buster — 121

15. *Back Stage*	135
16. *The Hayseed*	143
17. *The Garage*	152
18. Arbuckle Thereafter	158
19. Keaton Thereafter	172
20. Al St. John and Alice Lake	188
Afterword	195
Selected Bibliography	201
Index	205

Introduction

It was 1916 when Roscoe Arbuckle left the Keystone Studios, where in a few years he had risen from bit player to international star with creative control over his films. The moving picture's entire history was less than thirty years old. Narrative film had existed for a little more than a dozen years. Countless important ideas and innovations were causing the motion picture to evolve very rapidly, and the medium was being embraced as at least a potential art form in many circles.

Roscoe Arbuckle is one of the few comedians of this period to reach such a lofty level of artistic success. The ideas he had for presenting his character and creating his films dared to explore new avenues. Arbuckle could sometimes be a bit conservative, not wanting to stray too far from the slapstick that he had helped establish as being the quintessential method of presenting comedy on film. But within that context, he added an important human element to his character and a nuance to his direction that went beyond his aptitude for performing slapstick gags.

Charlie Chaplin, of course, is the master of exploring early cinema's ability to convey ideas through physical humor. But Chaplin's work was embraced early, has survived, and has been carefully studied. Even later scandal never fully diminished the understanding that Chaplin is perhaps the single most important figure in the history of screen comedy. While Arbuckle once enjoyed popularity at or near Chaplin's level, Arbuckle's best work only recently surfaced, and it is only lately that he has been considered among the cinema's truly great comedy pioneers.

Even now, there are many areas of early cinema that remain unexplored. This is understandable. Film is just over 100 years old—a period considered modern when applied to literature. Cinema evolved rapidly and in many directions.

Until recently, one of the many unexplored areas was the Joseph Schenck–produced series of Comique comedies starring Roscoe "Fatty" Arbuckle and featuring his apprentice Joseph Frank "Buster" Keaton.

There have been many fine books on Keaton's life and work, but these texts generally concentrate on his solo films, giving little more than casual mention to his appearances in support of Arbuckle. They are politely acknowledged as his introduction and initial training, but do not receive the same analysis as those films over which Keaton had full control.

The books written about Arbuckle are usually biographies that try to make sense of the scandal that ruined his career, lamenting what might have been. While some authors will claim that Arbuckle's work would not likely have been transcendent, most agree that his comedy is timeless as well as being important to the development of screen comedy. Although their two-reelers feature Arbuckle at the height of his career, past books have given more attention to his Keystone productions for Mack Sennett.

There is a good reason. For decades, only a few of the films Arbuckle made for Schenck existed, the others being among the 90 percent of lost movies from the silent era. The subjects covered had been limited to the films that were available and accessible. These accessible films were not always in the best of condition, were sometimes hampered by distracting scores tacked on by public domain distributors, and were small in number in comparison to the Arbuckle Keystones or the Keaton solo films. As a result, any discussions of the Comique series in which Arbuckle and Keaton appeared together were fleeting accounts.

According to film historian and preservationist Paul E. Gierucki:

> The films of Roscoe Arbuckle are in a horrible state of preservation. They survive primarily by way of the aging paper prints stored at the Library of Congress (originally deposited there for copyright purposes), preservation materials struck from incomplete or deteriorated 35mm nitrate release prints stored in a handful of archives, smaller gauge prints released for home use and, of course, the materials saved by the unsung heroes of film preservation—the private collectors.

Many key Arbuckle films are missing, presumed lost. Those titles which do exist are usually found in the form of battered release prints, heavily edited reissues, or duped out reduction copies which are so far removed from the original material that it is difficult to make out any of the action. There are exceptions to this rule but, sadly, those instances are fewer than one might imagine.

Comedy legends Charlie Chaplin and Harold Lloyd had the foresight (and funds) to preserve their own films and the better portion of their works survive. The films of Buster Keaton were preserved by Raymond Rohauer. While many historians question Rohauer's procurement tactics and editorial practices, he is directly responsible for those films being available today. Roscoe Arbuckle had no such savior. Rohauer did locate and preserve the Arbuckle films in which Buster Keaton appeared, later giving Keaton top billing in the reissue credits, but stopped short of gathering the non–Keaton titles. A tragic oversight.

WH Productions, owned by cowboy star William S. Hart, was reissuing the old Arbuckle-Keystones while Roscoe was busy making new comedies for Paramount. Eventually, because of the ban on Arbuckle films, these reissues ceased too. The films were no longer available, save for a few rogue screenings, and those prints slowly began to decompose and eventually vanished too.

I discovered several different news articles where Arbuckle mentions a film vault in which he allegedly stored pristine prints of all of his films. The location of the vault and the disposition of that cache, however, remain a mystery. Even if the vault were to be found at this late date, assuming that the contents had not been sold off or destroyed many years ago, the original materials contained therein would likely be little more than dust.

The chief problem regarding the survival rate of Arbuckle's post–Keystone movies was that he went from being among the most beloved comedians in films to one of the most hated men in America upon being put on trial for rape and murder in 1921. The scandal forced his films off the screen. Arbuckle's career never really recovered, even though he was acquitted after three trials and issued a formal apology by the jury. After his films were withdrawn, many were allowed to deteriorate. Keystone films have a reasonably good survival rate overall, primarily due to reissues throughout the twenties, and even as novelties strewn with obtrusive music and sound effects in the thirties and forties. As a result, it is by those films

Arbuckle's contribution to cinema has been judged. What little of his post–Sennett work survived is all we could use to assess why he was so tremendously popular from 1917 to 1919. Without the complete Schenck series to examine, film historians could not fully appreciate the extent of Arbuckle's genius.

Fortunately, by the end of the twentieth century, more films from this series were discovered, and restored. At the time of this writing, all but one of the Arbuckle-Keaton Comiques have been rediscovered— there are several with Arbuckle but without Keaton still missing.

These films were initially deemed significant by archivists due to their being the first appearances of Keaton. To see Keaton's earliest screen work, and to be able to assess how he gradually became more familiar with playing to the camera and creating gags that were essentially cinematic is necessary to having a comprehensive understanding of his enormous contribution to the film medium. Keaton is a comedian who truly used the motion picture's technological capabilities to enhance comic ideas that were at one with film.

But the real revelation with the discovery of the Arbuckle-Keaton films is our clearer understanding of Arbuckle's genius. While a fair amount of his creativity was evident with Sennett, his subsequent work for Schenck extends the level of his achievement even further.

Among the films that had long been available from this series, even as far back as 8mm and 16mm home movie collecting, are *Coney Island* and *The Garage*. These short subjects were considered funny movies that were interesting as early examples of Keaton's work, as well as two of the few representative titles of Arbuckle away from Sennett. But when examined within the context of this entire series, each of these subjects possesses a greater significance in the evolution of Arbuckle's comic and cinematic ideas.

It is likely that the Comique films will remain the most important of Arbuckle's career, even if more of his currently elusive post–1920 feature film work is discovered. It is these films where Arbuckle's genius culminates.

The Arbuckle films examined in this text clearly display every facet of his creativity as a comedian and filmmaker. The structure of each film may have offered some consistent similarities, and Arbuckle's penchant for slapstick was certainly a mainstay, but the films also show a greater substance than could be found in any other comedies of the time (with the obvious exception of Chaplin's concurrent productions for Mutual and First National). Arbuckle flirted with parody, delineated a beloved character whose humanity went beyond the limits of mere buffoonery, and offered clever, subtle pantomime with remarkable grace. At the same time he never strayed far from the slapstick of his Keystone roots, believing that it was expected by his audience.

Arbuckle was a big man, and he realized his size would be an imposing factor in each scene. Unlike a lot of larger men, Arbuckle uses his girth without relying on it. He doesn't settle for mechanical gags about fat men getting stuck in doorways. He instead attempts to incorporate his character as another part of the action, realizing the largeness of his very presence will be enough to enhance the gag without calling unsubtle attention to his size.

However, just as we should not overlook the fact that these are Arbuckle's films, our praise of Arbuckle does not mean Keaton's contribution to this series of comedies was negligible. There have been many heated discussions as to just how much Keaton contributed behind the camera. Keaton has stated that whenever Arbuckle was doing a solo turn on screen, it was he who was calling the action behind the camera. There are some clever bits of visual surrealism that are claimed to be definitely Keaton's creation, but Arbuckle had some substantial ideas in this area as well.

It is likely that Arbuckle's vision heavily influenced Keaton, who grew from this experience and evolved into perhaps the greatest comedy filmmaker in motion picture history. Keaton always clearly cited Arbuckle's influence, but the clarity of this testimonial is much sharper with the availability of these comedies showing his apprenticeship under Arbuckle's guidance.

Arbuckle was also wise enough to surround himself with exceptional supporting players. Al St. John, Roscoe's real-life nephew, was brought over from Keystone. And while St. John had some success in solo shorts during the twenties, and later won a new generation of fans as a grizzled western sidekick named Fuzzy St. John, it can be argued that some of his best work can be found in these Arbuckle films. St. John was an acrobatic stunt expert, a trick bicyclist, and one of the most agile, fearless slapstick performers of his time. Walter Kerr, in his book *The Silent Clowns*, said that St. John was "a man of thyroid eyes whose ankles seemed to extend to his shoulder blades."

It should also be noted that Arbuckle was quite magnanimous

with his supporting players. He would give screen time to Keaton, and to St. John, and not even appear in the scene. Few starring comedians would give up this much of the spotlight. It was an action that inspired fierce loyalty, especially on the part of Keaton.

Keaton had been involved in slapstick stage productions with his parents since he was a small child. His ability to take a fall was evident from the beginning, as his parents would toss him about the stage and the child would perform spectacular stunts to shocked audiences. He was introduced to Arbuckle, a movie veteran, just as the Schenck productions were about to get under way. Immediately proving himself capable of comic stunts at the level of a seasoned veteran like St. John, Keaton suddenly found himself a part of Arbuckle's new stock company.

While Arbuckle was certainly a cinematic visionary for what he contributed to the comic film, Keaton's talents emerged in this area as well. Keaton not only studied comedy, but also the filmmaking process, something that Arbuckle knew only rudimentarily. Roscoe was fully capable of staging the action and handling the camera, but his interest was chiefly character, story, and gags. Keaton understood that cinema offered qualities not available on stage and coaxed Arbuckle into trying a few cinematic ideas that went beyond then-standard levels of filmmaking.

Arbuckle was openminded to Keaton's ideas, but limited in his understanding. While he appreciated Buster's clever cinematic touches, he did not think audiences were especially impressed. Arbuckle felt the average audience was more interested in laughs, while Keaton believed the more sophisticated moviegoer who embraced such heady projects as D.W. Griffith's massive *Intolerance* (1916) was to be considered as well. Keaton's technological curiosity was so strong, Arbuckle once said of him, "He lives inside the camera."

Keaton was the apprentice, while Arbuckle was the master. However as we examine the films, they slowly evolve from the slapstick Arbuckle favored to featuring more of the subtlety and quiet cleverness as per Keaton's vision.

This is not to say that the films in this series were worthwhile only when Keaton had greater input. Some of the first films before Keaton's having as big a role are quite impressive. The available films Arbuckle made while Keaton was overseas in the army are among his most interesting (*Love*, made during this period, is one of the finest of all Arbuckle films).

Arbuckle did favor the chaotic, frenetic slapstick of his Sennett roots, and only augmented his rough comedies with more delicate, subtle approaches. Keaton was more artful and cerebral in his presentation, as is evident with his later solo films. But Arbuckle's comedies provided the necessary training ground for Keaton to better understand how to present his own personal vision, especially since Arbuckle indulged his ideas.

The fourteen short comedies in which both Arbuckle and Keaton appear are incredibly important to the history of cinema. Two of the medium's true geniuses are working together—one at the height of his powers, the other at the outset of his career. This book offers an analysis of their collaborative efforts, as well as introductory chapters on each comedian for a greater appreciation of who they were upon joining for these outstanding productions. In examining these films for this text, the writer admits to a frequent ladling on of superlatives. But the significance of these comedies is at such a level.

When Arbuckle graduated to feature pictures, the comedy unit was placed in Buster's capable hands. Keaton went on to produce such brilliant short films as *One Week*, *Cops*, *The Haunted House*, *The Balloonatic*, and *The Playhouse*, as well such classic features as *The General*, *The Navigator*, and *Steamboat Bill, Jr.*

Both Arbuckle and Keaton's careers ended sadly—Arbuckle almost immediately upon moving to features—but all that was undreamed of when these two comic artists collaborated for this impressive and significant series of short films.

1

Roscoe "Fatty" Arbuckle

It is unfortunate that so much attention has been paid to the scandal that ruined Roscoe Arbuckle's career. His significance to screen comedy's development is reasonably well appreciated, like that of Charley Chase or Raymond Griffith, but generally overshadowed by the 1921 death of Virginia Rappe, and rarely placed in its rightful spot alongside Charlie Chaplin, Buster Keaton, and Harold Lloyd.

In a May 10, 2001, article for *Time* magazine, film critic Richard Corliss stated:

> With a face as soft and pat-able as a baby's behind, he used his bulk with grace and reckless assurance. His screen character was baby like too: not so much innocent as pre-moral, and given to pranks performed so dexterously that he never lost the affection of his huge audience—at least, not until the 1921 scandal.

Arbuckle was an amazing performer and had a real understanding as to how he could most effectively present a character in the movies. Too often slapstick comedians are concentrated on simply for their ability to be acrobatic. While that is definitely part of their talent, the better slapstick comedians, such as Arbuckle and Keaton, offered much more.

Along with being adept at performing physical comedy, Arbuckle was able to convey a character that went beyond the most basic externals of bulging eyes and big reactions. There was a definite human element to his character, even early on, and he added greater nuance as he refined his directorial vision and presented more subtle touches of cleverness to his slapstick Keystone comedies.

In assessments of Arbuckle, it is easy to stumble into what is perhaps the greatest cliché in the analyses of slapstick comedy, and that is to state that an overweight performer shows a "ballet-like grace" and to marvel at his or her agility.

Any knowledge of slapstick comedy that attempts to be comprehensive would reveal that virtually every overweight performer who engages in slapstick, from Arbuckle, to Oliver Hardy, to the Ton of Fun trio, to Curly Howard, all the way to Chris Farley, had the necessary agility to perform physical comedy. If a heavier person who does comedy is merely capable of lumbering about slowly with a sweaty effort, he or she does not likely choose slapstick as their forte.

Arbuckle, however, is different. He is more than just "a fat man with ballet-like grace." Arbuckle also offers a gentle dexterity to his movements the same as Oliver Hardy would some ten years later.

There is something else about the overweight comics that seems to be overlooked in most studies of screen comedy. They portray the fat man as an outcast, one who is innocent, well meaning, and endearing, but dismissed for being too large, too overbearing, too crowding, and too different from that which is considered the norm. They also have their particular traits that set them even further from the mainstream.

The consistently popular Jerome Howard of The Three Stooges is a good example. His Curly character's bizarre little quirks, gestures, and noises have become very much a part of his character's enduring popularity, even finding their way into the mainstream of popular culture, long after their creator's passing. Through at least three generations, Curly has become embraced by fans who related to his being the perennial outcast, frequently saying the wrong thing, his reflexive outbursts of frustration, and his shrill expressions of delight.

But what the Curly character also appeared to have was a tangible self-esteem and the ability to persevere. He would frequently stand up to the abusive leader, Moe, always fight back against the heavies in his movies, and exhibited no shyness around women (his cheerful "Hiya, Babe!" was very much a part of his endearing persona). Curly did not hold in his frustrations, he let them out in a most uninhibited manner. He did not contain his happiness or amusement, but exhibited these positive emotions with a similar series of hoots and hollers. Audiences laughed then, and new generations continue to do so, giving his character the ultimate in collective positive attention. Fans have generally embraced him as the most popular of the Stooges.

Roscoe Arbuckle learned, long before Jerome Howard ever stepped onto a movie set, that presenting the fat man as an endearing character would mean more than merely performing knockabout gags with a "ballet-like grace."

Arbuckle never used his size as the mere butt of a gag. He would not submit himself to gags where his character was stuck in a small opening, for instance. But he did realize his being much bigger than his diminutive supporting players added a visual contrast that could work for laughs. When Fatty enters a room, his presence is so large and imposing that it receives immediate attention. Often filmmakers used this situation to present the fat man as bombastic and intrusive. Arbuckle knew that his fat man character could have more substance and win over the audience with more than just rough slapstick. But first he had to acquaint himself with acting for the movies.

Although stage-trained, Arbuckle soon adapted his broad performance to feature the sort of precise nuance that could be appreciated only by the intimate motion picture experience. It made this large man appear very gentle, playful, innocent, and easily loved. Arbuckle, in fact, is second only to Chaplin in his ability to create so beloved a character.

Arbuckle entered films at Mack Sennett's Keystone Studios in 1912, after having spent years on stage as a singer and comedian. Arbuckle was a bit intimidated by the cinematic process, and at a loss as to how one could be funny with pantomime. As with most theater actors, Arbuckle had little respect for the infant cinematic medium. He had marginal interest in the idea of committing his performances to film, but as an actor on the stage, and like most performers from the theater, Roscoe was initially wary of the "flickers."

Sennett's comedy was very broad. He enjoyed poking fun at authority, and his most noted creation was a group of outrageous stunt performers acting as harried policemen, led by popular Sennett comedian Ford Sterling. This dig at law enforcement was borne out in a series of wild knockabout slapstick comedies in which the Keystone Cops offered far-from-helpful aid.

Arbuckle's initial venture with Sennett was as a Keystone Cop.

He was not familiar with the working method for movies. He didn't understand retakes, expressing himself without dialog, or how to take proper direction for film acting. Naturally, no direction is issued during a performance in the theater, only during rehearsals. The movies were different, however. Sennett would direct as the cameras rolled, and film actors would be going about their business while listening to his instructions. The stage-trained Arbuckle kept turning to look at Sennett, thus spoiling the shot, causing extra retakes, taking extra time, and sending the budget-minded Sennett into fits of frustrated anger. These retakes were a financial hindrance to the studio. After one day on the job, Arbuckle was about to be fired.

One of Keystone's most beloved stars was Mabel Normand, whose talent with pantomime and acrobatics allowed her to be every bit as adept at knockabout slapstick as any male on the lot. Small, petite, and irresistibly cute, Normand was as beloved by her Keystone colleagues as she was by the moviegoing public.

Mabel was, and remains, one of the most significant female performers of early cinema, and one of its first comedy directors. Her understanding of screen comedy during cinema's infancy has been given only a modicum of attention, despite the fact that she was at one time known as The Female Chaplin.

In Arbuckle, Mabel saw an unrefined raw talent that simply needed a bit of experience in front of the camera. Mack was skeptical, but Mabel's keen eye insisted that pairing her diminutive frame opposite the enormous Arbuckle would be a fascinating study in contrasts, and great for the visuals of silent cinema. That Arbuckle was also agile and capable of good slapstick made the idea especially attractive. Sennett relented, but never truly warmed up to Arbuckle. For that matter, Arbuckle never warmed up to Sennett.

Like most overweight men, even those who pretend to emotional security, Arbuckle was uncomfortable with his bulk. Sennett would casually refer to him as Fatty, a nickname that found its way into his screen billing. Arbuckle hated the nickname, and would always politely correct fans who addressed him this way by stating, "My name is Roscoe, Roscoe Arbuckle." Mabel would never call him Fatty, but would instead affectionately address him as Big Otto, which was the name of a circus elephant that was used occasionally on the Sennett lot. Mabel's affectionate moniker did not offend Arbuckle.

It didn't take long for Sennett to realize that Mabel's assumption was correct. Not only did Arbuckle adapt to the motion picture very quickly, his films opposite Mabel were instant hits with moviegoers. Theater owners were writing to Sennett, asking for more product featuring "Mabel and Fatty." For his part, Arbuckle soon became more involved, and it was not long before he was directing his own movies.

The first several of these were typically crude Keystone slapstick endeavors, interesting today only as curios. However as Arbuckle and Normand looked deeper into the possibilities of adding more character and substance to their comedies, the films gradually evolved into a more refined presentation of the rough slapstick that Sennett was noted for producing.

By 1916, Arbuckle was the most successful star on the Sennett lot. Chaplin had started there in 1914, quickly became the hottest attraction in films, and left for Essanay Studios a year later in a quest for a larger salary and more creative control.

Sennett thought actors, even his best, were replaceable. Losing a Fred Mace or a Ford Sterling would net a Charlie Chaplin or a Roscoe Arbuckle. Losing Chaplin or Arbuckle would later net Harry Langdon or Ben Turpin. It was a bit shortsighted on Sennett's part, but he did not believe any comedian was bigger than the business.

Arbuckle and Normand costarred in several one and two reel comedies for Sennett, each achieving a greater level of popularity and success than the previous one. One particularly interesting 1915 short was *Fatty and Mabel at the San Diego Exposition* in which the two comedians appeared as a bickering couple doing some sight-seeing at a popular event. The actual event is a backdrop, used effectively by Arbuckle as director.

As Fatty and Mabel ride through the San Diego festival area, they coyly flirt with others milling about. Fatty points to Mabel as he makes faces at the crowd flirting with the women, while admonishing his date. Mabel smiles at male admirers, quickly points to Fatty beside her, and wrinkles her nose and shakes her head, as if to state, "We aren't together." While just a simple bit, it captures the delicate character nuance that Arbuckle liked to present within the context of typical knockabout comedy. And it was this personal touch that separated the great comedians from those that were merely amusing clowns.

Realizing his success, and seeing how Chaplin's emergence beyond the trappings at Keystone resulted in his being the screen's highest paid actor in films, Arbuckle grew restless. Not wanting to lose another top drawer comedy star, Sennett tried to keep Arbuckle happy by giving him as much creative control as the budget-minded producer could allow. This was quite an extension for Sennett, who would often dismiss actors as merely working stiffs who were replaceable. This may be true for those who specialized in stunt work, but someone like Arbuckle, whose talents extended from in front of the camera to behind the scenes, such a loss would be noticeable.

With greater creative control, Arbuckle decided to explore some of his more excessive ideas, realizing that Sennett would have the final say.

Fatty and Mabel Adrift is an exceptionally fine achievement featuring Arbuckle and Normand as newly married lovebirds. Al St. John is the angry rival for Mabel's affections. The film opens with a noted and clever bit where Fatty, Mabel, and Al's faces are framed by hearts. Cupid shoots an arrow connecting Mabel and Fatty, while Al bursts into tears as his heart-frame shatters.

In an effort to get even, Al arranges with some henchmen to set Mabel and Fatty's honeymoon cottage adrift in the waters. When the newlyweds awaken to find themselves floating out to sea, their faithful dog is sent, with a note, to swim for help. While waiting to be rescued, Fatty and Mabel battle the ever rising waters. They are saved just in time by a coast guard version of the Keystone Cops.

While not eschewing the broad slapstick that was Sennett's trademark, Roscoe's direction again allowed for the sort of nuanced performance that added charm to the characters. There is a brief, delightful bit of pantomime by Arbuckle when he first discovers the cottage is at sea. He opens a window, water rushes in, and soon it is knee-deep. Fatty sticks his hands in his pockets, shakes them out, and water splatters away. It is done very naturally and casually, and with such delicacy, that it is one of the most amusing quick shots in the film. That it is done as a throwaway, without calling attention, makes it that much more charming, and it further demonstrates the discernible human element that separates Arbuckle's work from that which limits itself to slapstick buffoonery.

When *Fatty and Mabel Adrift* was compiled in Robert Youngson's 1960 anthology *When Comedy Was King*, Youngson's narrator made note of a bit where Arbuckle's shadow bends over Mabel to kiss her good night, and instead kisses the dog. Arbuckle the director's choice to shoot this by using his shadow on the wall is what makes this bit so successful.

He Did and He Didn't (1916) is another extraordinary Arbuckle short, because he chooses to play against type while examining the on screen Fatty and Mabel relationship. It isn't boyish, innocent Fatty the rascal. Roscoe plays an impatient, disgruntled, angry married man. Mabel plays his wife as the long suffering victim of his harmless bluster. The conflict occurs when an old school beau of Mabel's comes to visit, raising her husband's jealous ire.

The opening scene is immediately telling. Roscoe is attempting to button his collar, which is fitting too tightly around his neck. And while Keystone Fatty the boyish clown would have made this scene amusing and endearing, Roscoe the stressed businessman is instead impatient and cursing. It isn't amusing, it is unnerving, and Mabel effectively uses her beautiful doe eyes to display the long suffering wife character most effectively. This is an unhappy marriage, and the arrival of Mabel's old beau only adds to the tension.

In a 1916 interview for *Caricature*, Arbuckle stated:

> We have tried to get some fine photographic effects here. I have always thought there was room for beautiful scenic achievements in comedy as well as the kick and the custard pie. Film standards change so fast and film styles come in so often that the director whose ideas were heralded as the climax of brilliancy six months ago is old fashioned now. And if he fails to discard his old ideas and keep at least two laps ahead of the procession—you know what is going to happen to him.

One particular photographic effect is during a dinner sequence when Roscoe chooses to use a long shot that fades into a medium shot of himself, Mabel, and her old beau at the table. It is very dark, with lights showing only their faces. A closeup of jealous Roscoe suspiciously staring down the old beau is initially very dramatic until, characteristic of Keystone Fatty, Roscoe quickly sticks out his tongue.

The extent to which Arbuckle challenges his and Mabel's characters in *He Did and He Didn't* can be presented by a chilling dream sequence in which Roscoe attempts to strangle Mabel, and she retaliates by shooting him dead.

He Did and He Didn't is an example of Arbuckle the filmmaker experimenting to the point where he allows Arbuckle the actor to extend beyond his established range, while Mabel effectively plays against type as well. It is one of Roscoe's most fascinating, and most courageous films as well as one of his most brilliant.

Arbuckle soon decided to take advantage of Sennett's New York studio, going there with a crew in early 1916 to shoot films with a different backdrop than had been available in California.

According to Karlton C. Lahue and Terry Brewer in their book *Kops and Custards: The Legend of the Keystone Films* (University of Oklahoma Press, 1968):

> Arbuckle had assumed a great deal of responsibility toward the end of his stay with Keystone. With a natural touch for comedy, he wrote, directed, and starred in many of the Keystones. His judgment was respected by Sennett, and Roscoe was given a freer hand than any other comic on the lot. He was allowed to do whatever he thought best, which usually made scads of money for the firm.
>
> The rotund comedian spent one week just to shoot the kitchen scenes for *Fickle Fatty's Fall* (1915). He used over 10,000 feet of film for that sequence. One scene called for him to flip a pancake over his shoulder and catch it behind his back. He started at 9:00 am and performed the feat on the first rehearsal. Setting the cameras, the confident fat man set out to do it once more and complete the sequence. The cameras rolled all day, but it was not until 4:00 that afternoon that Roscoe was able to do it again correctly while the cameras were turning.

When Mabel Normand was injured in a stunt, her recovery was slow. Arbuckle needed a replacement, and found a Brooklyn-born actress named Alice Lake, who had already appeared in some Vitagraph pictures. Lake was very spirited and outrageous, the very sort of actress Roscoe needed in his company. Becoming especially uninhibited at times, Lake was said to occasionally remove her clothing and dance topless on the set. Her presence was appreciated in that Mabel chose to move on to more prestigious feature pictures upon her recovery.

The Waiter's Ball is one of Arbuckle's funniest films for Sennett, offering some of his best gags, including the rhythmic broom fight between Fatty and Al St. John, who is once again cast as his rival.

The opening sequence shows a busy Arbuckle as a cook in a seedy restaurant. While the sanitary conditions of the kitchen leave much to be desired, Arbuckle takes great care in preparing each dish. With the sure hands of an expert juggler, Arbuckle prepares dishes, tosses silverware about, and keeps a rhythmic pace with his myriad of duties. As he tosses a knife into the air, it lands on the counter behind him, point down. A bowl of soup is prepared and tossed to waiter Al St. John, who catches it without spilling a drop and places it on a table for the customer. It is not the first time Roscoe used food preparation as a backdrop for comic bits, and it would not be the last.

Soon the rivalry between Al and Fatty is established. Al sweeps papers from the floor into the kitchen area. Fatty sweeps them back out. Soon they are engaged in a back-and-forth battle of swatting each other's backside with the brooms. When Al's broom breaks on Fatty's ample posterior, Fatty offers his broom and gets another from the kitchen for himself so that the battle can continue.

The film then moves into the reason for its title. Al wants to take his girl to the ball, but it is semiformal and he has no suit. He steal's Fatty's much larger clothes, forcing Fatty to steal a dress and go masquerading as a woman to catch Al. The result is a wild slapstick battle on the dance floor.

The magazine *Film Flashes* reviewed *The Waiter's Ball* with a full article at the time of its release, even acknowledging the role of the cook as among Arbuckle's favorites.

> Roscoe Arbuckle has a scream in his play, *The Waiter's Ball*. With his usual generosity, he gives his company a chance for a little glory, and the comedy as elucidated by Al St. John, a coming young comedian, Corinne Parquet, Arbuckle's new leading lady, and our own old favorite Kate Price, gets many a laugh over the screen.
>
> The cast in full is a good one. There is Roscoe Arbuckle as the cook, Al St. John as the waiter, Corinne Parquet as the cashier, Joe Bordeaux as her bad brother, Robert Maximillian as the proprietor, Kate Price as the dishwasher, and Alice Lake as the fair customer.

The Waiter's Ball is a great example of what Arbuckle could accomplish with full creative control. Working within the framework of the usual Keystone structure that featured wild gags concluding with a slapstick melee, Arbuckle also offers intimate character nuance and slight-of-hand pantomime along with St. John's thrilling acrobatic stunts. The gags are not simply a haphazard selection of unrelated bits.

While history has not recorded which film was being done when Arbuckle was approached by Paramount representative Lou Anger, who had gotten past the studio guards and found his way to Roscoe's set, it was certainly one of his very last Keystone efforts. Speculation leads us to believe it may have been one of the lost films, such as *The Bright Lights* or *The Other Man*. Lou Anger was interested in what

Arbuckle had to offer, and sought to sign him to a comedy series for producer Joseph Schenck and Famous Players-Lasky, which released through Paramount Pictures. Anger offered the restless Arbuckle the opportunity to leave Sennett and venture to a major studio where Roscoe would be given his very own comedy company, over which he would be in full charge.

Arbuckle was flattered, but loyal. He longed to branch out as Chaplin had, but he had close friends on the Sennett lot, and already enjoyed a certain creative control.

Anger not only offered Arbuckle a higher salary and full creative control, he promised that if Roscoe's short films were successful, he would eventually be starred in feature length pictures. Full creative control would mean that unlike at Keystone, Arbuckle would have final say. While Roscoe enjoyed free rein while creating his films at Keystone, it was still Mack Sennett who had the final word. But the mention of a feature film was especially enticing. That was the level of prestige every movie actor desired. Arbuckle made the decision to leave Sennett and sign with the Joseph Schenck productions at Paramount. He was given his own production company, Comique Film Productions, and was in full charge.

Sennett could not hang onto Arbuckle any more than he could Chaplin or Ford Sterling. Paramount would not only allow Arbuckle full control and supervision over his own comedy company, they could feasibly offer budgets that far exceeded Sennett's. The further promise of eventually starring in features, something Chaplin had not yet accomplished on a regular basis, was also enticing.

Arbuckle's leaving Keystone was reported in the show business press. The October 7, 1916, issue of *Motography* stated in an article headlined "Arbuckle to Leave Keystone":

> Roscoe Arbuckle ... divulged the startling news that after January he will no longer be a Keystone comedian but will begin work with his own producing company. The output of this company will be one two-reel comedy each month. This famous funmaker claims that you cannot make people laugh for five reels so he is going to make them "simply scream" for two.
>
> The name of Mr. Arbuckle's concern will be the Comique Film Corporation and J. M. Schenck of the Loew enterprises will be associated with him. The company may later try producing some dramas but at first will stick close to comedies. Mr. Arbuckle will direct most of the

productions himself. Another of his hobbies is that he wants to develop new people.

Arbuckle said goodbye to his many friends at Keystone, and left for Joseph Schenck's productions. He took both Al St. John and Alice Lake with him. It was where he would make the finest films of his career.

2

Joseph Frank "Buster" Keaton

So much has been said about Buster Keaton's work, it seems there is little left to discuss. This series of early films with Arbuckle, the first in Keaton's career, are perhaps the only movies in his filmography that have received little attention. Even the frequently dismissed two reelers Buster made for Jules White at Columbia Pictures from 1939 to 1941 are given thoroughgoing treatment in Ted Okuda and Ed Watz's *The Columbia Comedy Shorts* (McFarland, 1986).

There is much more to say about Roscoe Arbuckle's career prior to the Comique series, as he had already made several films. These are Keaton's very first. He was only 21 years old and his background was the stage.

Buster Keaton has been lauded as a comic genius for decades, and it is probably the James Agee essay *Comedy's Greatest Era* in *Life* magazine that first reminded audiences of this fine performer.

In his popular 1949 essay, James Agee stated:

> Keaton's face ranked almost with Lincoln's as an early American archetype;it was haunting, handsome, almost beautiful, yet it was irreducibly funny. No other comedian could do as much with the dead pan. He used this great, sad, motionless face to suggest various related things.

Several of the many film historians and analysts who have assessed Keaton's work have referred to a certain beauty, like that of a majestic equine purebred, in his athletic prowess within the context of physical comedy.

Buster Keaton had no formal education. His abilities were purely intuitive. He had a creative mind and a mechanical inclination that accepted challenges and was fascinated by new ideas. The motion picture was a newfangled technology that interested Buster.

When he joined Arbuckle's company, Keaton was no stranger to knockabout comedy, despite never having been near a movie set.

As a very small child, Keaton starred with his parents in an act called The Three Keatons, in which his father would throw him around the stage like a human broom. This is where he learned to take hard falls without getting injured. Child welfare organizations would hound the Keatons, so they would pretend that Buster was actually a midget to throw the welfare representatives off the track.

Only once did Buster get injured. His father had been drinking, his timing was off, and he ended up knocking Buster cold.

Buster had his own ideas about comedy, and longed to try them out. While still appearing with his parents, Buster would rehearse and perfect his own ideas offstage with the intention of incorporating them into the act. He had an instinctive ability to use props in a variety of amusing ways, and, according to his autobiography, learned early on that "the more seriously I took things, the funnier it was." However it should be noted that in films this was not really employed until he began starring in his own series. In the films with Arbuckle, Keaton smiles, laughs, weeps, and offers many other significant facial gestures that he would eschew by 1920.

Buster went out on his own as a solo act in 1917 when he was only 21 years old. He was enjoying some real success when he met Lou Anger, who was connected with Joseph Schenck productions. Anger invited Keaton to the Arbuckle set, where Roscoe was preparing his first Comique production, *The Butcher Boy*. Always interested in talented people, Roscoe took a liking to the young man, and invited him to watch the filming. Buster was fascinated by the process of performing gags for a camera that would shoot a moving picture. After spending his life on stage, to have a tangible photographic account of his work was something Buster found intriguing.

During rehearsals, Arbuckle and Al St. John were going through their paces with various knockabout bits when Roscoe invited Keaton to join the action. He told Buster that he was going to throw a sack of flour in his direction, and that Buster should do a fall upon being hit.

Having an instinct for timing and a long experience with pratfalls, Buster turned around just as the flour sack was about to come in contact, took the hit, lifted his feet high in the air, and did a solid fall.

Arbuckle and St. John, both veterans of slapstick comedy, were quite impressed. Arbuckle hired Keaton to appear in *The Butcher Boy*. Not only was Keaton to repeat the flour sack fall, he was also allowed to incorporate some of his own comedy ideas into the picture.

Keaton was currently appearing in J.J. Shubert's *The Passing Show* on stage, receiving $250 per week, $300 when touring. He took a large cut in pay to join the Arbuckle troupe. In his autobiography, Keaton recalled:

> From the first day on I hadn't a doubt that I was going to love working in the movies. I did not even ask what I'd be paid to work in Arbuckle's slapstick comedies. I didn't much care. I say all of this, but I must admit being quite surprised to find just forty dollars in my pay envelope at the end of my first week as a movie actor. When I asked Lou Anger about it, he said that was all his budget permitted him to pay me. Six weeks later, I was increased to $75 and not long after that to $125 a week.

Keaton told his theatrical agent that he was taking a large cut in pay to work in moving pictures. He was told to learn everything he could about the movie business, as movies were the coming thing. However it was difficult to break the news to his father. Joseph Keaton had offers for his family act to appear in movies, but like most stage performers of the time, Mr. Keaton dismissed the moving picture as a silly novelty.

Buster, however, remained most fascinated by performing for the camera and having it preserved on film, just as Arbuckle originally had been when he left the stage for the movies. Keaton was gadget-oriented as well, and wanted to know more about the technological aspects of filmmaking, something that interested Arbuckle only tangentially. Keaton was intrigued by the camera and the editing process, and how photography and cutting could enhance a gag's impact more so than on the stage.

In a 1958 oral history for Columbia University, Keaton stated:

I had to know how that film got into the cutting room, what you did to it in there, how you projected it, how you finally got the picture together, how you made things match. The technical part of pictures is what interested me. Material was the last thing in the world I thought about. You only had to turn me loose on the set and I'd have material in two minutes, because I'd been doing it all my life.

He got permission to bring home a camera, and literally took it apart and put it together again, carefully examining just how it worked and how each of its separate parts functioned. He also came up with possible ideas for his performance in the film. Unlike many slapstick comedians of the teens, Keaton was a thinking man. He approached each gag intuitively, concentrating on what exactly would work best. It is a trait that Arbuckle shared, adding subtle nuance to boorish knockabout.

Keaton saw the motion picture as a fascinating way to present comedy ideas that could not be done on stage. Along with the physical humor at which he was most adept, Keaton realized the technology of the motion picture presented even more opportunities. He truly wanted to use the film medium as more than merely a way to shoot the movie.

Thus, it was by the time of his first screen appearance, in *The Butcher Boy*, when Buster Keaton already considered himself an actor in the movies.

3

The Butcher Boy

Directed by: Roscoe "Fatty" Arbuckle
Written by: Roscoe "Fatty" Arbuckle, Joseph Anthony Roach
Produced by: Joseph M. Schenck
Cinematography by: Frank D. Williams
Film Editing by: Herbert Warren

Cast

Roscoe "Fatty" Arbuckle
Al St. John
Buster Keaton
Josephine Stevens
Arthur Earle
Agnes Neilson
Joe Bordeaux
Charles Dudley
Alice Lake

Filmed at the Colony Studios in New York, NY.
Released by the Comique Film Corporation on April 23, 1917.
Distributed by Paramount Pictures.
Running Time: Two Reels
Black and White—Silent

The Butcher Boy is usually noted for being Buster Keaton's film debut, but it has the added significance of being Roscoe Arbuckle's first film for his new unit.

3. The Butcher Boy

Over Labor Day weekend in 1916, just after leaving Sennett, Arbuckle had a semi-serious setback that involved pain, illness, even drug addiction (what is it about the Labor Day weekend that caused Roscoe Arbuckle such bad luck?).

After some annoying discomfort, Arbuckle discovered that he had developed a painful carbuncle on his leg. When he sought medical help, the carbuncle was mistreated by an intern, which almost resulted in amputation. The pain was so great, the intern prescribed heroin as a painkiller. Arbuckle became addicted, lost a great deal of weight, and was drifting in and out of coherence. He checked into a sanitarium, but it would be months before he would be well and able to go before the cameras with his initial film at his new studio.

Shortly after his recovery, and once he had gained enough strength, Arbuckle went on a cross-country promotional tour to meet and greet exhibitors. His signing with Paramount continued to be big news. The January 27, 1917, issue of *Motography* stated:

> Arbuckle ranks today uniquely in the field of comic productions and possesses the added faculty of directing the pictures in which he stars. The secret of Arbuckle's great popularity is the fact that he makes his audiences laugh at him as well as with him, never fearing to be made the victim of a joke himself instead of insisting upon always being the one who plays tricks upon others. The fact that Arbuckle directs his own pictures is important because he will set tasks for himself to do that no other director would have the moral courage to ask him to perform.
>
> The Arbuckle comedies will be released to all exhibitors the same as all other short reel subjects handled at the present time by Paramount Pictures Corporation without being influenced by the feature branch of the program.

Arbuckle's good will tour was also covered by the showbiz trade press. He embarked from Los Angeles, and on February 27, 1917, he appeared at the Hotel Sherman in Chicago along with Adolph Zukor, president of the Famous Players-Lasky Corporation and other prominent people. There were roughly 150 people present, many of whom were exhibitors, exchange men, and representatives of the daily and trade press. Zukor made a speech indicating, "The greatest art of all is to make people laugh, and we didn't feel that Paramount could furnish an absolutely complete art to the public until it had acquired the best comedian on the screen."

Arbuckle was well paid for his work at Comique.

Just over a week later, Arbuckle was in Boston, and then New York to greet another host of exhibitors. Along with special presentations at which he appeared, Arbuckle also toured the theaters of Buffalo, New York, appearing for ten minutes at each to sign autographs, meet exhibitors and fans. Arbuckle's full tour ran from February 17 until March 7, 1917, and was referred to in the trades as "one of the biggest publicity stunts ever pulled off in the film industry."

As with any first film at a new studio for an established star, *The Butcher Boy* falls back on a lot of safe, tried-and-true gags and styles that Arbuckle had used successfully with Sennett. Just as Chaplin's first few Essanay productions reworked many ideas he'd tried at Keystone, Arbuckle's first few Comiques followed the same two-parter structure as his films with Sennett.

While any critical consensus can now, in retrospect, appreciate Arbuckle's creative addition of subtle nuance to slapstick comedy, his chief interest was simply to be funny. He understood how his creative vision would be appreciated by those who were just beginning to understand cinema as an art, but remained keenly aware of his audience, realizing many of his biggest fans were children. Now that he was enjoying an even greater level of creative control than he'd had with Sennett, Arbuckle carefully balanced deft performance and outrageous slapstick.

Arbuckle's move to Paramount continued to be heralded in the motion picture trade press as something of an event. *Motion Picture World* stated:

> "Fatty" Arbuckle, the funniest man on the screen ... has entered into a contract with Paramount Pictures Corporation. These pictures will be distributed by Paramount, but not on the Paramount program which includes pictures only by Famous Players Lasky and Morosco companies.... Arbuckle is to form his own unit, Comique....
>
> "One of the most important factors in screen comedy is speed," declared the Rotund One. "By that I do not refer to speed in the slang sense of the word as applied to vulgarity, but the speed of plot and action. Keep things jumping and your audience will be with you at every moment."

The constant references to his girth (fat comedian, Rotund One, huge size, etc.) were cause for some concern. But Arbuckle was a tremendous success and tried to look past such adjectives and appreciate the accolades contained therein. In an interview at the time, Arbuckle stated:

> If I didn't do anything but weigh 320 pounds and wear queer clothes I might get six laughs. In a half-hour picture-play, I've got to get sixty or go out of business. People ask me if I ain't afraid of getting thin. If I knew how to lose 150 pounds I'd show them! I didn't choose to weigh sixteen pounds when I was born. I weighed 180 pounds when I was only twelve years old, but I didn't wake up in the night to tell myself how glad I was. Not on your life! I didn't want to be fat then and I don't want to be now. And if I couldn't be funny without being fat, I'd get another job.

The Butcher Boy initially appears to be a plotless series of gags, but soon finds its way into a story about rival suitors vying for the attentions of the same girl—a very standard Arbuckle plot device. Arbuckle two-reelers were often separated in this fashion, with the first reel very gag oriented, while the second begins to propel the narrative more specifically.

The film opens with a wide-angle shot of a general store as each of the major players is introduced with a title card. Josephine Stevens appears as Amanda, the store owner's daughter with whom Fatty is infatuated, while Al St. John is billed as Slim Snavely, a rival for her affection.

Al St. John had been hired by Arbuckle from Sennett, with the promise that he could assist in the direction of the Arbuckle comedies, and also star in his own series under Arbuckle's supervision. A nephew of Arbuckle, St. John was a trick bicycle rider and amazingly acrobatic athlete whose presence in Arbuckle's films was a real asset. Ironically, Uncle Roscoe was initially against Al being hired by Sennett; Arbuckle's wife, Minta Durfee, intervened.

Josephine Stevens came from a theatrical background. Her father was Benjamin D. Stevens, who had been one of the best known general managers in the theatrical world since the turn of the century.

The first comic bit in *The Butcher Boy* is the familiar gag where Fatty weighs meat while casually resting his arm on the scale, and charging the customer based on the total. This gag was also used by W.C. Fields in *It's a Gift* (Paramount, 1934), but while there is an underlying chicanery to the Fields character, Arbuckle's is presented as wholly innocent. The Fields character simply pretended not to realize he was cheating the customer, but the audience was aware that he knew exactly what he was doing. Fatty, however, is too innocent and boyish to be so underhanded. It is a genuine mistake.

This brief gag is a good example as to how the same bit can be performed from different perspectives and in different contexts.

Within the first moments of *The Butcher Boy*, Arbuckle repeats his agile knife-tossing bits from *The Waiter's Ball*. He fastidiously wraps the meat after cutting it, then casually tosses the knife into the air. It lands, point down, sticking safely to the counter behind him. While it appears quite effortless, Arbuckle was noted for spending as much as an entire day rehearsing business like this so that it would be perfect when filmed.

Enter a customer, played by a debuting Buster Keaton. He has brought in a pail which he would like Fatty to fill with molasses. His payment of loose change, however, is in the bucket, which is filled with gooey molasses before he is able to retrieve the money.

Fatty dumps the sticky matter into Buster's hat, gets the money, and dumps the molasses back in to the bucket. Buster's hat now sticks to his head. He cuts the hat off, but gets his foot stuck in a puddle of molasses on the floor. Fatty tries to help Buster extricate his foot by pouring hot water on his shoe, as Buster writhes wildly.

Fatty flirts with Amanda, angering Slim. Slim starts a brawl. Buster, standing nearby, is smacked hard with a large sack of flour thrown in the battle between Fatty and Slim. Soon he is also involved in the fight, and, within seconds, the store is filled with a thick cloud of flour.

The proprietor realizes his daughter is the reason for this battle, so he arranges for her to be shipped off to boarding school. Slim is angry. Fatty weeps.

In an effort to reunite with Amanda, Fatty hatches a scheme to get into her boarding school by dressing as a female and enrolling as a student. Slim has the same idea, and is helped by Buster and Joe (Joe Bordeaux, another former Sennett player).

It initially appears that Fatty and Slim do not recognize each other as "girls." They are hastily assigned to the same dormitory room, where a conflict between them escalates from sticking out tongues to wrestling around the room. The fight is stopped by a headmistress, who turns Fatty over her knee and spanks him with a hair brush. Again, Fatty cries.

Slim and his henchmen kidnap Amanda. Fatty's dog, Luke, enters through an open window. He alerts Fatty, who tries to thwart the kidnapping. Luke chases Slim, who runs from the dog through various bedrooms filled with screaming pajama-clad boarders.

Buster and Joe end up in the administrator's quarters and are soon joined by Slim. All three are held at gunpoint while Luke guards the door. The police are called and the three of them are arrested.

Fatty and Amanda leave the school and head off to be married, turning and winking to the audience as they leave.

It is clear from the outset of *The Butcher Boy* that Arbuckle is very aware of his audience and of the Fatty character. Development of this character was unnecessary as it had already been established with audiences. And it was the moviegoers who were foremost on Roscoe's mind. In an interview syndicated in the press at the time, he stated:

> I endeavor to cater to the masses as well as the classes, not forgetting the kids. Children like the purely physical comedy—the fall and the knockdown—and the more exaggerated the action, the more they laugh. The average person watchinga comedy on the screen does not

want to be compelled to think—to figure out a piece of business—so that there is always a little hesitancy in dealing with satire and the little subtleties that are enjoyed by the clever people.

The Butcher Boy is a wild slapstick romp with appropriately broad characters played by appropriately broader actors. St. John and Keaton are genuinely acrobatic when performing their overwhelming pratfalls. Arbuckle uses the rudimentary approaches of the camera, with establishing shots at the outset, medium shots to document the action, and closeups to allow for character nuance. The close shot of Fatty causally weighing meat while absent-mindedly resting his arm on the scale is a good example. Another is where Fatty is shown sneaking bites of errant sausage and pepperoni, exhibiting the sort of playful naughtiness that made his character that much more endearing. This is the human element that Arbuckle understood to be a very significant part of an actor's appeal, especially one who performs regularly in a series. Chaplin revolutionized comedy in cinema with his presentation of a universal character. Arbuckle built from his initial appeal as a childlike character and concentrate on subtleties to put across more substance to this persona.

Much has been discussed about the agility of Arbuckle's body, but not enough concentrates on his amazing dexterity. There is a very defined gentleness in his more concentrated movements and gestures. Arbuckle had a background in juggling (as had W.C. Fields) and the dexterity of either performer extended into his character presentation. In Arbuckle's case, the contrast is between a fat man who seems as though he would be rather clumsy and ham fisted, and his actual dexterous movements displaying an unusual gentleness and rhythm.

Al St. John's tall, skinny body contrasts nicely with the larger framed Arbuckle. He is virtually a prop in some scenes, even to the point of being mistaken for a coat rack by Fatty. St. John's extraordinary leaps and flips are far better seen than described. Although said to be rather brittle boned and easily injured, St. John remains a most fearless slapstick tumbler.

It is understood that the fact this is Buster Keaton's entry into the world of cinema is what makes The Butcher Boy most notable today. It is probably the chief reason the late Keaton archivist Raymond Rohauer took the trouble to restore it. Arbuckle's significance is, unfairly perhaps, less noted than it should be, while St. John is usually dismissed as amusing support. Realizing that this film is important as an Arbuckle movie, and that St. John's support was an essential ingredient to its success, does not negate the historical significance of it being our cinematic introduction to Keaton.

For those familiar with Keaton's solo work, it is most interesting to see him performing variations of gags that would be revamped, and further honed, in later films when he was the star. His sticky bit with the molasses also found its way into television appearances some 40 years later.

And while he is merely support in *The Butcher Boy*, Keaton's debut did not go by unnoticed by the press when the film was released in April of 1917. The *New York Daily Mail* stated: "Newcomer Keaton can take a fall and still come up swinging for laughs."

That same article went on to state: "The spectacle of Fatty as a kittenish young thing in his ruffled pinafore and short socks will undoubtedly delight the Arbuckle fan."

The Butcher Boy was a most anticipated release, and was covered extensively in the trades. Most reviews echoed the rave offered by the *New York Daily Mail*.

Motography stated, in a review by George W. Graves:

> Fatty Arbuckle's first Paramount is a winner. It has even more laughs than the most sanguine hopes of the slapstick bug had probably cherished. After the star himself, Al St. John comes in for a round of applause. He doesn't keep any laughs from Fatty, but he makes plenty for himself. Josephine Stevens is a lucky find for the girl, and Buster Keaton makes his first appearance in pictures a praiseworthy one.
>
> Without resorting a moment to the vulgar, *The Butcher Boy* is a continuous round of laughs from start to finish. If the Arbuckle comedies keep up this pace some of the other slapstick makers will have to look to their laurels.

Various syndicated reviews called *The Butcher Boy* "a rollicking two reels of roundhouse and romance" and stated that "Fatty's latest will set audiences to uncontrollable laughter."

Keaton remained fascinated by the film medium. Cinema was still in its infancy, and Keaton had many ideas as to how to use the magic of the moving picture to enhance visual comedy. Arbuckle was quite settled and comfortable with an established method. He understood the power of creating character nuance within the context of wild knockabout comedy. This had been an innovation itself, so he tried to be open-minded to Keaton's maverick filmmaking ideas.

Along with having a creative mind regarding comedy, Keaton

also had a technical capability and interest. He liked machines and the use of objects and props. Arbuckle was very much prop-oriented, often realizing that improvising with an object found on the set could result in a nice piece of comedy. Keaton was more calculated. He already began imagining the big picture where the camera, the editing process, and whatever technical effects were possible could play a part in the presentation. This offered far greater possibilities than the stage, and Keaton's very active mind was exploding with ideas.

It is certainly possible that Keaton made suggestions on *The Butcher Boy*. However he was on the set of his first film, and was likely too new to the process to explore more than a handful of creative options. While green to the power of cinema, Keaton learned fast, and exerted more influence as he became more comfortable. With his first films, his contribution was limited to gags he had perfected on stage. Keaton's understanding of film's technology, and its ability to create a certain magic, allowed him to think beyond gags. He wanted to create sequences that were funny, and purely cinematic. Buster Keaton's ideas would continue to challenge cinema for many years.

The Butcher Boy was initially set up for a print run of 75 units. However its popularity was underestimated, as was Arbuckle's built-in audience craving to see the next wild slapstick effort from their beloved Fatty. More prints were ordered, and *The Butcher Boy* was eventually released to 200 theaters and earned strong box office returns, despite being a short subject set to open for the featured programs. Some newspaper ads contained as big an announcement for this two reeler as for the accompanying feature picture. Arbuckle was billed Roscoe (Fatty) Arbuckle, relegating his dreaded-but-established nickname to a parenthetical addendum.

Silent film historian David Pearson, an expert on the Arbuckle films, stated:

> Roscoe really didn't like the nickname under any context, but being a showbiz professional—and that by 1916 the name "Fatty" was already locked into the public's mind—Roscoe sort of shrugged and went with the flow. Regardless, the Roscoe correction, while low key, was always there. His billing was always as Roscoe (Fatty) Arbuckle or Roscoe Arbuckle, but never as Fatty Arbuckle.

Joseph Schenck collected 25 percent of the film's net receipts, while the others received a smaller percentage. Still, as things progressed, Roscoe stood to make as much as a million dollars during his first year at Paramount.

In an interview at the time with Mary B. Mullett of the *New York Sun*, Arbuckle reflected on his current success:

> Every moving picture star on earth claims to get $10,000 a week. Some of them do, too. But when I was on a salary, I think I was the only star that didn't shout about earning half a million a year. What's the use? If audiences don't like you they'll think you're lying about your salary. And if they do like you it won't be because of what you get but what you do. Now that I'm working for myself I realize that I'll earn what I'm worth; no more. I haven't been my own producer, director, and general boss long enough to know whether I'm going to make a million dollars or ten cents. And if I did know, I wouldn't tell.

The success of *The Butcher Boy* pleased Arbuckle, and Keaton's fascination continued well past the shooting days. On many nights, Buster could be found at the Strand theater, watching himself on the screen, and critically assessing his own performance. He concentrated on how *The Butcher Boy* played as a film, how the different audiences reacted, what they laughed at. Buster continued examining the actor-to-screen process and imagined the seemingly endless possibilities of this process. He then started to concentrate as to how he could do better in the next picture.

4

The Rough House

Directed by Roscoe "Fatty" Arbuckle, Buster Keaton
Written by Roscoe "Fatty" Arbuckle, Buster Keaton, Joseph Anthony Roach
Produced by Joseph M. Schenck
Cinematography by Frank D. Williams
Film Editing by Herbert Warren

Cast

Roscoe "Fatty" Arbuckle
Al St. John
Buster Keaton
Alice Lake
Agnes Neilson
Glen Cavender
Joe Bordeaux
Josephine Stevens

Filmed at the Colony Studios in New York, NY.
Released by the Comique Film Corporation for Paramount Pictures on June 25, 1917.
Distributed by Paramount Pictures.
Running Time: Two Reels
Black and White—Silent

There has been some historical confusion as to whether *The Rough House* is actually Arbuckle's third Comique production, following *Reckless Romeo*, which was released May 21, 1917.

4. The Rough House

A Reckless Romeo, was long thought to be a lost film until a print was discovered in a Norwegian archive in 1999 and subsequently restored. It was initially believed to be an early Comique production in which Keaton was featured in a brief bit, but further study appears to indicate that Keaton is not in *A Reckless Romeo* at all, and that it was filmed as early as 1916. Some filmographies offer *A Reckless Romeo* as a Keystone title and a possible Comique title, wondering if one was a remake of the other, and pondering why the same title was used twice.

It was not. There is only one *A Reckless Romeo*, and it was filmed before Arbuckle entered his Comique series. But it was released by the studio distributing the Comique two reelers.

According to comedy film historian Brent Walker:

> *A Reckless Romeo* was a Keystone comedy produced in Fort Lee, New Jersey, between July and September 1916; later sold outright to Paramount to fill in Arbuckle's release schedule.

While not one of the movies discussed at length in this text, *A Reckless Romeo* is still significant for its cinematic maturity on the part of Arbuckle. As a masher whose exploits are caught by a newsreel camera, Fatty is taken aback when he attends a movie with his wife and mother-in-law some time later and discovers his flirtation is being presented on screen. In a typically delightful bit of pantomime, Fatty indicates himself, and then the screen, as if to say "Hey, that guy looks like me," in an effort to play off this awkward situation.

A Reckless Romeo is really quite similar to an earlier Sennett production, *Fatty's Tintype Tangle*, in which a roving tintype photographer gets a shot of Fatty with another woman, causing confusion to stem from an innocent situation. However in *A Reckless Romeo*, it is not a tintype photo that gets Fatty in hot water, it is the film medium itself. Arbuckle progresses by using cinema against cinema with his old tintype premise. He examines the moving picture as a recorder of time and events, presenting the cinematic process at another level and uses it within the context of his two-reeler. It serves as a method for creating a comic situation within itself. It is quite brilliant.

According to Keystone expert Brent Walker:

> *A Reckless Romeo* is actually a remake of two earlier Keystones—*The Tale of a Black Eye* (1913) with Fred Mace, and a few months later *Fatty*

Arbuckle behind the camera.

at *San Diego* (1913, with Arbuckle). Both films, like *A Reckless Romeo*, featured a story told by the lead character to his wife about the source of a black eye (received while flirting) being exposed as a lie when the wife (Alice Davenport in the former, Phyllis Allen in the latter) goes to a theater and sees a newsreel that captured the real events leading up to the black eye.

A Reckless Romeo was the third Keystone to feature this plot. It was one of Mack Sennett's favorite plot lines—he used it as late as 1932's

Candid Camera. And, of course, Sennett also used variations in other films using a still photo, like *The Star Boarder* and *Fatty's Tintype Tangle*, though not the actual plot.

Sennett always had a firm input and final say on Keystone story lines, which was partly why Arbuckle left Keystone and Sennett after making *A Reckless Romeo* and a subsequent unfinished film.

This was a particularly creative period for Arbuckle, where other interesting films like *Fatty and Mabel Adrift*, *The Waiter's Ball*, and *He Did and He Didn't* offer new, exciting ideas. Several of the films from this period are unfortunately lost, and it would be most fascinating to see what innovations are offered by such elusive Arbuckle Keystones as *The Bright Lights* and *The Other Man*.

The Rough House once again uses Arbuckle's two-part structure where the first half of the film is very gag oriented and the second introduces a discernible narrative. However in this case the first half is screamingly funny, while the second is merely amusing, albeit admittedly interesting. Arbuckle was very adept at making a seamless transition between the two very different reels that employed a complete short, but with *The Rough House*, it is the earlier footage that is decidedly the best.

Now that he was enjoying such absolute freedom as a comedian and filmmaker, Arbuckle would frequently indulge himself. As stated previously, Arbuckle shared Keaton's fascination with objects and props. Often during the filming of an already rehearsed sequence, a prop on the set would inspire Arbuckle to come up with another gag to build atop the one already worked out. As Keaton stated years later, "sometimes things just started to happen." This spirit of improvisation marks the entire film.

In a two-part article for *Film Threat* in June of 2002, movie historian Phil Hall stated:

> The Arbuckle films offer a brisk, surreal and, admittedly sometimes incoherent approach to comedy. Plotlines shift abruptly to support a truckload of gags and routines which, although screamingly funny, nonetheless bear no resemblance to the purpose and point of the film's initial direction and goal.

In a syndicated interview at the time of *The Rough House*, Arbuckle stated:

> I make up my own plays. I don't write them, I make them up as I go along. I have a general idea in my head when we begin, but I don't

have a written scenario or even synopsis. I try out every scene I can think of, working out the business by actually rehearsing it. And all the time I'm rehearsing out there, I'm trying to devise funny little twists that will get a laugh.

This spirit of improvisation works especially well in *The Rough House* as it is a veritable textbook of different types of comedy. And even though it is produced very early during Arbuckle's Comique tenure, it shows how he has evolved from the Sennett method and continues to come into his own as a filmmaker—something he made clearly evident with his last few Keystone productions.

Here Arbuckle experiments more with building gag sequences, while his keen eye for visual presentation within the frame is also more evident. Keaton is, perhaps, the more imaginative cinematic technician, even this early on, but Arbuckle certainly understood that communicating visually was more than merely a series of gags. He realized just how those gags were framed made a distinct difference as to their effectiveness. And the all important human element was certainly used most effectively.

The Rough House is the house where Mr. and Mrs. Rough live. This play on words extends to the fact that there is a great deal of rough activity going on in the household as well. Fatty is Mr. Rough.

For a comedy that eventually explodes into many wild slapstick situations, *The Rough House* begins very slowly and artfully with one of Arbuckle's most inventive and most cleverly performed sequences.

Fatty is carelessly smoking in bed and a fire starts. The blaze is, at first, quite small and manageable, but Fatty reacts in a very relaxed, nonchalant manner. He slowly rises, inspects the fire, and carefully decides just what measure to take in putting it out. Not realizing its potential danger, Fatty casually strolls into the kitchen, fills a small teacup with water, just as casually returns to the bedroom, and splatters the few ineffective drops of water on the growing blaze. He repeats this action two more times before his inquisitive wife and mother-in-law discover the now out-of-control fire and respond accordingly. When the ladies react in horror, something snaps in Fatty and he joins in their histrionics, suddenly appearing to realize the danger of the situation. He hurriedly borrows a neighbor's garden hose, and puts out the fire.

During the portion where Fatty is hosing down the fire, Arbuckle chooses to use this prop in a most outrageous piece of pantomime.

While it is a simple garden hose, Fatty reacts as if it were a fire hose, with a force so strong, it is capable of propelling the big man around the room. This study in contrasts, with a simple, narrow garden hose having such an impact on a large framed man, is another example of how Arbuckle used the visuals of cinema for comic effect. Just as he realized his slapstick battles with skinny, lanky performers like Al St. John and Buster Keaton would offer a humorous visual contrast, he also realized the incongruity of a garden hose being strong enough to overpower a big man would have a solid comic effect. As it is, this bit punctuates the sequence perfectly. Fatty evolves from confused, to unconcerned, to frantic, and finally to helpless. While he does eventually gain control of the hose and aims the water towards the burning bed, the absurdity of this entire sequence culminates in having effectively introduced the tumultuous existence of Mr. Rough.

There has been some discussion as to just when Buster Keaton started offering enough suggestions on the Arbuckle films to establish him as a co-director. While Keaton's influence became clearly more evident a few films later, some historians argue that Keaton was already at this level by this, his second film. Keaton himself has stated that by the time of *The Rough House*, he had become Arbuckle's sole writing staff. While entirely possible, there is greater probability that Keaton's suggestions were still just that. Many feel that the burning bed sequence is so typical of the type of comedy Keaton would do when starring in his own series, it appears obvious that he is at the helm. While one can certainly imagine Buster Keaton performing this scene, it would seem to this writer that Arbuckle himself created and staged this sequence, and it impressed Keaton to the point where its influence can be found in his own films a few years later. Keaton always acknowledged how much he learned from his apprenticeship with Arbuckle. It would seem more likely that during this early stage, Keaton was more interested in what he could do with his own character and in his own scenes than to suggest staging any set pieces that Arbuckle was to perform himself. His further study into the technological mechanics of cinema and how that could be used to enhance the humor and offer more unusual possibilities was likely on his mind as well.

Soon after the burning bed highlight, another very important sequence occurs. It is one that continues to generate heated discussions among film buffs.

Seated at the breakfast table, Fatty coyly flirts with the pretty female servant (Alice Lake). He sticks two forks in two rolls, and walks them along the table in a waddling fashion as an obvious homage to Charlie Chaplin.

Of course this immediately recalls Chaplin's delightful Dance of the Rolls in his classic 1925 feature *The Gold Rush*. Since *The Rough House* had been a lost film for many decades, it was not known that Arbuckle did a variation of this bit first, eight years earlier. This discussion was always a tricky one, because while there was an indication such a scene existed, there was no immediately available footage to verify it (some sources mistakenly thought this bit occurred in *The Cook*, a later Arbuckle Comique film). Now that we have this footage available to us, we can determine that Arbuckle's bit is, at the very most, a portent for what Chaplin would do in *The Gold Rush*. Fatty is merely being coy and flirtatious in this scene, and his playing with the forks and rolls is very brief, more of an aside. Chaplin, however, did an entire little dance with the forks and rolls in *The Gold Rush*. It was a specific scene, not an off-the-cuff extra. But, like Fatty, Charlie was also doing it to impress some ladies.

Did Chaplin see this bit in Arbuckle's film and get the idea? Had Arbuckle seen Chaplin do this on the Keystone lot when both were employed there a few years earlier?

We can only speculate as to who was the originator, but Arbuckle did do it on film first, and Chaplin, of course, did much more with it in 1925.

While *The Rough House* is so titled because Fatty's name is Rough in the movie, it serves as a double meaning regarding the roughhousing that occurs during the first reel. This roughness really gets going once Buster arrives on the scene. As a grocery delivery boy, Buster comes riding up on a bicycle, tangles with a clothesline, and takes a hard backward fall off the bike. Upon entering the house, Buster slips and falls on the wet kitchen floor. This results in a slapstick battle between Buster and Al, who is hired kitchen help. Their battle escalates to the point of involving Alice the servant girl, who gets caught in the middle of the action and sustains an injury to her ankle.

Meanwhile, Fatty is preoccupied in the dining room eating breakfast, oblivious to the melee that is occurring in his kitchen. Fatty sticks a fork in a juicy grapefruit, which splatters him in the eyes. Momentarily blinded, Fatty reaches for something to wipe his eyes.

4. The Rough House

He finds a pastry, wipes away the sting, and messily smears icing over his face.

The battle between Al and Buster continues, moving from the kitchen in to the dining area where Fatty is comfortably seated. Buster is chasing Al with a knife, causing the frightened cook to fly into Fatty, who topples the entire dining room table. From a standing position, Al leaps up and dives behind the piano, hiding from the angry errand boy Buster. Al is spotted by Buster, who throws the knife, but resourceful Al manages to catch it in his mouth without causing any injury (Arbuckle staged this by having St. John hold a knife in his mouth and spit it out. The final few seconds were shown in reverse and edited into the film immediately after Buster throws the knife. For 1917, the effect is impressive).

The chase then continues into the dining area once again. Fatty is seated atop a table as Buster and Al chase around it. The table propels with the chase, spinning Fatty around as Buster chases Al. This makeshift merry-go-round amuses Fatty, who merrily laughs and applauds as he enjoys the ride.

The merry-go-round bit is especially amusing. While it fits neatly within the context of the action, it is still inspired enough as to come out of nowhere. The chase between Buster and Al has become rather angry and gruesome (Buster is wielding a knife, for gosh sakes!), while still maintaining a discernible level of outrageous slapstick amusement. When suddenly the chase goes around a table where Fatty is sitting, propels it in a circular motion, while Fatty reacts as if he were a child enjoying a ride, the outrageousness spills completely into the comic vein. It really is a marvelous little bit, and it shifts the viewer's perspective while blending neatly within the proceedings. One can also be comfortable in assuming that Arbuckle could very well have thought of that bit during filming, realizing the spinning table would work well as a prop.

This craziness finally subsides when Al is ejected from the house, while Buster laughs derisively. However when Buster leaves to return to the store from which he makes his deliveries, Al attacks him and their battle resumes. They are noticed by the nearby police officer on the beat, and are taken down to the station.

Back at home, tranquility is being restored at the home of Mr. and Mrs. Rough. Fatty is consoling the injured servant girl, who had become unfortunately involved in the fracas between Buster and Al, and is now complaining of an injured ankle.

Fatty bends over and rubs the girl's ankle just as his wife and mother-in-law return home The tranquility is suddenly disrupted and another thread of violence begins as the mother-in-law starts choking Fatty. The wife orders the servant girl out of the house, twisted ankle notwithstanding.

Due to the Roughs' lack of kitchen help, Fatty is ordered by his wife and mother-in-law to act as both cook and servant for two distinguished dinner guests set to arrive that evening.

This essentially concludes the knockabout first half of the film. Arbuckle, as director, has effectively used a series of slapstick situations, from artful and subtle to wild and outrageous. Within this framework, he has introduced the characters, established their personalities, and made the viewer aware of the situation. It is now time to introduce the narrative element.

Some critics have complained about Arbuckle's trademark twoparter structure, feeling the change in gears midway through the film is jarring. Actually, one of the more impressive things about this presentation is how well Arbuckle is able to blend these halves into a comfortable unified whole. The first section sets up the situation where the kitchen help are no longer employed, which forces Fatty to act as both cook and servant for the dinner guests. That this setup takes up a full reel and is filled with exciting slapstick makes it perhaps a bit too lively, causing the narrative second reel seem a bit too relaxed by comparison.

Back to Buster and Al, who are allowed to avoid a jail sentence for their disorderly conduct by becoming cops themselves (recruitments are low). This silliness is another way of mocking authority in the Sennett tradition, something Arbuckle also enjoyed doing if perhaps more subtlely than his former employer. Oddly enough, this same premise was used as part of a skit on a professional wrestling program as late as the 1990s. This bit is even referred to in the booklength wrestling exposè *The Death of WCW* (ECW Press, 2004) by authors R.D. Reynolds and Bryan Alvarez, who cite the Arbuckle film while describing the wrestling skit.

Back at the Rough house, Fatty is preparing lunch for his wife and her guests. This gives Arbuckle another opportunity for his always amusing food preparation gags. In one particularly inspired bit, Fatty slices potatoes by pushing them though the blades of an electric fan.

Another standard Arbuckle plot device is then introduced. Supposedly safe strangers turn out to be dangerous ones, as the allegedly distinguished dinner guests sneak into a bedroom and steal jewels. The cop on the beat sees this through an open window and confronts the crooks. Reinforcements are called, so naturally Buster, Al, and Joe Bordeaux are on their way (Bordeaux being a staple in the Arbuckle Comiques as third banana support).

The slapstick bits while Buster, Al, and Joe are hurrying towards the Rough house (on foot) include taking a short cut by rolling down a hill, and climbing a fence on which Buster's belt gets caught. When these reinforcements finally arrive on the scene, they run into the crooks, quite literally, and ultimately capture them.

The Rough House is a very funny movie, and truly impressive in the way Arbuckle the director paces the film so that relaxed scenes blend with frenetic ones, and how he manages to pack so many solid laughs in just two reels. The gentle subtlety of Fatty's initial reaction to the burning bed is delightfully delicate. The battle with the fire house has him flailing wildly. Fatty flirting with Alice by sticking forks in buns and imitating the Chaplin waddle is clever and amusing. The chase, and battle, between Buster and Al explodes on the screen and covers nearly every other player. Fatty's dinner preparation features more clever sleight of hand. The return of Buster and Al as cops, and the apprehension of the crooks, ends the film with more wild slapstick. Through all of this, Arbuckle paces the film along very nicely, never offering a disruption to the comic rhythm, and providing big laughs in both the wilder and gentler sequences. It is all quite exceptional.

There is some unusual experimenting that could be considered indulgent, such as when Buster, Al, and Joe suddenly appear, then disappear, in the police station. Of course this bit is quite primitive, having been in some of the very first experiments with the moving picture process at the turn of the century. Arbuckle seems to be using it simply because he can. Rather than have Buster, Al, and Joe enter the area and leave it, he has them simply appear and disappear. It is interesting, even rather amusing, but ultimately pointless. It does not, however, serve as a detriment to the effectiveness of *The Rough House*.

This is the first notable appearance of Alice Lake in an Arbuckle film (she had a tiny bit as one of the boarding school girls in *The Butcher Boy*). Standing at a petite five feet and one inch, Lake became a mainstay of Arbuckle's troupe, appearing in nearly all of his comedies (she did leave for Metro before Arbuckle switched to features). Having been brought over from Sennett, as were St. John and Bordeaux, Lake had a flair for comedy that was often used to full advantage in the Arbuckle Comique productions. A free spirit off screen, Lake was known to dance topless on the set between takes. There has also been some discussion of her being romantically involved with Arbuckle while Roscoe was still married to Minta Durfee. Alice's nickname was The Laughing Lady.

Overall, *The Rough House* is one of the wildest, funniest, and most impressive of all the Comique comedies. It uses more ideas and styles effectively, and shows continued improvement in its humor and in Arbuckle's direction.

This is interesting in that *The Rough House* comes along so early in the Comique series. Roscoe was still evolving into his greater creative freedom. He was still relying pretty heavily on the Sennett knockabout style, while also continuing to offer greater substance to the Fatty character. It is fascinating to see this style evolve on film. *The Rough House* includes the more relaxed bits like the burning bed routine, and soon explodes into a knockabout free-for-all. Then it settles down to some semblance of a narrative. It is disjointed, but still manages a certain rhythm, and exhibits several styles of comedy within its two reels. *The Rough House* notably features Arbuckle experimenting on screen with his many ideas, which will later influence many, especially co-star Keaton, and be central to the development of motion picture comedy.

Arbuckle stated in a *New York Sun* interview:

> By the time I'm through [making a movie] I have about 15,000 feet of film—and all I need is 2000 feet. I've got to skim the cream off that milk. I go over all the films and pick out the best scenes. Then is the time I write the story. I make the scenario from the scenes I intend to use. When I have it finished I take the reels, find the scenes I want, cut them out, and put them in numbered pigeonholes. I write the titles that connect up these scenes and then everything is in shipshape order for making up the necessary two reels.

Arbuckle also stated that had he been given a written scenario, he wouldn't even know how to film it. He needed the freedom of improvisation.

In a similar interview around the same time for *Photoplay*, co-star Alice Lake weighed in on comedy experimentation.

> I've noticed this about comedies. The gags that seem funniest at the studio will often look dead on the screen, while something which hasn't made you smile on the set will make you shriek with laughter when you see the picture.

As Arbuckle continued to enjoy his creative freedom, he was now at the top of his game. And while he enjoyed exploring different kinds of ideas, Arbuckle still felt most comfortable relying on the wild slapstick that pleased his audience.

Al St. John was enjoying his own freedom to offer creative input. Alice Lake was satisfied with steady employment in one of the most popular comedy series of the era.

And Buster Keaton was preparing ideas for his next turn in front of the moving picture cameras, realizing that the infant medium had endless possibilities, which he was all too eager to explore.

5

His Wedding Night

Directed by Roscoe "Fatty" Arbuckle
Written by Roscoe "Fatty" Arbuckle, Joseph Anthony Roach
Produced by Joseph M. Schenck
Cinematography by George Peters
Film Editing by Herbert Warren

Cast
Roscoe "Fatty" Arbuckle
Al St. John
Buster Keaton
Alice Mann
Arthur Earle
Alice Lake
Jimmy Bryant
Josephine Stevens

Filmed at the Colony Studios in New York, NY.
Released by the Comique Film Corporation for Paramount Pictures on August 20, 1917.
Distributed by Paramount Pictures.
Running Time: Two Reels
Black and White—Silent

To state that *His Wedding Night* is probably one of the weaker two reelers in the Comique series may give the reader the wrong idea. This is not a bad film, except when compared to the other Arbuckle

5. His Wedding Night   47

comedies made during this time. It still features many creative ideas in an effort to satire melodrama. It also features Roscoe Arbuckle at the height of his creative powers. A weaker Arbuckle film was still superior to nearly all of the comedies being made around the same time by other screen comedians. One of the most interesting aspects to *His Wedding Night* is how many amusing ideas can be found even in that which can be considered a lesser Arbuckle Comique two reeler.

His Wedding Night opens with Fatty entering the store where he doubles as a soda jerk and gas pump attendant. Fatty enters the store by hanging his coat on Al St. John, who stands very still like a mannequin. Donning an apron, Fatty takes his place behind the soda fountain.

Roscoe often revisited food preparation bits. Such scenes are the highlights of either of the previous Comique productions, as well the earlier Keystone short *The Waiter's Ball*.

With *His Wedding Night*, Arbuckle as director takes full advantage of the accessible props for preparing ice cream sodas. While much of this could be improvised, especially when Arbuckle introduces offbeat props into the mix, the actual presentation relied on perfect timing as well as the proper visual experience. The camera had to be stationed correctly in order to get the full action in the shot, while Arbuckle had to perform without obscuring the viewer's vision of the piece. Roscoe is said to have spent as much as an hour filming just one brief gag in these situations. And since Roscoe was always interested in presenting a good deal of movement within the frame, there is a definite rhythm to this sequence as there had been with all of Arbuckle's food preparation routines.

At the soda fountain, Fatty tosses scoops of ice cream into the air, and catches them behind his back. He sloppily licks the spoon and sets in back into the drink to stir. He wipes the drips from the glass with a hair brush. All of this is done as if it were a dance, with Fatty bopping about the materials, responding to the customers' requests while deftly maneuvering the props to create sodas. It is all quite delightful.

A pretty customer comes into the store and begins dousing herself with the free sample perfume. She doesn't merely spray it on, she actually pours it all over herself, causing Fatty to put out a $4-per-ounce sign.

An African American woman comes in and asks for some facial

powder. Fatty ponders the various possibilities, and finally offers her a tin of charcoal, causing her to go away satisfied.

In these more enlightened, more sensitive times, such an offensive gag forces the writer to act as an apologist for comedy of a long ago era.

This gag is certainly a prime example of being politically incorrect by today's standards. However we must remember, even if only historically, that humor stemmed from ethnicity quite commonly in early movies, and always preyed on the most notorious stereotypes. African American, Hispanic, Asian, Irish, German, and Italian stereotypes abound in early comedy films. Max Davidson, for instance, was a very popular comedian during the 1920s, playing a character that was a Jewish stereotype. Gino Corrado and Henry Armetta played comical versions of stereotypical Italian Americans throughout the 1930s and 1940s.

A gag such as the charcoal-as-makeup bit will elicit groans from today's audiences, but in 1917 it was just another comic bit that elicited no such reaction. Even in the wake of D.W. Griffith's *The Birth of a Nation* (1915), and the subsequent protests by the NAACP as to how African Americans were depicted, when it came to slapstick comedy, stereotyping was part of the territory. There is a truly offensive racially charged scene in the later Arbuckle two reeler *Out West*, but this gag, while disquieting, seems pretty harmless in its historical and cultural context. It certainly could be considered offensive, and can also act as catalyst for more detailed discussion.

There is an Alice in *His Wedding Night*, but this time it is not Alice Lake. Miss Lake does appear briefly in this film, but she is not the heroine. That honor goes to actress Alice Mann, who appears in the first of a handful of Arbuckle Comique productions. Alice is the pharmacist's daughter who is smitten with Fatty as he is with her. Their flirtations are disarming and cute, and do an excellent job fleshing out Arbuckle's ideas for character nuance. Fatty is presented as very gentle, playful, coy, innocent, and harmless. He delicately places a ring on Alice's finger and daintily kisses her hand. She reacts favorably, and the two are engaged. They share an ice cream soda with two straws.

Later, while Fatty is preoccupied at the gas pump outside the store, Al, his rival, enjoys watermelon with Alice. Here Al does a funny bit with the watermelon, as the rind stretches to either side of his head. He frowns, scratches his ears, and pulls out watermelon seeds.

Meanwhile, a chauffer-driven car pulls up. Fatty, seeing an opportunity, quickly changes the price-per-gallon sign to a higher rate.

Al makes a play for Alice. Surprisingly she is not repulsed by his homely, elastic, freckled mug, and simply shows him Fatty's ring. Al reacts big to this news, and bursts into tears in much the same way when his heart is broken in one of Arbuckle's most noted Sennett productions, *Fatty and Mabel Adrift*.

Al, the bully, attacks Alice. He puts his hands around her neck and chokes her, while she tries to fight back. While such a scene can easily be quite uncomfortable to viewers, it is played here with such over-the-top slapstick style, it appears more outrageously humorous than uncomfortably violent.

Fatty comes to the rescue. He picks Al up over his head and throws him across the store. Al jumps back and clings to Fatty, biting on his ear. With Alice's help, Fatty douses Al with various creams from the soda fountain. The pharmacist kicks Al out of the store.

That problem solved, and along comes Buster, racing on his bike with Alice's wedding dress. He is riding at top speed, and balancing the dress box on his head. When he arrives at the store, he crashes and flies over the bike stand in a spectacular pratfall.

A wonderfully subtle bit follows as Buster enters the store and steps up to Fatty's soda fountain. A twitch in Buster's eye is mistaken by Fatty as a sly wink. So, instead of an ice cream soda, Fatty serves him a beer, much to Buster's delight. While not essentially a gag that figures prominently in the context of the film, this is nevertheless a very clever sequence that shows another side of Arbuckle's creativity.

Buster is soon up in Alice's room. She is excited about seeing her dress, and asks Buster to model it. Not at all put off by this request, Buster not only agrees, he accepts the request with remarkable glee. Initially he begins throwing off his clothing, but Alice asks that he change in another room.

At the same time, Fatty is watching the store, when a stereotypical sissy enters and begins dousing himself with sample perfume. Fatty notices how much the customer is bathing in the perfume, and offers him a small tub and a towel. Fatty then stands back, and sprays the man with seltzer.

Tired of customers taking advantage of the free samples of perfume, Fatty fills the perfume bottle with chloroform. A pretty woman comes in, tries a sample, and is knocked out cold. Fatty playfully steals a kiss from the unconscious woman, and as she begins to awaken, he sprays her with chloroform again so that he may steal another.

This bit is another that some viewers find bothersome, perhaps due to their concentrating too much on what happened in Arbuckle's life a few years later. Within the context of the film, and with an understanding of the Fatty character, it never appears as though there is any truly malicious intent. It is all quite playful, almost childishly innocent, and quite amusing. Not above tossing in ideas on the spot, Fatty also kills a fly by quickly spraying it with chloroform perfume as it lands in his hand.

Upstairs, Buster is now wearing, and modeling, Alice's wedding gown, delightedly camping it up for Alice, who is pleased with how the dress looks. This presents another side of Keaton, who prances and flails about the room in a most demonstrative and amusing fashion.

Meanwhile, nearby, Al and two henchmen are making plans to kidnap Alice and force her into marriage. They steal a horse and buggy, and set out to execute their plan. Noticing, through an upstairs window, Buster parading around in the gown, they run upstairs and hastily throw a sheet over him, believing him to be the prospective bride. Buster's wild attempts to fight back are for naught, and he is brought to the justice of the peace while the buggy owner looks on helplessly from nearby.

The injured buggy owner is shaken, but not completely out of it. He staggers into the store and alerts Fatty and the pharmacist to Alice's plight. They react big, and immediately take off for the justice of the peace in an effort to save her from Al's clutches.

Lacking in good transportation (this is before everyone simply had a car parked out front), Fatty and Alice's father borrow a mule-driven cart to hurriedly reach their destination. However the mule is stubbornly uncooperative. Fatty dangerously stands behind the mule and pushes against it. In reaction, the mule sits on Fatty's head, trapping him until Alice's father helps him out. Finally things are situated, and the two of them are on their way.

Back at the store, Alice comes downstairs, surprising the buggy owner, who explains that Fatty and her father have headed for the justice of the peace to save her. Alice realizes she must reach her father and Fatty before they commit a huge error. She runs outside, finds Buster's delivery bicycle and uses it to hurry towards the others.

Al is at the justice of the peace's quarters, forcing him at gunpoint to perform the marriage ceremony. Al's henchmen hold Buster, who is still covered and thought to be Alice. Fatty comes bursting in and stops the ceremony. He carries Buster, also believing it to be Alice, into another room and requests the justice marry them immediately. Just as the ceremony is about to begin, Alice runs in and reveals Buster to a surprised Fatty. Buster offers an embarrassed laugh, but an angry Fatty picks him up and throws him into the next room for a melee with Al and company. Fatty does marry Alice and all is well.

Despite its being a somewhat weaker effort among the Arbuckle Comique productions, *His Wedding Night* is still briskly paced and very funny. It does a nice job of parodying elements of the standard melodrama, which was already old fashioned and ripe for satire by 1917. Fatty is the hero, Alice the damsel in distress, and Al the villain. Buster Keaton's part is smaller, but he makes his presence quite known as he camps it up madly and appears to enjoy a bit of scenery chewing during his relatively brief time on camera.

The chief problem with *His Wedding Night* is its structure. The pace is uneven and jumpy, first offering a relaxed tempo and then crashing into a set piece of explosive slapstick. The amusing subtlety of Fatty and the woman who has fainted is edged off the screen by Fatty and Al's brief but gigantic slapstick brawl. The nuance of Buster parading in the gown is offset by a slapstick melee that is very big and obtrusive. *His Wedding Night* is funny and creative, but lacks the steadier tempo that even the two-parter efforts like *The Butcher Boy* and *The Rough House* were able to offer.

There is an interesting comparison-contrast in Roscoe casting Fatty in the role of melodramatic hero. Heroes of this period were often boyishly pretty, slender, and acrobatic. Fatty was a big man, heavy set, whose boyish features were more cherubic than pretty. He was indeed acrobatic, but not in the same sense as, say, a Douglas Fairbanks. He was capable of wild pratfalls, showing an outrageous clumsiness via the ability to take a fall as well as any athletic feat that could be found on the screen.

In a May 2001 article for *Film Threat*, movie historian Phil Hall stated:

With his oversized derby and too-tight clothing wrapped around his 265 pound body, Arbuckle is the too-visible central focus, and his coyly mischievous fondness for rude pranks and challenging authority provides an endless stream of confrontations. Arbuckle inevitably charges into the status quo-disrupting situations alike the proverbial bull entering the china shop.

And while there is much of the original Fatty in Arbuckle's performance, it still offers another level in placing the big man in the context of stereotypical silent movie hero.

Al St. John is, once again, the perfect comedy villain. His thin, wispy build, squinty eyes, high brow, defined cheekbones, wicked smile, angry grimace, and generally ugly nature combined to make him a most amusing representation of comic evil. When accosted by Fatty, he sells the gag with his usual wild falls that would have seriously injured a lesser man.

Fatty is presented as especially strong here. When he lifts and tosses St. John, it is not merely tantamount to a familiar pro wrestling maneuver. Fatty lifts St. John high into the air and heaves this tall, grown man across the store. Al responds by jumping back upon Fatty and biting his ear. St John does not merely get up and run at the bigger man; he literally leaps back on him from where he'd been thrown, flying across the store as if defying gravity itself. As with any of St. John's stunt work, it is really quite impressive.

Keaton's campy, crazy performance is amusing, but perhaps more interesting than funny. Coming to this film after familiarity with Buster as The Great Stone Face, one is taken aback by Keaton's blatant reactions. For years, studies on Keaton indicated the upcoming Comique production *Coney Island* as the only time The Great Stone Face ever smiled on screen. With the eventual discovery of more Comique films, we find that Buster smiled quite often before settling into his own niche once he was in full creative control of his own two reel series and Arbuckle moved on to feature pictures in 1920.

His Wedding Night would not be the last film in which Buster went completely against what we consider his most noted persona (with the understanding that this "stone face" persona was not to emerge for a few more years). The following *Oh Doctor* presents him in another offbeat role where he exhibits blatant gestures and a more uninhibited presentation than he would later display.

Another interesting aspect about *His Wedding Night* is the structure of the film. While it can be said that it does not clearly separate

5. His Wedding Night

its two reels as do *The Rough House* or *The Butcher Boy* by opening with a reel of gags and then settling into a narrative, it can also be claimed that no real narrative exists at all. The thread of Fatty and Al as rivals for Alice, leading up to the confusion and eventual conclusion, exists throughout the film. There are gags along the way, some of them unrelated to this specific thread. They are there to use the store background and the available props at the soda fountain. Of course this allows Roscoe access to many props within the context of a food preparation sequence. This is an area where Arbuckle feels most comfortable and noticeably creative. His juggling background is perfect for flipping the scoops of ice cream in the air, and catching them in the glass behind his back. His interest in props that work in contrast to the action is evident in his using a hair brush as a cleaning tool for a messy, overflowing milk shake. Arbuckle enjoyed physical nonsequiturs like this, and his dedication to each gag was passionate.

In a *New York Sun* interview, he stated:

> If work and worry would make me thin, you'd have to hunt for me with a microscope. How long do you think it takes to make a picture that you'll laugh at—maybe—for a half an hour? It takes me a solid month, and it costs $40,000 in cash.

This is Alice Mann's first of three appearances with Roscoe Arbuckle. Little is known about her, chiefly due to the fact that most of her films were not made for major studios and have since been forgotten or lost. In fact, two of the three films in which she appears with Arbuckle—*His Wedding Night* and *Oh Doctor*—were lost films until recently. For the most part, she had been known for her appearance in another Arbuckle Comique, *Coney Island*, which is one of the few that has been rather readily available over the years, including via 16mm and 8mm home movie distributors, as well as VHS and DVD.

Ms. Mann nabbed some good roles in feature pictures after her three film stint with Arbuckle's Comique productions. She had leading roles in such films as *The Water Lily* and *Fruits of Passion* (both Triangle, 1919); *Perjury* (Fox, 1921) opposite William Farnum; and back at Paramount, and Famous Players-Lasky, for *West of the Water Tower* in 1923. Before appearing in the three Comiques, she was support in three of the Otto comedies for Lubin productions in 1916. This series, popular with rural audiences, was written and directed by Edward McKim and starred Davy Don as Otto. While Ms. Mann's brief career included support in comedy shorts and plum roles in feature pictures, she is forgotten today. If she is known at all, it is due to her appearances in the three Roscoe Arbuckle comedies.

An interesting bit of trivia is the claim that Virginia Rappe is one of the women in the chauffeur-driven car to which Fatty attends. Film historian Joan Myers, who has researched the life and career of Rappe, told the author:

> The jaw line and the eyes certainly look like her. Plus the hair—she kept her hair long, parted it in the middle, and put it into a roll sort of affair at the back of her head, sometimes with waves over the ears. *His Wedding Night* was filmed in New York. She had relatives and friends in New York so it's possible she could have been there at the same time it was filmed—however, she also did *Paradise Garden* that same year, which was definitely filmed in Los Angeles. I know she was in Los Angeles from May 1916. But she did a lot of traveling from about 1912 on, so she's very hard to pin down at any one time. It's really hard to say what films she may have been in, other than the few that survive.

Comedy film historian Richard Roberts, however, stated that he used frame blowups of this scene and carefully compared them to several stills of Ms. Rappe. His conclusion is that it is definitely not Virginia Rappe.

Interestingly, the car in this scene belonged to Arbuckle. According to Robert Young, Jr.'s *Roscoe "Fatty" Arbuckle: A Bio-Bibliography* (Greenwood Press, 1994):

> The 1917 Rolls-Royce Silver Ghost touring used in the film was Arbuckle's personal property. It was the bonus he received from producer Joseph M. Schenck when he agreed to having his own producing company under the aegis Paramount. For years it was understood the deal was solely sealed on a handshake. However, a signed contract is on film in the archives of Paramount Pictures. Arbuckle and Schenck, of course, did shake hands when the deal was made in Atlantic City, and when the comedian drew his hand away he found the key to the car in it.

As stated previously, *His Wedding Night* was, for many decades, a lost film. A print was eventually discovered, and subsequently restored by during the latter part of the 20th Century, some 70-odd years after its initial release. Its restoration was possible by using the only surviving elements, found in the Narodni Filmovy Archiv of Prague. It was released in a DVD package from Image Entertainment in 2001.

6

Oh Doctor!

Directed by Roscoe "Fatty" Arbuckle
Written by Roscoe "Fatty" Arbuckle, Jean Havez, Joseph Anthony Roach
Produced by Joseph M. Schenck
Cinematography by George Peters
Film Editing by Herbert Warren

Cast
Roscoe "Fatty" Arbuckle
Al St. John
Buster Keaton
Alice Mann
Alice Lake

Filmed at the Colony Studios in New York, NY.
Released by the Comique Film Corporation for Paramount Pictures on August 20, 1917.
Distributed by Paramount Pictures.
Running Time: Two Reels
Black and White—Silent

It is sometimes stated that Roscoe Arbuckle really exhibited the depth of his acting ability when he began starring in feature films after 1920. While this prestigious move was a major boost to Arbuckle's career, and would likely have evolved had the 1921 scandal never occurred, it was certainly not the first indication of his acting ability.

As early has his first Keystone work, Arbuckle showed real talent as an actor. His "Fatty" character was not simply a bombastic presence who was prone to pratfalls. Fatty had the aforementioned human element, some depth of character, and the subtle nuance that Roscoe gave Fatty which allowed him to be more endearing to audiences than would one who was merely a practitioner of knockabout slapstick gags. Despite his films being dismissed by the more snobbish critics as vulgar slapstick excursions, there is always substance of character lurking from within the knockabout trappings. *He Did and He Didn't* is a Keystone film that has been discussed as allowing Arbuckle to especially extend beyond his established range as an actor and filmmaker.

Oh Doctor! is another long lost Arbuckle short that turned up decades after its initial release. While generally considered another of the weaker Comique efforts, *Oh Doctor!* is nevertheless a fascinating take on drawing room farce from Arbuckle's perspective, with a completely offbeat role for Buster Keaton. Roscoe Arbuckle's acting is interesting in that he casts himself in a rather offbeat role, as he had in *He Did and He Didn't*.

Instead of his usual role as a working class Everyman, Arbuckle this time presents Fatty in the title role. Casting Fatty as a physician with the wealth and success that his usual characters are seeking to achieve, Arbuckle presents a different perspective. This wealthy man has problems as well, only different ones than the struggling, working class Fatty of the other films. Instead of a wife and mother-in-law hoping that he reaches a higher level in society, Fatty has a wife who is materially satisfied and a pampered, obnoxious son who appears to be the bane of his existence. Buster Keaton plays the son with blatant gestures in a role that seemed more suited to Al St. John. Al instead plays the equally offbeat role of a nattily dressed con artist (a portent to the clean cut type he'd play in his much later Tuxedo Comedies for Educational Pictures).

Oh Doctor! opens with Dr. Fatty, his wife, and his son arriving for a family outing at the race track in their car. As Fatty exits the car, he accidentally kicks his pampered son in the face, who pitifully wails to his mother.

Once at their seats, this dysfunctional family prepares to watch preparations for the first race. The son is continues to be obnoxious, pulling and tugging at his father's sleeve. Fatty yells at the son and shoves him down, causing him to wail to his comforting mother again.

6. Oh Doctor!

Al the sharpie and his girl, the vamp, enter in another car. The vamp leaves the car and heads for the race, but the car catches Al's jacket as he exits and drags him several feet though a large puddle.

Meanwhile, the vamp has taken a seat near the doctor's family, and is seated next to his wife. Fatty is smitten with the vamp, but pantomimes he is with his wife by pointing to her, and to the ring on his finger. He wants to trade places and sit next to the vamp, so he sticks a pin in his son, who hollers and cries, causing the alarmed wife to swap seats.

While his wife is preoccupied with calming down the son, Fatty flirts with the vamp. Al shows up to claim his seat, curtailing Fatty's flirting.

A bookie quietly gives Al some race info, which Fatty strains to overhear. Al sneaks off and places a side bet, so a spying Fatty does likewise.

The trusting Fatty bets his entire bankroll. His wife exclaims, via a title card, "If we lose we're ruined," but Fatty is confident.

The race is on, and Fatty's horse comes in a very distant last.

The son laughs, "Pop when that horse went the wrong way that was funny." Fatty socks him and down he goes, bouncing up crying. He laughs again once they get home, so Fatty shoves him over the kitchen table, and he lands comfortably in a chair. Fatty walks over and kicks his shin.

Worn out from the event, and upset about the loss of money, Dr. Fatty retreats to his office.

Meanwhile, Al and the vamp arrive home, upset over also having lost all their money. They discover Fatty's business card, and create a scheme to get him to the house, whereupon Al states, "I'll do the rest."

The vamp phones Fatty and reintroduces herself. "Please come quickly, I swallowed a bottle of shoe polish by mistake." The doctor hurries to her home.

Once at the home of the vamp, Fatty flirtatiously conducts an examination, complete with cocktails. With Fatty out of the house, Al calls on his wife and steals an expensive piece of jewelry. When he leaves, he is pursued by Buster, who follows him home. Realizing the theft, Buster hurries to nearby phone and calls his mother. She goes to the address to retrieve her necklace, not realizing Fatty is there with the vamp. Upon her arrival at the door, Fatty hides. The two women prepare to hit each other with vases, but Al gets in the way and is knocked cold.

Fatty finds an errant police uniform, left behind by a cop who had been keeping time with the servant girl. Fatty puts on the uniform and disguises his face by applying hairs from a brush with molasses to create a mustache. Al awakens, grabs the necklace, and is pursued by Fatty to the roof. The necklace is eventually retrieved after the inevitable free-for-all, and all is well.

Oh Doctor! has some very funny moments, and is one of the most fascinating Arbuckle-Keaton films, despite being one of the weaker efforts. Roscoe, Buster, and Al are all working in offbeat roles. Roscoe plays a blustery society doctor who is in danger of losing the material things that success has brought him thus far. It is perhaps closer to his role in the Keystone production *He Did and He Didn't* than any of his previous Comiques. Al is a smooth, well-dressed, wealthy sharpster who lives in a nice place with an attractive vamp accomplice. Buster is an annoying, wailing, tattling, pampered rich kid. And through each of these offbeat roles, the actors are able to experiment.

Al envelopes his role very nicely. He is not the freakishly ugly rival for the pretty girl's affections. He is a settled, low-key crook with nice clothes and handsome features. This was something of a portent to the character he would play in his own series for Fox (1921–1925) and Educational Pictures (1924–1929). Film historian Tommie Hicks Jr. believes St. John may have starred in more Fox-produced silent comedy shorts than any other comedian.

Buster has a role that seems unsettling to longtime fans of The Great Stone Face, but as an actor he appears to enjoy camping it up in such an uninhibited fashion. It is interesting that the most unusual roles Buster played in the Arbuckle Comiques—in *His Wife's Relations* and *Oh Doctor*—were featured in the most elusive films. Neither of these was readily available until the end of the 20th Century, which is why some biographies indicate *Coney Island* as the only film in which The Great Stone Face smiled.

Roscoe is especially amusing as the doctor. He manages to convey his unhappiness with his marriage and family, but at the same time realizing that rocking the boat at all could cost him the success he enjoys. While he is not the angry, jealous, tension-ridden married man of *He Did and He Didn't*, this is still not the harmlessly boyish Fatty. There is a comic mean streak evident. When the bad wager threatens him financially, he is ready to go to whatever means necessary to get it back. One of the most amusing occurs when he is en route to the vamp's home. Fatty sees a street vendor addressing a crowd about a miracle antibacterial soap. Worried about a possible loss of patients, Fatty steps out of his moving car and lets it run into the crowd, causing several injuries. He then goes about the crowd and hands out his card. He retrieves his auto and is again on his way.

Taking on drawing room farce is an interesting choice for Arbuckle. He is able to flesh out very different characters for himself and his two most noted supporting players. He has room for good slapstick gags. And he can work through the structure of a plot that is more than merely a series of gags with a narrative conclusion.

Roscoe also flirts with a bit of the macabre. In one sequence the doctor is in his office reading the mail. A closeup shows us a letter from the local undertakers asking for a list of any critically ill patients, so that they might prepare for the ultimate outcome. This sort of black humor attracted both Keaton and Arbuckle, and it is said that many such gags they discussed off screen were never filmed.

In playing a character who is wealthy, Roscoe was able to dress Fatty accordingly. This time he is not clad in bib overalls and a tiny hat. He is well dressed as befitting a doctor. Off screen, Arbuckle was particular about his sartorial appearance. Just as he never depended on his girth to be funny by using cheap gags where he is stuck in a door or window, he always presented himself off screen with appropriate attire. He was said to own fifteen pairs of shoes. Arbuckle believed there was nothing so repulsive as an overweight man who was poorly, or sloppily, dressed.

Oh Doctor! is certainly an interesting movie, and does contain some solid laughs, but is not among the better Comique productions. What sets it apart is its attempt to do a few things differently, showing Arbuckle experimenting as a filmmaker. These experiments do not fail. The drawing room situation works well, and the three actors cast in offbeat roles truly rise to the occasion. It is especially interesting to see Buster Keaton play the sort of character that is the antithesis of what he is known for doing.

As with his previous films, *Oh Doctor!* received solid bookings throughout the nation, and was a big hit with audiences. The critic for *Variety*, however, appeared to be a bit disappointed as he noticed the film was a low comedy with "no pies or messing" and wondered if it was perhaps an experiment. But the review, reporting on a screening at Loew's Victoria in New York City, did indicate that "it was thoroughly enjoyed before an audience of nearly 3000 people." And it was the audience that was always most important to Arbuckle. If there was any experimenting in *Oh Doctor!* the favorable reaction it received from theatergoers indicated it was successful.

In an interview, Arbuckle remained thoughtful about his continued success:

> I'm in the manufacturing business, and what I'm making is laughs. If you figure that every laugh I get is worth at least a thousand dollars, you'll understand why I get up every morning at seven o'clock to try and be funny.

7

Coney Island

Directed by Roscoe "Fatty" Arbuckle
Written by Roscoe "Fatty" Arbuckle
Produced by Joseph M. Schenck
Cinematography by George Peters
Film Editing by Herbert Warren

Cast

Roscoe "Fatty" Arbuckle
Agnes Neilson
Al St. John
Buster Keaton
Alice Mann
Joe Bordeaux
Jimmy Bryant

Filmed at the Colony Studios in New York, NY, and Coney Island in Brooklyn, NY.
Released by the Comique Film Corporation for Paramount Pictures on October 29, 1917.
Distributed by Paramount Pictures.
Running Time: Two Reels
Black and White—Silent

With *Coney Island*, Roscoe Arbuckle really hits his stride. Although the previous Comiques offered a fair share of brilliant moments, *Coney Island* set a new standard with more sustained character-driven situations, better gags, and an even greater abundance of clever ideas than can be found in Roscoe's previous efforts. Perhaps location filming allowed for stronger inspiration, or maybe it was simply a natural creative evolution, but *Coney Island* stands out as a particularly funny, wonderfully outrageous two-reeler.

Arbuckle opens the film with an establishing shot of Luna Park at night. When seen in its original blue tint, this is a particularly attractive series of shots, showing the lit up park against the dark background of the night. Impressive now, it certainly must have thrilled audiences in the fall of 1917. Looking beyond this series of establishing shots, it appears that Arbuckle's eye for interesting cinema had evolved quite noticeably from merely placing a lot of well choreographed slapstick action in the center of the frame.

The film's situations all derive from character. First, Buster and his girl (Alice Mann) are seen rubbernecking at the Mardi Gras parade, standing tiptoe and peering over the massive throngs in an effort to see the parading exhibits. Arbuckle crosscuts between footage of an actual parade, and Buster and Alice's attempt to find a place where they can see it. As with his old boss, Mack Sennett, Roscoe realized that real life events could be handily used as a backdrop in the context of a comedy short.

Arbuckle has established that Buster and Alice are a couple out on a date. This is not a marriage, nor does it present the romance of a particularly long-term relationship. This is a very typical date, with the boy trying to show the girl a good time, and the girl trying to have one.

Meanwhile at the nearby beach, a bored Fatty is sitting in the sand with his domineering wife. While she reads a magazine, Fatty mopes with a pail and shovel like a listless child.

This is, quite obviously, a married couple. The wife is stern, unmoving, domineering, and self-centered. She is reading a magazine article and wishes not to be disturbed. The husband is very likely exhibiting a feeling he has quite frequently.

Arbuckle's first shot of himself as Fatty is perfect. Putting him in the center of the frame, Arbuckle shows Fatty toying with a pail and shovel in a most childlike manner, with a dull, angry expression that speaks volumes. After flipping the sand into the air and catching it in the pail a few times, Fatty glances at his wife, who is still satisfied with her reading, and continues to appear bored and dejected, as if he'd rather be anywhere else.

7. Coney Island

Roscoe enjoyed stereotyping the situations of his characters, especially couples. With Fatty and the wife, we do not see any real complexities of the marital experience. We are simply shown the stagnant relationship that has resulted in dull predictability and bored indifference.

An element of dominance is shown early. Fatty gets up to wander around, but his wife pulls him back by the sleeve as one would an errant child. In order to escape this close proximity, Fatty devises a scheme. He tosses his hat and gets up to retrieve it, stating to his wife that the wind blew it off. The ruse fails, as the wife insists he stay put, regardless of his hat. Fatty realizes he must be sneaky. He lies down, rolls over to his hat, and retrieves it without his wife noticing. She continues to peruse her book, while Fatty continues to sit dejectedly.

Seeing a dog (Luke, in his first appearance since *The Butcher Boy*) digging a hole in the sand, Fatty gets an idea. He quickly digs a hole in the sand with both hands and buries himself, effectively hiding from his wife. When she finally looks up and notices him missing, she is not alerted to the huge mound of sand under which he rests quietly, keeping still so as not to be discovered. When she wanders to find him, Fatty rises from the sand and sneaks away.

This first bit with Fatty presents him as an endearing childlike character, which is how much of his audience accepted him. His smooth moonfaced look could resemble that of a big baby, and Arbuckle used this to present the Fatty character as such. Since this childlike effect was embedded in the viewer's consciousness when approaching an Arbuckle comedy, it was not off-putting to see Fatty engage in misbehavior, which he does repeatedly in *Coney Island*. His sneaking away from his wife is similar to a bored, errant child sneaking away from an overbearing parent in order to enjoy the nearby amusements. Arbuckle has Fatty bury himself after seeing a dog burying a bone—childlike mimicry augmented for the desired effect.

This idea itself is clever enough, but Arbuckle punctuates the gag by having Fatty raise a toy periscope out of the mound of sand, making sure the wife has wandered on, before rising up and scurrying off.

In his presentation of the stereotypical married couple, Roscoe shows the male as little more than an overgrown child who needs his id satisfied by immediately accessible amusements, while the wife is a domineering shrew. Although this stereotype is hardly indicative of every married couple, it is a perfect basis from which to garner slapstick comedy, which is Arbuckle's intention.

While searching for her husband, Fatty's wife runs into Al, an old friend. Al is headed toward the amusement area to look for girls. Fatty has gone there, too, but is more interested in having a good time without his wife. And, naturally, it is there where the wife decides to look for him.

Here the setup is perfect. Alice and Buster are together on a date, but not having much fun. Fatty is looking for fun as would a curious and mischievous child. Al is looking for fun too, but more as a wily girl chaser with one thing on his mind. Both Fatty and Al want to satisfy the id, but from decidedly different perspectives. And meanwhile, the wife is looking for Fatty, as if he were a lost child who has wandered off. A comedy of errors has been established with the vast opportunity for gags to be derived from the characters, their loosely related situations, and the amusement park backdrop.

Al notices Buster in line for an amusement ride with pretty Alice. Buster hasn't the money to buy two tickets for the ride, so Al confidently approaches and gets tickets for himself and Alice, who wanders off with a new suitor. The fickle girl leaves a rejected Buster alone. Buster decides to buy one ticket and follow Al and Alice on the Witching Waves ride, where a cart is propelled across a rippling floor that simulates the waves of the sea.

Here Arbuckle has set up the initial conflict. Alice is presented as fickle and will go with whichever man who has the means to provide the most fun and best opportunities. The smitten, undaunted Buster wants Alice, despite her fickleness, and schemes to get her back while keeping a close eye on her and Al. Al is playing yet another in a long line of creeps who move in on other men's women.

It is also here where the viewer can determine how Arbuckle likely realized that an amusement park would serve as a great place for slapstick. The Witching Waves ride is fast paced and provides plenty of opportunities for Al, and a pursuing Buster, to flip and fly in their inimitable acrobatic fashion. From this, the narrative is furthered when the ride proves to be a bit too much for Alice to handle. On a ride that only simulates boating on the water, Alice becomes seasick, and must rest on a nearby park bench. Al leaves her to get ice cream cones for each of them, believing the treat will perhaps settle her upset stomach.

With Buster still separating himself from the ride, and Al off buying ice cream cones, it is the perfect time for Fatty to come wandering by, deepening the conflict. His roving eye spots pretty Alice alone on the park bench with a sour expression on her face. He takes a seat beside the pretty girl and rests his hat upside down in his lap. In a delightful bit of pantomime, Fatty realizes her nauseated condition, and quickly moves his hat away from her.

Al returns with the ice cream cones. Fatty seizes the opportunity. He thanks Al and takes the cones, giving one to Alice and keeping one for himself.

Fatty takes a big bite of the ice cream and is punched in the belly by angry Al. Fatty's reaction to this blow causes him to spit a mouthful of vanilla into Al's face.

This bit of slapstick vulgarity is the sort that often raised the chagrin of various righteous groups who decried such gags as unsuitable for children. Arbuckle, very conscious of his younger viewers, felt adults were the chief problem when kids misbehaved. In a *New York Sun* interview he stated: "I like children themselves. When I don't like them it's their parents I dislike through them. It ain't the kids' fault when they're measly. It's mostly the mothers that make 'em so."

This quote is particularly interesting in that Roscoe is here presenting Fatty as the sort of errant child who is trying to avoid time with a wife that acts like an overbearing mother figure.

Arbuckle would continue to augment his clever subtleties with boorish vulgarity in a neat blend of various comic levels. Each of these remained in character, in context, and were well received by mass audiences who had little use for small fringe groups that attempted to create restrictions.

In perhaps an homage to the old Keystone tradition, a brief ice cream battle between Al and Fatty soon escalates. A jealous Al, his face covered with ice cream, begins arguing with Alice. Fatty wants to get rid of Al, but is not sure he can do so without help, Thinking fast, Fatty hits a nearby cop from behind, and blames it on Al. The cop, seeing Al for what he is—a classic carnival slickster who is no stranger to trouble, hauls the bully away.

With Alice now all to himself, and not bothering to realize the very real probability of his wife looking for him, Fatty decides to go on a wild water ride. He and Alice go flying down a steep slide in a cart and plunge into the water below. Separated from their cart, Alice splashes wildly and cries for help. Fatty is of no use. He is nearby in the water, battling with a giant fish.

It is now Buster who is able to seize an opportunity. He saves Alice, and is once again in the fickle girl's good graces. Buster also tries to help Fatty, but the laws of physics are too great, and he is pulled into the water. As Buster reaches for assistance, an ungrateful Fatty looks away and wanders off with Alice, leaving his rescuer behind.

Fatty and Alice's next venture is to rent bathing suits and go for a swim. No problem for Alice, who leaves to change, but there are no suits that will fit Fatty. Seeing a heavy set woman, he cagily sneaks over and steals her attire. He then carefully makes himself up, with great attention to detail, and poses as a woman to be near Alice.

Since drag goes back as far as Year Zero in comedy, Arbuckle's use of it is the stuff of time honored tradition. Arbuckle the actor appears to enjoy these sequences, truly coming to life as a character as a result of the costuming. In everything from *Miss Fatty's Seaside Lovers* to *The Waiter's Ball* to *The Butcher Boy* where Arbuckle put his Fatty character in drag, the highlight is watching how the actor and comedian uses the material to evolve into a different persona. The mannerisms are not exaggerated, and it is their subtlety that makes each scene so amusing.

What is even more amusing in *Coney Island* is that Arbuckle allows us to watch Fatty groom and primp. He does not merely throw on a costume and wig. He carefully places each item of clothing and accessory, adjusting it to its greatest effect, and gradually becomes the character as he dons each garment. It appears as though Fatty does not simply want to disguise himself as a woman, he wants to look as pretty as he possibly can. The transformation is expertly played, as Arbuckle uses each prop for a different element of the character, and he allows us to watch it evolve.

Arbuckle also refers back to his Keystone roots for a delightful pantomime during the scene where Fatty is changing into the woman's clothes. He coyly looks straight into the camera and indicates with a hand gesture that it is to move up, so as not to reveal too much. The camera moves up until Fatty is presented in the frame only down to his waist. This bit originally appeared in Arbuckle's 1914 Keystone two-reeler *The Knockout* in which Charlie Chaplin had a cameo as the referee of a boxing match. And while it was amusing in the Keystone film, it succeeds better here as Arbuckle has mastered greater subtlety in his pantomime. His face exudes modesty and embarrassment as he delicately moves his hand up, directing the camera thusly. It is not until the camera has reached an acceptable angle that he continues to change clothes.

Buster enters the bathhouse and sees Fatty donning woman's attire. He reacts by laughing, and is physically kicked out of the dressing room by Fatty.

Meanwhile, Al is brought in to the nearby local jail for hitting a cop. He is spotted by Fatty's wife, who happens to also be at the police station to report her husband missing. After noticing Al, she posts his bail, and shows him Fatty's picture in her locket. Al's reaction is big. "That's the guy that stole my girl!" With Al in tow, Fatty's wife hastily leaves the station and heads for the amusement park.

Buster is shown having donned a swimsuit himself, as he prepares to wrest Alice from Fatty. This shot of Buster shows the results of his lifetime of acrobatic stunt work. His arms bulge with well-defined biceps and triceps, and his shoulders and chest are equally ripped. He has the cut physique of someone who'd spent years training in a gym.

Fatty, now fully clad in women's attire, casually strolls into the men's area. Being perceived as a woman, he is sent to the women's area.

As Fatty enters the area where the women are preparing themselves, he looks around at the scantily clad ladies and starts to sweat. This sequence could be misrepresented easily in the hands of a less skillful comedian and director. But Arbuckle realized that Fatty's wholly innocent, boyish demeanor would register as innocent embarrassment rather than lewd or predatorial. He is not comfortable among the women, he realizes he does not belong there, and his tension stems from these innocent feelings.

Fatty takes off his hat to cool off, and inadvertently removes his wig. He realizes what he's done after having been spotted by one woman, but puts it back on too quickly for it to fully register.

Alice enters and recognizes Fatty (you can read her lips saying "Roscoe!"). They leave quickly and head to the beach.

Alice and Fatty are on the beach with Luke. Al and Fatty's wife are nearby and notice Fatty in drag. They do not realize it is him. Al actually starts to flirt with Fatty, who plays it up so as not to get discovered by his wife (who is looking at him carefully and noticing an odd resemblance). Buster happens by and is asked by Fatty's wife who the fat girl is. Buster, who saw Fatty changing, indicates that she is a he, and proves it by lifting the wig from Fatty's head.

Al is shocked as he recognizes his rival, and jumps on Fatty, starting a typically acrobatic slapstick battle on land and in the water. Seizing yet another opportunity, Buster snatches Alice and runs away with her. Fatty's wife calls the local police, who arrive in Keystone Cop fashion (while this may have been a heartfelt homage, Roscoe was hardly above using what had worked for him in the past).

The battle between Fatty and Al features some very funny ideas. At one point Al is shown standing in chest-deep water with his dukes up. Fatty emerges from underwater, and beneath Al. As Fatty rises, Al ends up atop his shoulders. They swim after each other in deeper water, and the fight continues. Al and Fatty are eventually caught by the cops and hauled away. Meanwhile, Buster and Alice sit on nearby wooden posts and laugh.

So Buster and Alice started out on a date and ended that way. During the course of their day we discovered Buster hardly had the financial means to date the young lady, while Alice was not so interested in Buster that such a thing didn't matter. She was willing to go off with whatever man won her over. But despite her fickleness, and perhaps because of his perseverance, they ended up together.

For their part, Fatty and Al resume fighting once locked up in jail. A cop comes in to break it up, as does another. One by one, Fatty and Al knock out each of the cops. But when Fatty and Al escape, Fatty is accosted by his wife. As she scolds, he opens a cell door, shoves her in and slams the door shut. Fatty and Al leave the police station together, vowing to never be troubled by women again. A pretty girl walks by, and Al starts after her. One comes from another direction, and Fatty goes after her, glancing back at the camera with a smile.

Coney Island is a wonderful, consistent, character-driven comedy filled with interrelating situations that come to a most satisfying conclusion. Fatty does not want to be imprisoned by his wife any more than he would like to be behind bars. Al has suffered enough arrests and beatings to have a change of heart also. But the instinct of man cannot be so easily overpowered.

There is an interesting, disturbing story regarding the filming of *Coney Island*, especially when one considers the troubles with which Arbuckle would be fraught in another four years. In his autobiography Keaton recalled that while Arbuckle was resting between sequences on the set, a young girl hired as an extra for the beach sequences entered Roscoe's room and held up two bathing suits in front of her, asking which would look better. She dropped one, revealing herself to be completely naked. Arbuckle immediately got up and left the room. As he went out the door, he ran right into the girl's mother. The girl was fired.

"I had enough sense to get out of there fast," Roscoe told Keaton. "The door knocked her mother down. She was all set to bust in. Daughter would scream. Ma would yell, 'Rape!' And here would come Pa with the shotgun."

In an oral history for Columbia University, Buster Keaton recalled in 1958:

> We used Coney Island for location. I remember making it very well, but it's nothing to write about. We just went down there, went on the concessions at Luna Park, and got in trouble—that's all there was to that.

The bit during the carnival sequence that was, for years, pointed out as Buster's only on-camera smile was the test of strength, where Fatty attempts to use a hammer to cause the pulley to rise up and hit the bell at the top. When Fatty does a pratfall, Buster laughs derisively. It is not the only time he smiles in films. It is not even the only time he smiles in *Coney Island* as he also laughs when he recognizes the fat woman in drag is his rival Fatty.

As production ended on *Coney Island* in mid–October of 1917, Roscoe decided he wanted to return to California and make his films there. He was allowed by Joseph Schenck to move his Comique company to Los Angeles to work in the enormous glassed-in stage in Balboa. Arbuckle moved into a home in nearby Long Beach and settled on the West Coast.

8

A Country Hero

Directed by Roscoe "Fatty" Arbuckle
Written by Roscoe "Fatty" Arbuckle
Produced by Joseph M. Schenck
Cinematography by George Peters
Film Editing by Herbert Warren

Cast

Roscoe "Fatty" Arbuckle
Buster Keaton
Alice Lake
Joe Keaton
Al St. John

Filmed at the Balboa Amusement Producing Company studio in Long Beach, California
Released by the Comique Film Corporation for Paramount Pictures on December 13, 1917.
Distributed by Paramount Pictures.
Running Time: Two Reels

Arbuckle left the East Coast and went to California to make films upon the completion of *Coney Island*. The first of his films to be shot on the West Coast was *A Country Hero*.

At the time of this writing, this is the only film in which Roscoe Arbuckle and Buster Keaton appear together that remains lost.

8. A Country Hero

The synopsis for A *Country Hero*, from the December 1917 *Motion Picture World*, is as follows:

> Fatty plays a village blacksmith in "Jazzville," an imaginary rural village. Rival between Fatty and Cy Klone, the garage owner, over the affections of a pretty schoolteacher. A city chap unites the two rivals when he tries to steal the girl. At annual village ball, amateur talent in vaudeville stunts: Keaton as a wriggling Fatima who charms a long black stocking from a cigar box like a snake.

The advance press information on A *Country Hero*, distributed by the studio, gave the following information:

> In this comedy [Arbuckle] assumes several brand new roles, including being a blacksmith, a chauffeur, and a farmer by turns. Needless to say, he has captured all existing medals for he leaves no stunt undone, and no laugh unlaughed. In the first place there is Fatty's encounter with a refractory automobile which exhibits all the obstinate tendencies of a balky mule as specified by the scenario. It runs up to Fatty's garage, known as the Spark Plug Garage, and defies all efforts of the entire cast to movie it one small inch further.
>
> Fatty, Buster Keaton, and Al St. John exert their combined and separable strength without avail. Finally, for some unexplained reason of its own, the machine starts with an explosion that could be heard from Long Beach to Los Angeles and the studio physician was busy for half an hour binding up the wounded. When the machine is at last repaired, Fatty is seen on the screen in an automobile race. He is in pursuit of the city chap who carries off the little schoolmistress. This portion of the film promises to be the most exciting in the picture.

The studio publicity also stated that the setting, Jazzville, was an exact reproduction of the little village of Smith Center, Kansas, where Roscoe was born.

Arbuckle told the syndicated press at the time, "I am confident that A *Country Hero* will make the film fan hold his sides with laughter. The rural atmosphere is one that never fails to have its humorous appeal and I feel that this picture will be no different."

Since A *Country Hero* is among the large percentage of lost films from the silent era, we can only assess it based on first hand accounts such as the *Motion Picture World* synopsis and the studio publicity. While there are many fine institutions that concern themselves with the preservation of filmed images, no print of A *Country Hero* has turned up at the time of this writing.

The idea of film preservation is hardly new. There were cries from forward thinking people and organizations during the motion picture's early days.

In Anthony Slide's book *Nitrate Won't Wait* (McFarland, 1992), he quotes a prophetic article from the first movie industry trade paper *Views and Film Index* (later retitled *The Film Index*) that was first published December 1, 1906:

> We often wonder where all the films that are made and used a few times go to, and the questions come up in our minds, again and again: Are the manufacturers aware that they are making history? Do they realize that in fifty or one hundred years the films now being made will be curiosities? In looking through the maker's catalogues, we observe specially important subjects of great public interest, such as President [Theodore] Roosevelt at gatherings, Veterans processions, Scenes in busy streets, Political meetings, Prominent senators, and a host of other subjects too numerous to mention, all of which are of value to the present generation; but how much more so will they be to the men and women of the future?
>
> We are making such rapid strides nowadays, the march of improvement is so great that we hardly keep in touch with what a few short years ago we though wonderful. A large section of a city is torn down, another built in a few weeks' time, and the former state forgotten except to the film or photograph. Perhaps the day will come when motion pictures will be treasured by governments in their museums as vital documents in their historic archives. Our great universities should commence to gather in and save for future students films of national importance.

Slide himself further stated in his text:

> Despite the urging of the trade press, film producers in the teens and twenties paid scant attention to the need to safeguard their films for either archival study or future commercial release. With an average of 6000 feature films produced in each decade, there was little, if any, need to resurrect an old film for reissue.

Audiences wanted to see the latest releases.

Of course we are fortunate to have such important silent screen milestones as *The Great Train Robbery*, *The Birth of a Nation*, and *The Gold Rush*. But a film like *A Country Hero* is terribly significant as being a part of Arbuckle's best work and Keaton's first, as with all of the films in the Comique series in which these two exceptional comedians appeared. While great strides have been made regarding film preservation, the lack of enthusiasm over older films has not changed among mainstream moviegoers. Often movies only a year old are dismissed as archaic. The moviegoing public often fails to realize that film does not age like bread—it ages like wine.

The vast amount of film, television, and radio broadcasts that have strong historical interest, but have been lost, is staggering. Collectors of television animation have indicated that may television cartoon shows are no longer available. One of these is a series called *The Beagles*, which enjoyed a season on Saturday mornings just as The Beatles were at the height of their popularity. The Beagles were two dogs who played rock music, and otherwise engaged in Abbott and Costello routines. Gags lifted directly from such Abbott and Costello features as *Abbott and Costello in the Foreign Legion* and *In Society* were interspersed with original songs that attempted a Beatlesque rhythm and vocal harmony. Sadly, all original episodes of this animated curio were reportedly taped over and no copies are known to exist.

Most of the films discussed in this very text were lost until the end of the twentieth century. Their discovery and eventual availability on videotape and disc made some of the most important silent comedies of either Arbuckle or Keaton's career accessible. Film historian and archivist Paul E. Gierucki has indicated that the Arbuckle filmography remains in some disarray, despite more recent efforts to uncover and restore his work.

A Country Hero could very well be discovered after this book's publication, but an assessment at the time of its writing is impossible, save for the following anecdotes that have been offered in other studies of Keaton or Arbuckle's films

Joseph Keaton, Buster's father, had always been against his son's involvement in motion pictures. Like many stage performers, Joe Keaton looked down upon the movies as lowbrow entertainment. The fact that his son chose a large pay cut to work in this infantile medium was well beyond the elder Keaton's comprehension.

Buster's success in the Comique productions did a little to change Joe's mind, so Buster was able to talk him into taking a role in *A Country Doctor*. While he appeared with Buster in subsequent films that are available, it is unfortunate that this film's status does not allow us to see Mr. Keaton in his motion picture debut.

According to Stuart Oderman's *Roscoe "Fatty" Arbuckle: A Biography of the Silent Film Comedian (1887-1933)* (McFarland, 1994):

> When Joe reported to the Keaton-Arbuckle set of *A Country Hero*, a tactful Roscoe quickly pointed out that Joe's famous "high kick" could be incorporated into the plot. Alice Lake, eager to support Roscoe and Buster, invited a reluctant Joe to play her father, adding that he could lift his shoe and kick her, if he wanted to. From that moment, Joe Keaton's attitude changed—not from distrust to acceptance of the motion picture, but to appreciation of Buster's talent and Buster's ability to direct his sequences. It was Roscoe, once again, being generous to an appreciative Buster.

In the same biography, Oderman also discussed the Comique films and their interest in pure comedy:

> Roscoe's job, at this time, as outlined by Lou Anger and Joseph Schenck, was very simple: to turn out a two reeler with a good story line and plenty of laughs every seven or eight weeks. Once Roscoe and Buster agreed upon a theme, a few sentences were submitted to writers Joe Roach, Jean Havez, and Herbert Warren for direction and embellishments. If what was being filmed proved to be less than satisfactory, based on a viewing of the daily rushes, it was never too late to make changes before the conclusion of the second reel. Something could be salvaged.

Arbuckle himself stated in a syndicated interview at the time:

> I think I've picked out the worst job in sight. If you don't believe me, try to be funny for thirty solid minutes yourself. After that you'll want to be a villain or a vampire just by way of a little relaxation.

The film's publicity also indicated that supporting player Alice Lake had been "for a long time a dancer of note. Consequently, at the opening of a new ball room at which a dancing cup was offered for the best dancing couple, Arbuckle promptly entered her in the contest, and she and her dancing partner came off victorious."

The write-up went on to state Arbuckle himself was a good dancer, but did not enter the contest himself.

Lou Anger, upon hearing that Alice Lake had won the dancing cup, indicated that she could take the first hour off from the studio the following day, allowing her to come to the set at 9 A.M. instead of the customary 8 A.M.

It was also announced in the press around this time that Arbuckle was exempt from being drafted into the army, due to his being overweight.

9

Out West

Directed by Roscoe "Fatty" Arbuckle
Written by Roscoe "Fatty" Arbuckle
Story by Natalie Talmadge
Produced by Joseph M. Schenck
Cinematography by George Peters
Film Editing by Herbert Warren

Cast

Roscoe "Fatty" Arbuckle
Buster Keaton
Alice Lake
Al St. John
Joe Keaton
Ernie Morrison, Sr.

Filmed at the Balboa Amusement Producing Company studio in Long Beach, California
Released by the Comique Film Corporation for Paramount Pictures on January 20, 1918
Distributed by Paramount Pictures.
Running Time: Two Reels

The western is central to the development of cinema. The film that is most often referred to as the first narrative motion picture is Edwin S. Porter's *The Great Train Robbery* (1903), which itself was a western.

9. Out West

Hollywood was out west. Films shot in Hollywood took advantage of the scenery that lent itself to western stories and themes. Some of the biggest stars of the silent era specialized in westerns, including Broncho Billy Anderson (who had a role in *The Great Train Robbery* and starred in the first successful series of western films), Fred Thomson, Tom Mix, and William S. Hart.

Throughout movie history, comedians have found western conventions worthy of satire. Laurel and Hardy, The Three Stooges, Abbott and Costello, W.C. Fields, The Marx Brothers, Joe E. Brown, Buster Keaton, Will Rogers, Bob Hope, Jerry Lewis, and Mel Brooks have all successfully poked fun at western movie clichés.

Arbuckle enjoyed satirizing conventional behaviors, and was an intelligent enough filmmaker to notice that such movie staples as old fashioned melodrama and romance were good fodder for slapstick parody. But what is most interesting about *Out West* is that as early as the teens, western conventions were already ripe for parody. Some of these same conventions appeared in serious western production well into the talking picture era, and were satirized by latter day comedians, but as early as 1918, Arbuckle already noticed the humor inherent in the standard western movie clichés. However, while many period reviewers pointed out its apparent attempt to satire the films of William S. Hart, it appears that *Out West* pokes fun at the western film in general and does not, for instance, parody specific scenes from specific movies (as Arbuckle would do in a later film, sans Keaton, entitled *The Sheriff*, which makes specific sport of action star Douglas Fairbanks. Unfortunately, this is yet another lost film).

Out West opens with Fatty as a drifter, stowing away on a westbound train. Peering out onto the top of the train, he spies some of the foremen eating in one of the train cars. He removes his tie and "fishes" for food from their table as the men are preoccupied reading the newspaper. Fatty gets a meal, but the foremen notice and chase Fatty along the top of the train, with the California desert in the background.

Realizing he has no hope, Fatty jumps from the train, deftly rolls a cigarette with one hand, and hops back onto the train's last car. He detaches the car from the rest of the train, allows it to slow to a stop, and enters the car to enjoy the remainder of the foremen's meal. But the conductor backs the train up onto the car, causing Fatty to take a wild pratfall and be thrown from the reattached train car.

Finding an out-of-the-way western town, Fatty enters the bar of Bull Bullhorn (Buster Keaton) whose "firewater cures all known ills." The first shot of Keaton as Bull shows him pouring a shot glass of said firewater, and dousing his eye. Bull notices a man cheating at cards, and casually shoots him dead, saying to his opponent, "You would have lost anyway." The dead man is tossed down a trap door that appears on a saloon floor.

Fatty is dry from walking through the California desert. He had been chasing mirages (shown via some rather impressive special effects), and was himself chased by Indians who refer to him as "big fat paleface" and shoot arrows at him stating, "Catch him! Plenty of food for winter!"

In rides a bandit named Wild Bill Hiccup (Al St. John) and his group of desperadoes, holding up the saloon for its money. The bartender tries to be brave, but is shot dead by Hiccup. Fatty, running from the Indians, comes charging into the saloon, knocking Hiccup down and subduing him and his gang with a series of wild, errant shots from two six shooters that appear to never empty. He goes outside and also shoots down the faraway Indians who had been chasing him.

Back in the bar, Fatty asks for, and gets, the open bartender job. On his first day, he joins some cowboys in shooting at a black man in a toying fashion. The man tries to escape through the trap door, sees the dead body in the cellar, and jumps back up into the saloon. He is made to dance by the bullets flying at his feet, and is rescued by a Salvation Army worker (Alice Lake) who happens into the establishment. She pats the black man's head while he kneels and sobs.

An angry Hiccup returns, embarrassed at having been run out of the bar by Fatty, and immediately tries to get a kiss out of Alice. Bullhorn tries to stop him and is tossed aside, almost swallowing his cigar. Bullhorn holds a gun on Hiccup, who breaks the gun and punches Bullhorn. Fatty tries to intervene by hitting Hiccup in the head with bottles, but they have no effect. He shoots him at point blank range, and it simply makes Hiccup mad. Finally he takes a feather from a feather duster and starts tickling the bandit. That works. Hiccup falls to the floor laughing helplessly as Fatty and Bullhorn continue to subdue him with tickling. Hiccup is forced to leave the bar, vowing, "They'll pay for this!"

Exacting his revenge, Wild Bill lassos and kidnaps Alice. Fatty attempts to chase him, but is held off by Bill's henchmen. At his hideout, Wild Bill tries to have his way with Alice, while Fatty heads out to rescue her. Meanwhile, Bullhorn engages the henchmen in a wild slapstick gunfight to keep them at bay.

Fatty enters the hideout through a window and immediately starts ticking Wild Bill so Alice can escape (including tickling his feet through his cowboy boots), while Bill giggles helplessly. Bullhorn's fancy shooting has subdued Bill's gang, Alice is rescued, and Wild Bill's hideout is pushed over a cliff, crashing into pieces.

As can be determined by the written assessment of the structure, *Out West* follows the pattern of a typical western film, using comedy to satirize the most noted clichés. The result is a very uneven two reeler that is at once hilarious and then, suddenly, a bit repetitious and, ultimately, less amusing.

It is perhaps necessary to first address the shameful taunting of the black patron; a bit of negative stereotyping that is very unsettling. It has already been noted in our discussion of *His Wedding Night* and the sequence where a black woman is shown purchasing a tin of charcoal as makeup powder, ethnic stereotyping was a staple in comedy of this era. But this is not the harmless-yet-dated stereotyping we generally see in old comedies. This scene presents a real cruelty that is unsettling to any viewer, and merits some attention.

While it is true that much of what is called offensive racial stereotyping in early movies is blown a bit out of proportion, the very real occurrences are fewer in number, and will stand out quite blatantly. This particular scene where the boys shoot at the black man in a wicked, toying fashion is such an example.

If one chooses to go out on the proverbial limb in apologist mode, perhaps it can be argued that this scene, as it appears in a satire, is in and of itself parodying the presentation of minority characters in the western film. But there is not enough substance in the sequence to effectively back up such a claim. It does not present the characters or the situation in what can be clearly determined as satirical. The scene simply happens, without any noticeable provocation. The black man is a servant. He is shot at by the good guys (Roscoe, Buster, and others) simply to observe his frightened reactions for the purpose of amusement. He falls through a trap door, sees the dead man, shrieks with fright, and jumps back up onto the bar floor. A closeup shows him praying with visible tears streaming down his cheeks. The others continue to taunt him. And somehow this is supposed to be funny.

Mel Brooks's *Blazing Saddles* (1974), another western satire, was successful at using stereotyped images for the purpose of comic parody. Brooks presented black men working a railroad being chided by white cowboys with lines like, "Let's hear a good ol' nigger work song," and the workers responding by giving them a jazzy version of Cole Porter's "I Get a Kick Out of You." The film goes on to reveal that it is, by all means, an anti-racist film with its intelligent black hero outsmarting the white western movie stereotypes of dumbbell cowpokes.

Using the 20/20 hindsight that the much later Mel Brooks film allows, there can be an argument that the scene with the black man in *Out West* is supposed to parody the treatment of minority characters in serious westerns, pushing the satiric envelope just past the edge with the closeup of the black actor (identified in some filmographies as Ernest Morrison, Sr., whose son, Sunshine Sammy, was in films with Harold Lloyd, was the central figure in the original Our Gang, and, years later, a member of the East Side Kids). Perhaps a more in-depth knowledge of scenes with minorities in pre-1918 westerns, too many of which are lost and therefore unavailable for assessment, would reveal such a thing. But as it exists, it appears to be an attempt at humor that may likely have been dismissed as silly, comical cruelty back in 1918, but is not at all funny during this more enlightened post civil rights era. A scene such as this is best used to prompt discussion about the treatment of minority characters in much of early cinema. The black man as servant is not treated as a human being, but as a veritable animal who can be cruelly toyed with by a group of people who are amused by his frightened reactions. If it were villains taunting the man, with Fatty and company coming to his rescue, it might have been less unsettling. But it is Fatty and Buster, the supposed good guys, the heroes of the picture, who somehow derive amusement by taunting this man. It is quite a disturbing scene.

The other uncomfortable stereotype involves Native American warriors who see Fatty as prey. Indians were portrayed as savages in most of the western films, even well into the more modern era of cinema, but in this two reel comedy they are shown to be cannibals. One doesn't quite know if the laugh is supposed to be the fact that Fatty is considered ample prey for a month's worth of food, or that the depiction of Indians as cannibals is a satiric look at the presentation of Native Americans in westerns. Again, this film is too early in movie history, without enough solid accessible evidence as to pre-1918 western films

In any case, as with the depiction of the black man, the presentation of the Native Americans is a very unfunny, uncomfortable one in this more enlightened area. Of course the writer hastens to add that editing out either of these scenes would be detrimental to our understanding of the good and bad in cinema's presentation of various minorities during the motion picture's infancy. Even the disturbing images are necessary, if only to provoke discussion and a more enlightened look at an uglier side of motion picture history.

Still, even without these off-putting presentations of African American or Native American people, *Out West* is one of the less amusing Arbuckle Comique productions. Its attempts to parody the young cinema's western clichés is indeed an interesting idea, but the subsequent comedy simply does seem not have the level of cleverness as can be found in any number of superior Arbuckle films from this period.

St. John is once again all blatant gestures and overplayed grimaces as the villain. And while he often plays over the top for comedic purposes, and his presentation here is in tune with the satiric context, he does little more than react. His stunt work is always good, his performance always enthusiastic, but usually he is given more substantial material with which to work. Here his series of grotesque faces and wild gestures are just that. They don't seem to work from the character in the same fashion as any number of his conniving bullies in these or the earlier Sennett pictures.

Keaton's bartender is little more than a supporting player whose presence is used in greater measure to fill in than to assist with the comedy. Even the slapstick finale in which he subdues the bad guys with some trick shooting is not of the caliber we have already come to expect. Keaton has a less interesting role than St. John or even Alice Lake. He may have as much or more screen time, but his role in *Out West* is still on the periphery. This would change rather drastically with the next film.

Alice Lake does well as the typical ingenue, and Fatty is great playing his usual boyish innocent who stumbles into trouble and extricates himself with a few tricky ideas.

While it is one of the weaker Comique productions, *Out West* is certainly not completely devoid of laughs. There is an amusing bit where a cowboy brings his horse into the bar for a bucket of water. As the horse drinks, Fatty playfully pours liquor into the bucket, causing the animal to literally stagger out of the saloon.

Fatty is also fun as he runs and hides from the train men who set out to catch him and throw him off. As he weaves about and dodges their clutches, his agility and his genuine sense of danger provide both amusement and excitement.

And the idea of attempting to satirize a central genre of the film industry as early as 1918 is bold and innovative. However it should be pointed out that while the western film may have been quite new, western stories had been around for some years, and in the teens many popular pulp westerns by the likes of Zane Grey, Bob Wister, or Clarence Mulford were being read by the masses. And the movies already boasted western stars like Broncho Billy Anderson and William S. Hart by the time Arbuckle made *Out West*.

The central gag here seems to be the fact that the evil, scary bad guy who is invulnerable to pain or even gunfire, turns out to be helpless when tickled. This probably sounded funny in discussion, and might be amusing enough for one scene, but Arbuckle chooses to use it again as the film's climax, when Fatty subdues the villain in the same way so that Alice can be rescued.

Tickling as a comic attack has been used countless times in slapstick comedy. Interestingly enough, perhaps the funniest and most noted example would be Stan Laurel and Oliver Hardy's own western satire; a feature from 1937 similarly titled *Way Out West*. The scene where a saloon girl tries to extricate a valuable deed from Stan's shirt pocket and unwittingly tickles him into helplessness in the process is among the highlights of this 65 minute film. But in the Laurel and Hardy feature it is not revisited, and is not overplayed. In *Out West* the tickling is used beyond its limitation as being mildly amusing. When it is used to subdue Wild Bill at the climax, it almost appears as if they'd run out of comic ideas and simply wrapped things up by lazily revisiting a gag from earlier in the two reeler.

Both Arbuckle and Keaton had a certain macabre interest in dark comedy, and *Out West* is a very dark film. The scene where Buster Keaton's character of bartender Bull Bullhorn casually shoots at a card cheat and nonchalantly kicks his body down a trap door and into a cellar may be funny due to its outrageousness, and could also be satirizing the lack of respect for human life in western pictures (or books). It can remind one of the rather spooky dream sequence in Arbuckle's fascinating Keystone two reeler *He Did and He Didn't* where Fatty attempts to strangle wife Mabel and, in self defense, she shoots and kills him. The killing in *Out West* is not a dream, but an impulsive action that seems to directly parody similar scenes in serious western films of the time.

A initial story credit for *Out West* goes to Natalie Talmadge who was then a script girl and secretary for Arbuckle. Her sister, actress Norma Talmadge, shot her films at an adjacent studio, and would frequently complain about the noise generated from the Arbuckle unit. It is likely that Natalie Talmadge initially came up with the idea of doing a comic western, perhaps in casual conversation on the set, and Arbuckle filled it in from there. This is the only writing credit of Natalie Talmadge's career. She would later become Mrs. Buster Keaton.

Some of the scenes for *Out West* were filmed at Horkheimer Brothers' Balboa Amusement Producing Company studios in Long Beach, California. Other scenes were filmed at Mad Dog Gulch, which was a western mining town built in San Gabriel Canyon near Los Angeles for this production.

Period reviews of *Out West* were generally favorable. In a review from February 9, 1918, critic L. J. Bournstein stated:

> Arbuckle's latest is a dashing, slashing, shooting tale of the west. This is bound to be a sure fire hit. Its burlesque on the familiar western dance hall with its two-gun man, made even some of the hardhearted and unrelenting reviewers and critics laugh. When this can be done, the subject must, indeed, be a humorous one. Al St. John, the popular contortionist and tumbler who has appeared in many of the Arbuckle successes is again very much in evidence in the part of the rascally bandit. But, as usual, he gets the worst of it.

Reviewer Peter Milne thought there were some areas lacking, despite the fact that he believed *Out West* to be a good film, stating in a review that was syndicated at the time:

> In *Out West*, Arbuckle offers a burlesque on the Western melodrama that possesses many laughable features. William S. Hart is the main target of Arbuckle's comedy. But while *Out West* is good when it comes to Arbuckle and his immediate support, consisting of Buster Keaton, Al St. John, and Alice Lake, it becomes noticeably slack when these peo-

ple recede from the foreground. The long shots of furious fighting possess no comedy value and are quite out of place, while Arbuckle as director has shown a marked tendency to cater directly to Arbuckle the star, sometimes to the detriment of incidental action of the scene.
However, *Out West* hands out a good supply of laughs and Fatty's popularity is never to be taken lightly.

Judging by these examples, it appears period critics recognized *Out West* as a satire, and the repetitive tickle attacks were not singled out as lazy wrap ups, nor was any mention made of stereotyping. Further study would be necessary to assume that perhaps the African American status back in 1918 was at such a level, a sequence such as the afore-described one in *Out West* offended none of the average moviegoers. Even placing it in its historical context, the scene, when viewed today, hampers the entire film.

While a lesser entry in the Comique series, there is some interest in *Out West*. Essentially, it is the darkness that is most intriguing, setting it apart from the majority of comedies made during the late teens. Author and film historian Jim Kline, in *The Complete Films of Buster Keaton*, agrees that *Out West* is an extremely dark comedy:

> Keaton and Arbuckle indulge in a brand of humor they both loved, gags built around killing and death. Extremely nightmarish, like a filmed dream, *Out West* is totally illogical, chaotic and amoral.

Responding to some of the darker scenes in *Out West*, Arbuckle said at the time that it was all for the sake of comedy. Having had experience on stage in both comedies and dramas, Arbuckle acknowledged that playing comedy was far more difficult, but still worth it. He told *The New York Sun*: "I'd a heap rather make people laugh than make 'em cry. It's a darn site harder to do."

10

The Bell Boy

Directed by Roscoe "Fatty" Arbuckle
Written by Roscoe "Fatty" Arbuckle
Story by Natalie Talmadge
Produced by Joseph M. Schenck
Cinematography by Elgin Lessley and George Peters
Film Editing by Herbert Warren

Cast

Roscoe "Fatty" Arbuckle
Buster Keaton
Alice Lake
Al St. John
Joe Keaton
Charles Dudley

Filmed at the Balboa Amusement Producing Company studio in Long Beach, California
Released by the Comique Film Corporation for Paramount Pictures on March 18, 1918
Distributed by Paramount Pictures.
Running Time: Two Reels

Rebounding from the less than stellar result of *Out West*, Arbuckle made one of the finest films of his Comique series with *The Bell Boy*.

Without a wasted moment, *The Bell Boy* is another of those

Comique productions that does an effective job of presenting each facet of Arbuckle's talent as a director, writer, and actor. Along with being very funny on a purely visceral level, there is a genuine brilliance to much of that which is contained herein. The film's use of objects as comic props and its concentration on visually presenting an idea are very obvious influences on Buster Keaton's later work. And with *The Bell Boy*, Keaton's status appears to have been elevated before the camera and behind it.

First, Keaton is raised in status by appearing in a veritable comedy team opposite Arbuckle. The large Arbuckle and smaller Keaton may call forth visual images of Stan Laurel and Oliver Hardy (who were to begin regularly making films together in another eight years), but really their teaming of ample and diminutive is perhaps more accurately comparable, as a precedent, to earlier teams in which Oliver Hardy was involved, such as the Plump and Runt series with Bobby Ray, that may have been influenced by this film (one of the Plump and Runt shorts, *Hop To It*, featured Hardy and Ray as bellhops and had some standard similarities to *The Bell Boy*).

However despite Keaton's elevated co-starring position, this is still an Arbuckle film (it is not called *The Bell Boys*). It is he who is the center, and who propels the action. While at this point it can certainly be assumed Keaton was making suggestions that Roscoe endorsed, it is still Arbuckle's final say, and his creative vision that is to be commended.

But this is not to indicate that Arbuckle wasn't generous with screen time for the other performers. Even in a 1918 issue of *Photoplay*, Arbuckle is pointed out as being quite understanding in regard to the supporting talents by which he is surrounded:

> Roscoe Arbuckle, like Charlie Chaplin, likes to dope out his funny stunts right in front of the camera, even if it is not in operation, but "Fatty" is more generous with his footage so far as his colleagues are concerned—he lets them "get" the laugh if it improves the completed product.

The Bell Boy opens at a hotel that features, according to a title card, "third rate service for first class prices." Fatty makes a memorable first appearance. Arbuckle stages his character's entrance by focusing on an elevator car coming down, with a smiling Fatty emerging. He then cuts to Al St. John as the angry manager, standing behind

Arbuckle and Keaton with Alice Lake on the set of *The Bell Boy*.

the counter and exhibiting his personality with his usual series of blatant facial expressions. When Arbuckle cuts back to Fatty, he is teamed with Buster.

The first slapstick mishap occurs when Fatty and Buster attempt to toss the luggage of a departing party onto the hotel's horse-driven street car. Fatty tosses the luggage towards the car's roof, only to have it fall back down on top of him. When Buster hoists a suitcase, he heaves it past Fatty, knocking him to the ground.

Back in the hotel, Buster is carefully cleaning what appears to be a clear window, only to reveal there is no glass at all. In his biobibliography of Arbuckle (Greenwood Press, 1994), film historian Robert Young, Jr. stated:

> Keaton introduced the gag of washing a glassless window and reaching through it in this film. A deathless bit of business destined for a long life, Arbuckle used it two years later when he cleans a car window in *The Garage*, and again, in a restaurant scene in his first talking picture *Hey, Pop* twelve years after that.

It has been recycled since in nearly every zany comedy where there is a scene calling for a small window to be washed. For thousands of young audiences, the gag is as fresh as it was in 1918.

Meanwhile, Fatty is mopping the floor in a seated position. He dunks the mop into the bucket, mops the small area between his legs, moves over a few inches, and repeats the action. Buster approaches the bucket and decides to do a bit of laundry, dunking in a pair of dirty socks.

An unusual man enters the scene, looking for a haircut and a shave, which is one of many services that Fatty usually provides. The man is tall, skinny, and is dressed completely in black with a black top hat. He has long hair, a pointy beard, and bushy eyebrows. His demonic appearance frightens both Fatty and Buster who jump behind the counter. Their pantomime indicates they believe this man to be Old Scratch himself, holding their forefingers up to their heads as horns. Their attitude towards this man changes abruptly when he makes his request. The customer begins speaking, using florid, swishy gestures as he explains what he wants. An amused Fatty dances about the man, mocking his fruitiness, and agrees to perform the haircut and shave.

The next sequence is, quite simply, one of the finest of Arbuckle's career. It was singled out in reviews of the period, and again by modern day critics when released on VHS and DVD.

As Fatty shaves the man and cuts his hair, he transforms him into a lookalike for General Grant. He stands back and inspects his handiwork, then performs some more hair cutting and shaving to reveal the man as Abraham Lincoln. Still not satisfied, his final act is to use his skills to present his customer as Kaiser Wilhelm. A few seconds of looking at that image causes Arbuckle to conclude the session with handfuls of shaving cream into the man's face, followed by a hot towel.

The writer is at something of a loss as to how he can accurately, through prose, present a sequence such as this, that is so completely visual. Perhaps we can correlate this scene to Arbuckle's many sequences featuring Fatty preparing food. The delicate dexterity and artistic intentions of Fatty the barber are neat supplements to the visual presentation of the man's face in various guises. Such a sequence offers even greater understanding as to Arbuckle's influence on Keaton's later work, as Keaton would take these bits of surrealism to other exciting levels once he began starring in and directing his own films. In any case, Roscoe Arbuckle's barber sequence in *The Bell Boy* is one of the cleverest and most delightful in all of silent comedy. Since Fatty is on camera doing a solo turn, it can perhaps be concluded that it is Buster Keaton directing this sequence as his assistant behind the camera.

Al returns with another group of hotel customers, including a new hire. Cutie Cuticle is the pretty new manicurist (played by Alice Lake). Fatty is immediately attracted to this gentle beauty. As he first meets and converses with her, Fatty looks to the camera (at us) and offers a sly wink. Self-referential asides like these helped make Arbuckle among the most beloved entertainers of his time. It emphasizes the all-important human element that set comedians like Arbuckle (and Chaplin) ahead of their counterparts during this era of filmmaking. Peering over cinema's fourth wall, Roscoe has Fatty respond directly to us, the audience, and with sly gestures such as these, Arbuckle handily and successfully connected with moviegoers of 1918.

Initially Buster and Fatty are rivals for Alice's interest and attention. They trip and kick each other at every opportunity, where they had before been working cohesively. Cutie, a manicurist who takes her job seriously, is repulsed by working man Buster's filthy hands and horrid fingernails. Fatty notices this, and tries to avoid offending Miss Cuticle by cleaning his own fingernails with the blade of a large barber shears, while simultaneously using the other blade to pick his teeth.

The next sequence is a wild slapstick melee involving the elevator, which is propelled, quite literally, by horse power. The horse that pulls the hotel's bus is also connected to the elevator, being responsible for its going up or down. This falls through with Alice trapped, as well as Buster, whose head gets caught between the elevator car floor and the door frame. Fatty tries to help by pulling on Buster's head.

Alice Lake recalled in a *Photoplay* interview four years later that this sequence resulted in an on-set mishap.

> The funniest looking accident we ever had was when Roscoe Arbuckle was making *The Bell Boy*. A crazy old elevator we were using fell to pieces and I was dangling in mid-air on the end of a rope. One of the boys was inside of what was left of the elevator and I was left whirling around in space while he was being rescued from the debris.

The first half of *The Bell Boy* is filled with many hilarious pieces, but as with many of Arbuckle's two-reelers, the second half shifts gears into a clearer narrative, and ultimately concludes with a slapstick free-for-all. This does not hamper the film, despite a more precarious linear structure.

As the film's second half begins, we have Fatty concocting an elaborate scheme to appear heroic to Cutie and ultimately impress her enough to win her hand. He convinces Al and Buster to pose as crooks and stage a phony bank robbery. He, then, will pretend to stop them, and, ultimately, look like a hero to Cutie Cuticle.

Buster and Al, in full criminal garb, enter the bank, only to discover that two actual crooks are pulling a real robbery. They try to stop the criminals by attacking them, but end up being overpowered. Al and Buster escape by leaping through windows with the criminals in pursuit.

Fatty enters and is hit by a thrown vase. He grabs one of the crooks, sticks the man's head in a vise, and tightens it. The outnumbered crooks break free and try to escape, and it is now Fatty, Al, and Buster pursuing them. The battle finds its way back to the inn, where the criminals are finally apprehended, and Fatty is rewarded by the police for his bravery. The idea was a success, as Cutie Cuticle embraces and kisses Fatty. However it was not the phony setup, it was Fatty actually apprehending two real bank bandits, becoming an actual hero, and being given a sizable reward. But the money means little to Fatty. His intent was to woo Cutie Cuticle, and when she kisses him, he dazedly tosses his reward money to Al and Buster.

In examining this film's structure, it is interesting to note how Arbuckle the filmmaker has evolved. Still believing that frenetic slapstick is the best way to conclude his comedies, Arbuckle's films still seem to flow better and appear less like two separate halves that are loosely pieced together. The characters and actions are consistent in *The Bell Boy*, and Fatty's decision to stage a robbery in order to act as a hero for the pretty manicurist is consistent with his initial attraction to Cutie Cuticle. He immediately gives her a great deal of attention, even to the point of slyly winking at the audience.

Arbuckle realized early in his cinematic tenure that offbeat ways of doing ordinary tasks could be amusing, and he could be quite creative in this area. His floor mopping sequence, where he is seated and mopping the small area of floor between his legs, is a good example.

When Buster Keaton started making his own films, he would come up with some extraordinary ideas from ordinary situations; another indication of his Arbuckle influence.

It is interesting to see Keaton in so lofty a co-starring role during much of *The Bell Boy*. While he is once again relegated to Al St. John's level of slapstick support towards the end of this short, he enjoys equal footing with Roscoe for the film's first half. However it does not appear that Roscoe and Buster were playing off of each other like Laurel and Hardy would. There is a set piece featuring Roscoe, and a routine featuring Keaton, and a few broad slapstick sequences featuring both of them. But they were not functioning as a team. Keaton was nowhere during Roscoe's brilliant bit in the barber shop (except, perhaps, behind the camera), while Arbuckle kept himself off screen while Buster performed his window wiping bit (revealing there to be no glass in the pane). When Alice Lake enters as Cutie Cuticle, there is some rivalry between Buster and Fatty for her attention, and this is similar to sequences featuring Fatty and Al in earlier films all the way back to the Sennett productions. This rivalry is forgotten when Fatty hatches the bank robbery scheme, as both Buster and Al agree to cooperate in helping Fatty appear as a hero to the manicurist.

The most interesting thing about the structure of *The Bell Boy* is its combining the gentler, more subtler acting nuances, and the clever visual sequences, with the customary broad slapstick. It appeared that Roscoe was listening to Buster's proclamations that slapstick gags can be enhanced within the context of the film medium. Buster maintained a keen interest in how comedy for the cinema allowed for an intimacy and a magic that would be impossible on stage.

Arbuckle still believed the average moviegoer would be disappointed without the customary violent slapstick that he knew his name represented. While he was not above experiments like the Sennett-produced *He Did and He Didn't*, and he had a real affinity for surrealism, Arbuckle often played it a bit more safely than the maverick Keaton.

Keaton's interesting ideas were respected, and often used. This became especially evident with the next film.

11

Moonshine

Directed by Roscoe "Fatty" Arbuckle
Written by Roscoe "Fatty" Arbuckle
Produced by Joseph M. Schenck
Cinematography by George Peters
Film Editing by Herbert Warren

Cast
Roscoe "Fatty" Arbuckle
Buster Keaton
Al St. John
Alice Lake
Joe Bordeaux
Charles Dudley

Filmed at Mad Dog Gulch, San Gabriel Canyon, Angeles National Forest, California
Released by the Comique Film Corporation for Paramount Pictures on May 12, 1918
Distributed by Paramount Pictures, Famous Players-Lasky.
Running Time: Two Reels
Black and White—Silent

    Even in a consistently brilliant series of comedies there will occasionally emerge a special effort that stands out ahead of the others. This is not necessarily to state that one particular film is far and away superior, but perhaps different in such a way as to make it a bit more exceptional. *The Music Box* (1932), for instance, is one of many truly brilliant Laurel and Hardy comedies, but this Oscar winner featuring Stan and Ollie delivering a heavy piano to a home atop a long flight of stairs is, and has long been, considered a standout film. The same can perhaps be said for Harold Lloyd's *Safety Last* (1923), which features a building climbing sequence that has permeated popular culture via a production still of Lloyd hanging from the hand of a large clock set high above the ground. Among their thirteen starring features, The Marx Brothers made a handful of true classics, but their political satire *Duck Soup* (1933) has long been considered an exceptionally intelligent, insightful, and perceptive achievement that was decades ahead of its time and continues to display real relevance.

And then we come to *Moonshine*, a Roscoe Arbuckle two reeler that predates all of these other standout films. Its direction is keener, its satire is smarter, the chances it chooses to take are greater, the challenges to the idea of comedy in cinema are more impressive, and its gags are more clever. It is a film that can elicit an oddly respectful awestruck reaction as much as laughter. It really is an amazing two reeler.

As discussed earlier in this text, Roscoe Arbuckle was a comedian whose ideas were all about creating comedy. He was well acquainted with the cinematic process, and tempered his gags so they would be effective within the camera's frame. But he did not care as much to explore the technological aspects of film very deeply, his genius as a comedian centering on the creation of comedy itself.

Buster Keaton was also a genius at creating comedy, and despite being merely a supporting player, he was given a reasonable amount of opportunity to contribute during this Comique series. But, as stated previously in this text, Keaton also had a technological curiosity that resulted in exploring ideas that were film-centric. Arbuckle did not always understand these ideas, but would never dismiss them. Roscoe found Buster's technology-based ideas about filmmaking to be interesting, inspiring, and he encouraged Keaton to speak up whenever an idea came along that might help the scene.

With *Moonshine*, Arbuckle explored further into his own creative processes moreso than perhaps any other film since the brilliant Keystone two reeler *He Did and He Didn't*. Slapstick is certainly not absent from *Moonshine*, but Arbuckle concentrates almost completely on satire here, not only using physical comedy but also the visual pres-

Keaton, Arbuckle, and Al St. John pose on the set of *Moonshine*.

entation of setting and set design to enhance the atmosphere of each segment. There simply appears to be more to *Moonshine* than the other Comiques.

Keaton, for his part, came up with some purely cinematic ideas here that were not only successfully incorporated, they are among this film's highlights. One particular gag of several people leaving a small car, which will be discussed in detail later in this chapter, can be considered well ahead of its time.

To adequately assess *Moonshine*, the author found it necessary to screen the film three times—once to watch and appreciate the total film, a second time to concentrate on Keaton, and a third to concentrate on Arbuckle. Each factor cannot be underestimated, as one is not more adroit than the other.

While Arbuckle had extended his range, as an actor and a filmmaker, beyond knockabout slapstick in other films, and was not above experimenting, he continued to stick fairly close to his cinematic roots. Charlie Chaplin, by his 1916–1917 Mutual productions, had weeded out just about all of the Keystone roughhousing and replaced it with a subtler approach, fewer and more elaborate gags, and greater depth within his character. Arbuckle offered some remarkably imaginative visual ideas in each of his Comique two reelers; even an excellent film like *The Bell Boy* ends with a Sennett-like slapstick free-for-all.

In no film in the Comique series is this more evident than *Moonshine*, which offers a greater maturity in Arbuckle as a film satirist, cheerfully and effectively breaking down the fourth wall.

Fatty and Buster are once again acting as a team. This time they are cast as revenuers, who are trying to ferret out moonshiners up in the hills. The rural setting, the casting of comic actors in wildly stereotypical roles for this setting, the humor deriving from their extended characterizations, the gags contained therein, and the offbeat situations all combine cohesively, netting remarkable results.

Rather than examining, and satirizing, movie making behind the scenes, *Moonshine* turns the humor inward and makes fun of itself, of the cinematic process, of the fact that this is a piece of celluloid make believe.

There are written accounts indicating that while Arbuckle enjoyed this type of self-referential satire, he was a bit apprehensive about using it throughout an entire film. It was Keaton who convinced him to try it. Arbuckle argued that his name represented knockabout slapstick, and his fans might be disappointed if one of his films was too cerebral.

In an interview a couple of years earlier for *Caricature*, when discussing the remarkable, offbeat Keystone production *He Did and He Didn't*, Arbuckle had said: "I believe in comedy that makes you think, and I believe that the time has come to put it on—and that is what I am going to do."

This was in reference to one of Arbuckle's most ambitious and daring Sennett productions, which had crossed boundaries in the way of performance for its two stars—Arbuckle and Mabel Normand—and showed greater depth in scenario and direction.

Moonshine not only satirizes motion picture production, it also digs at popular melodrama, using a more sophisticated cinematic approach than Arbuckle may have been completely comfortable doing. Keaton had always insisted that cinema's more sophisticated audience, the ones who appreciated something like D.W. Griffith's epic achievement *Intolerance* (1916), should be considered when one made a comedy, and certainly Buster's later solo films bore this out. When working with Arbuckle, Keaton's vision was held slightly in check. Although it was respectfully encouraged, Keaton's ideas were also used sparingly within the context of Arbuckle's own vision. Roscoe could certainly come up with something as visually remarkable as the barber bit in *The Bell Boy*, but committing an entire movie to Keaton's penchant for offbeat satire must have seemed a bit daunting. Arbuckle perhaps realized there was enough wacky comedy in *Moonshine* to please his less discerning longtime fans, despite the heady structure that would be more likely to charm the intellectuals who frequently embraced Chaplin with one arm while dismissing Roscoe with the other.

Keaton had been contributing, even if only at the level of offering suggestions, on a regular basis almost from the beginning. His salary had increased from $40 per week to $250. He was acting as an assistant director, helming scenes in which Arbuckle does a solo turn. And now, with *Moonshine*, it appears his vision for satire and its ability to sustain a complete film was to have the sort of influence on Arbuckle as Roscoe's initial status as a comedian for films had on Buster. It was the quintessential give-and-take relationship where these artists were now effectively learning from each other.

Keaton recalled in his autobiography:

> I became his assistant director. He came up and said, "From now on, you're assistant director." You fell into those jobs. He never referred to me as the assistant director, but I was the guy who sat alongside of the camera and watched the scenes that he was in. I ended up just practically co-directing with him. He was considered one of the best comedy directors in pictures at the time.

The opening gag in *Moonshine* features the sort of comical incongruity both Keaton and Arbuckle enjoyed, with Fatty and Buster driving through the backwoods in a chauffeured limousine. As the car stops, the old circus gag of several dozen people leaving the limo is used. The cinematic trickery is unusually impressive in that this gag is shot by showing the entire car in a long shot, as the army of passengers emerges from the car in one continuous shot.

This was Keaton's creation, and his idea for filming it. Keaton got the idea of shooting the gag by masking one side of the camera's lens, rewinding the film, and masking the other side of the lens. The effect remains dazzling, even in this post–CGI era of special effects extravaganzas, and is far ahead of its time.

Al St. John is once again the villain of this picture, playing a scowling mountain man who is in pursuit of barefoot hillbilly girl Alice Lake. In their first scene together, Alice is shown relaxing on a hammock when Al approaches and starts tickling her foot. Alice clearly does not like Al, and finds his attentions annoying, but she is also very ticklish and laughs in spite of the negative feelings she has for her tormenter. She kicks him in the face, and he shakes her out of the hammock. She beats him up, and he scurries off. Her father then approaches her, saying, via title card: "Wait until you're married to start hitting him."

One particularly interesting thing about this scene, which is designed to set up the relationship between Lake's and St. John's characters, is how Al is filmed as he approaches Alice. It was reportedly Keaton's idea for Roscoe to shoot Al's face in closeup, using it for comic effect. St. John walks directly towards the camera until his face takes up the entire screen, then grimaces at the viewer in an obvious takeoff of Harry Carey's glowering closeup in D.W. Griffith's one reel drama *Musketeers of Pig Alley* (1912). When Griffith used the close up in his early Biograph production, it was an innovation. Griffith realized such a shot would be intimidating to the audience and enhance the actor's presentation of being evil and scary. It was most effective and is still being used as a method of cinematic character definition nearly a century later. Keaton uses it in essentially the same way, but his is for comic effect. St. John offers one of his trademark grimaces as his face takes up the entire frame, and his attempt to intimidate the audience instead results in our laughing at him. It sets up his character as a comic foil every bit as effectively as Griffith presented his intimidating punk in the 1912 drama.

Alice Lake recalled in an interview for *Photoplay* a couple of years later that working barefoot had its hazards. She recalled a horse she was trying to mount stepped on her foot (she admitted to not being a very good horse woman). Fortunately she was standing on a sandy surface and no bones were broken, but she suffered with her foot for weeks afterward. She stated that it was one of only three times she was injured in all her years of working in slapstick.

As with most of the two reelers in which a facially contorting Al

St. John is interested in a girl, Fatty, naturally, ends up being St. John's rival for Alice's affections. When Fatty sees Alice's father violently spanking her with a switch, he comes to the rescue—of her father. Fatty scolds Alice for defiance towards her parent, and throws her into the water. She emerges, embraces Fatty, and proclaims her love for him. This causes her father to react incredulously (a close up reveals that he appears to be saying "Well I'll be damned!"), as Fatty explains, via title card, "This is only a two-reeler, we have no time to build up to love scenes." The father then replies, "In that case go ahead, it's your movie."

These types of quips, stepping outside the box and destroying the fourth wall, were typical of the Bob Hope Bing Crosby *Road* series at Paramount Pictures during the 1940s. Here they are presented via title card, but no less effectively.

Meanwhile, Buster finds the moonshiners' hidden still, but forgets the "open sesame" password by the time he finds Fatty. They finally get it open and discover the contraband. An eventual battle between revenuers and moonshiners ensues. While holding a gun on Buster, Al gets something in his eye and drops his gun. Buster politely retrieves Al's gun, gives it back to him, and then helps him with his eye. Once his eye is cleared, Al continues to accost Buster with his usual blatant grimaces. In a parody of one of the Arbuckle's unit's own players, Buster, the Great Stone Face, starts mimicking Al's trademark facial expressions.

Fatty, captured by the moonshiners, is taken to their rustic cabin where they decide to lock him in the cellar. Fatty is taken to the cellar and discovers it to be a neat, well furnished suite with comfortable chairs and couches, an adjacent kitchen, even a piano. Alice comes in wearing a formal gown to serve Fatty a meal. At the same time, the moonshiners are enjoying dinner upstairs in the rustic cabin setting, all clad in formal attire.

In an effort to escape, Fatty fakes his death by shooting a gun in the air and pouring ketchup on his own head, getting the idea from a copy of *The Count of Monte Cristo* which is resting handily on a table next to his chair.

The moonshiners discover the "corpse" and Fatty's "remains" are dumped in the river, as he swims to safety. He climbs on a rock, raises his arms and shouts, via title card, "And now the world is mine!" The film then cuts to a shot of Buster, seated on a nearby river bank, applauding and yelling, "bravo" at Fatty's performance.

11. Moonshine

Buster and Fatty finally subdue the moonshiners and Alice is prepared to go off with her hero. Fatty reneges, admitting to her that he is already married, and, for once Buster gets the girl as Fatty wanders off alone. As he wanders off, he is shot from the back in the same way Chaplin concluded his two reel Essanay classic *The Tramp*.

Moonshine is a remarkably skillful comedy, pushing well past the established edge to experiment with some truly offbeat ideas. While Arbuckle's comic genius was the axis, this time we can assuredly give relative newcomer Buster Keaton a substantial amount of credit. He was far more open to trying surreal cinematic ideas, while the veteran Arbuckle took some precautions to avoid confusing his audience. Arbuckle felt that after five steady years of a prolific output, and having achieved perhaps the second highest level of stardom in comedy films at that time, his vast audience expected certain things from his product. He believed that his name represented something. Even when making the offbeat *He Did and He Didn't* for Sennett, Arbuckle was clear in interviews regarding his making a movie in a different comic style, indicating that some knockabout was necessary due to what the Keystone name represented.

Often it has been believed that *Moonshine* is Keaton's film. Since so much of it seems offbeat for Arbuckle, credit is frequently given to Buster as to the film's concept and execution. It is Roscoe Arbuckle who is credited for writing and directing *Moonshine*. Keaton's contribution is certainly significant, but Arbuckle was the still master and Keaton the apprentice. The film may have been more collaborative than the others, but it is Roscoe who had the final say.

Keaton was not a veteran, he had not yet achieved stardom, he was still a supporting player with a wealth of interesting ideas and a craving to explore them. That he worked under the tutelage of a comedian and filmmaker like Arbuckle who encouraged ideas and input from his fellow players was beneficial for his own development. At this point, nobody was aware that Keaton would soon emerge as a brilliant filmmaker in his own right, taking what he learned from working with Arbuckle and expanding upon this vision and his own ideas. With *Moonshine*, we get an idea of what was soon to come.

Reviews from the period seemed appreciative, but curiously did not call any attention to the offbeat style. Critic Peter Milne stated in his widely syndicated review at the time:

There is much in this two-reel burlesque of the once popular moonshiner picture to amuse. Fatty Arbuckle and Buster Keaton as detectives arrive in the mountains and attempt to apprehend the band of moonshiners headed by Al St. John, and in which Alice Lake thrives. There are plenty of good gags while the comedy of Fatty and the athletic funny business of his two supporting principals is excellent. The first reel is all that a comedy should be.

It has originality, a plentiful supply of gags which bespeak the inventive genius of Arbuckle and his partners-in-fun, and is so obviously a burlesque of the old moonshine picture that it registers with every scene. The second reel slows up to a certain extent but no one can complain that it is the least bit tiresome.

The review in *Motion Picture Magazine* stated:

Fatty Arbuckle has a good time leaping around mountains and hanging perilously over cliffs in this, his newest comedy, as the redoubtable Doug [Fairbanks] himself. *Moonshine* is a takeoff on Kentucky mountain dramas with their everlasting secret stills. Many deliciously funny and original comedy stunts are interpolated. For instance, when Fatty hangs his side partner by his toes from the limb of a tree to dry after his ducking in the rapids. Because of equally original bits of funny business, this is the best comedy Fatty has done in some time.

The New York Times stated: "*Moonshine* is a roughhouse farce, much better than slapstick comedy. It was made to make spectators laugh, and certainly succeeds."

This indication of the spectators laughing was quite accurate. Comments from theater owners that played *Moonshine* offered such comments as, "Best comedy Fatty ever made," and noticed, "He is not afraid to let someone else get a laugh."

One of the truly unfortunate details surrounding *Moonshine* is its current print status. At the time of this writing, a poor quality 16mm print is the most complete version currently available. A few scenes exist in 35mm, and they have been restored, but only these fragments are in what can be considered excellent condition.

The only available complete print of *Moonshine* was a dupey 16mm copy from which Kino was able to put the almost the entire film on DVD. Some time later, the clear 35mm fragments turned up on a more complete collection of Arbuckle-Keaton films from Image Entertainment.

Much of the outrageous self-referential comedy in *Moonshine* was an interesting harbinger to what Keaton would be doing once in charge of the studio and making his own films. The breathtaking cinematic achievement of, say, *Sherlock, Jr.* would be possible in a few years as a result of Keaton's training with Arbuckle at Comique, and the freedom he was granted to explore and experiment with his innovations.

Despite his being cautionary about how far he'd allow his films to stray from that which had been successful, Arbuckle's open minded approach to Keaton's innovative ideas combined beautifully with his own particular brand of comic genius. *Moonshine* is a perfect example.

12

Good Night Nurse

Directed by Roscoe "Fatty" Arbuckle
Written by Roscoe "Fatty" Arbuckle
Produced by Joseph M. Schenck
Cinematography by George Peters
Film Editing by Herbert Warren

Cast
Roscoe "Fatty" Arbuckle
Buster Keaton
Al St. John
Alice Lake
Kate Price

Filmed at the Comique Film Corporation studios (formerly Balboa), Alamitos and Sixth streets in Long Beach, and Arrowhead Hot Springs Health Resort, Lake Arrowhead, California
Released by the Comique Film Corporation for Paramount Pictures on July 8, 1918
Distributed by Paramount Pictures, Famous Players-Lasky.
Running Time: Two Reels
Black and White—Silent

    Roscoe Arbuckle had an interest in setting and context when preparing his comedies. Though notoriously without a script, the basic structure was still necessary, and often humor was derived from just where Arbuckle chose to set his comedies.

12. Good Night Nurse

The hospital setting is a good one for slapstick comedy. Scary procedures with the potential for pain can result in some very funny if a bit unsettling slapstick sequences. The sanitarium presented in *Good Night Nurse* appears to engage in every possible cure for any conceivable malady from alcoholism to mental illness to surgical needs. Arbuckle explores all of the possibilities.

Arbuckle also revisits the dream sequence to add a bit of avant garde surrealism to the proceedings. A dream sequence served Arbuckle well in what may be his best Keystone production, *He Did and He Didn't* (1916). In the Keystone two reeler, Arbuckle dreams a truly macabre set of circumstances that include murder. However in *Good Night Nurse*, the dream reveals Fatty's subconscious desires, and is one of the highlights of the series. *Good Night Nurse* features a dream sequence that is far less macabre that the horrific events in *He Did and He Didn't*, but in either case he is relieved upon waking, and each is just as interesting in its exploration of cinema's avant garde.

One of the more notable examples of avant garde in early cinema is the Edwin S. Porter film version of Winsor McKay's mind bending comic *The Dream of a Rarebit Fiend* (1906), which uses some of cinema's first visual effects to present the nightmare that exists in the head of the central character. Using cinema for the purpose of presenting surreal imagery was the method used by some of the first films that could be considered primitive examples of the science-fiction genre, especially George Meliès college classroom staple *A Trip to the Moon* (1904). Arbuckle had an interest in surrealism and offbeat ideas. He used dreams in his films to convey the character's subconscious desires.

Good Night Nurse maintains the structure that had noticeably evolved up to *The Bell Boy*, and doesn't offer two separate ideas within the same film. The series of ideas presented in *Good Night Nurse* maintains a steady pace. It contains all of the now standard Arbuckle comic traits: absurdity, visual cleverness, wild slapstick, and a nod to the cinematic avant-garde with the dream sequence. It is one of Arbuckle's most interesting and most effective films.

Good Night Nurse immediately uses setting for comic impact. The film opens during a heavy rainstorm, as a drunken Fatty stumbles along a city street, trying to light a cigarette with matches that are wet from the pouring rain. While Fatty is too intoxicated to be affected by the rain, inanimate objects, in this case his matches, are thwarted by the elements.

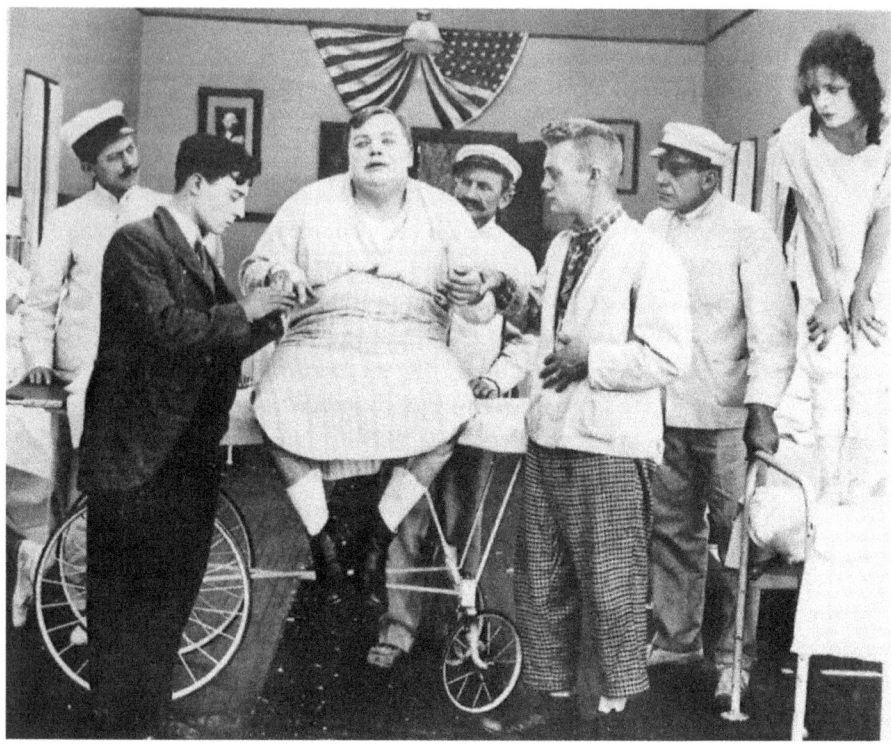

Arbuckle is flanked by Keaton and Al St. John as Alice Lake looks on from the far right.

A woman with an umbrella comes blowing by, propelled by the strong winds, and bumps into Fatty. He kicks her away, but she comes sliding by again. This time he stops her, and tries to use her umbrella, turned inside-out by the winds, as a shield to light his cigarette. It doesn't work. As the wind picks up again, Fatty grabs the woman's dress in an effort to hold her steady, but the dress rips off of her body. She gives Fatty a high kick in the chin, knocking him down, and sails off.

The opening to *Good Night Nurse* bumps along with rhythmic slapstick, the stormy backdrop adding to the discomfort of the players and the sloppiness of their knockabout antics. The harmlessly sadistic nature in which Fatty treats the "woman," who is actually Buster Keaton in drag doing a stunt bit, and her violent reaction to his tearing of the dress, open the film with appropriate slapstick

12. Good Night Nurse

bombast. It is typical Arbuckle silliness, and it effectively gets things rolling.

It also continues to use the setting of a rainstorm. The elements may not affect a big man like Fatty, but this diminutive woman is at the mercy of the strong winds. While Fatty is grounded, he is beset by the surroundings via his matches being too wet to light and the woman slamming into him as the winds propel her.

Another standout gag features a drunk, even more inebriated than Fatty, needing a way home. Fatty asks the man his address, writes it on the man's shirt, pastes a few stamps on his head, and plops him atop a mail box.

An organ grinder, his female accomplice, and their monkey come by and Fatty requests they play the national anthem. They oblige, and the cop on the beat removes his hat in respect. Using it as an appropriate shield, Fatty is finally able to light his cigarette. Pleased with this accomplishment, he invites the organ grinder and company to his home.

Meanwhile at the house, Fatty's wife is looking into placing her errant husband into a sanitarium whose specialty is, according to an advertisement, curing hopeless drunks. The problem is, Fatty is in such good "spirits" while dancing about his living room to the tune of the organ grinder's music, he takes little notice of his wife's scolding. Early the next day, she has him at the sanitarium, ready to be admitted.

Once Fatty and his wife arrive, they are met by a heavily bandaged man on crutches (a barely recognizable Al St. John), happily announcing that he has been cured. Fatty finds this intimidating enough, and makes an attempt to sneak away. Of course he is caught by his wife and brought to the attention of the doctor.

Buster is the doctor of the sanitarium. If the heavily bandaged "cured" patient was not intimidating enough, Fatty notices that Dr. Buster's smock is splattered with what looks to be human blood. Buster is also equipped with such operating tools as a saw and a drill. Again Fatty tries to sneak away, and is retrieved by his wife.

While Fatty is being admitted, a very cute, and very unstable, female patient (Alice Lake) comes bursting into the room, jumps into Fatty's arms, and starts kissing him. He enjoys the attention, but with his wife nearby, has to pretend to be upset. The patient is taken away by an orderly (Al St. John), and Fatty is given a room of his own.

During a routine initial examination, Fatty eats the thermometer. Buster decides that he must now operate, and it is a typical Arbuckle free-for-all as the doctor, nurse, and orderly attempt to wrestle Fatty onto a stretcher and into the operating room. Once there, Fatty starts praying, and is given ether from a large container. His world blurs and he falls asleep.

At this point in *Good Night Nurse*, Arbuckle is maintaining his typical pace with a good solid comedy taking satiric shots at the medical profession. Buster the doctor appearing as though he works in a slaughter house and Al's grimacing stint as orderly (as well as his cameo as the heavily bandaged patient who has been "cured") are offset by Alice's wild appearance as a completely unstable patient. This allows Alice to offer perhaps her most uninhibited performance in an Arbuckle short, drawing from the natural gregariousness and the fearless quality she was said to possess off screen.

It is here that *Good Night Nurse* takes a surreal turn. As the ether knocks out Fatty, it shows the doctors from his perspective, their images blurring as he enters a stupor that, for once, is not from the consumption of alcoholic beverages. He awakens much later in his room, immediately looking under the covers at the rest of his body and making sure it is all there.

Suddenly, Alice rushes into Fatty's room insisting she is not crazy, and begs him to help her escape the sanitarium. As with most men, Fatty is a sucker for beauty, and Alice's irresistible cuteness overrides the fact that she is completely unstable.

The two sneak out of the room, using the old gag where Fatty puts his shoes on two crutches held outward and a sheet over everything to appear as though he is on a stretcher. The two are caught, and a feather pillow fight causes another free-for-all as a veritable blizzard feathers fly about and obstruct everyone's view.

Finally, Fatty escapes with Alice tucked into a pillow sack. Once they reach safety, he lets her out and she starts crying. When asked the matter, Alice wails, "Help me get back in!"

Reacting big to her fickleness, Fatty falls into a nearby pool as Alice scurries off and returns to the sanitarium. Meanwhile, Buster and Al are running about the grounds in an attempt to locate and capture Fatty for what they believe to be necessary surgery.

Realizing he is unsafe on the grounds while being pursued, Fatty sneaks back into the sanitarium and steals the uniform of a heavy set nurse. After putting it on, he begins camping it up flirtatiously for Dr. Buster, who responds in kind. When the nurse returns and recognizes her uniform, she takes the hat and wig from Fatty, revealing him to Buster and Al. He is pursued once again.

Fatty runs outside and scurries off the grounds. He ends up running right into a special foot race that is in progress, for men over 200 pounds. Still pursued by Buster and Al, he gets into this race and is soon way ahead of the others. As one of the participants drops from exhaustion, he is inspected by Buster and Al, making sure it is not the patient they are chasing. Still being pursued, Fatty wins the race and the cash prize. He is finally caught by Buster and Al, tries to fight his way out, but is subdued. Suddenly he awakens in the operating room from the effects of the ether. It had all been a dream.

As stated earlier in this chapter, *Good Night Nurse* is not like earlier Arbuckle Comique productions where each reel represents two separate ideas that form a whole. The opening of *Good Night Nurse* features typical Arbuckle slapstick in an effort to set up the remainder of the film. This setup not only offers the outrageous slapstick in the rainstorm scenes, as well as the clever visual bit of Fatty trying to light a cigarette in the pouring rain, but also some delightfully wacky physical comedy once Fatty and the musicians get to his home. As the organ grinder plays, Fatty dances and gyrates to the music, falling down repeatedly in his drunken stupor, and making the sort of ruckus that finally decides for his wife that he needs professional help. These delightfully funny opening sequences effectively set up the body of the film, which takes place at the sanitarium.

Good Night Nurse not only retains its pace with a more effective structure than perhaps any of the previous Arbuckle Comique productions, it also features the surreal dream sequence where Arbuckle can indulge his penchant for offbeat ideas. While Buster Keaton greatly admired and would be influenced by Arbuckle's surreal nature, he also had many innovative ideas of his own. But in *Good Night Nurse*, Buster is best examined as a performer, and his performance here is exceptional. One of the film's many highlights is the scene in which Fatty in drag as the nurse coyly flirts with Buster the doctor. The series of flirtatious gestures from Fatty are met with red-faced gyrations from Buster, and the pantomime here is delightful. Keaton appears to be having a hard time keeping a straight face as Fatty blatantly vamps.

The drag bit was seasoned territory for Roscoe, who realized the big laughs it received from his fans, and noted the comments made by critics of the time. Pure burlesque of the hoariest sort, and something that Arbuckle performed with gusto, the drag bits really brought out his uninhibited comic spirit. During the teens, when slapstick bombast was most typical in screen comedy, Arbuckle's drag bits were especially well received. The very idea that Roscoe would not only perform in drag, but would vamp in the most outrageous manner, was enough to delight the massive throngs of Arbuckle fans who, as Roscoe often stated in interviews, came to realize that his name meant something in the way of a certain style of comedy.

Interestingly enough, at least one character in the popular comedies Charlie Chaplin was making at Mutual, which set the bar for any other comedian of the era, actually appears to have been inspired by Roscoe's drag bits. In Chaplin's *The Rink* (1916), Chaplin stock company actor Henry Bergman, an overweight man not unlike Roscoe, appeared in outrageous drag in much the same way as Arbuckle had been doing at Keystone (*The Rink* being released before the Comique series got underway). Bergman, in fact, went so far as to actually play a female character in *The Rink* (the nagging wife of Eric Campbell, Chaplin's chosen comic heavy in the Mutual films). Henry Bergman's style was similar to Arbuckle's in execution, and thus it can be considered likely that he (and Chaplin) were paying some attention to what Roscoe had been doing at Keystone.

Chaplin's Mutual period is said by many to be the quintessential example of his having weeded out most of the Sennett-inspired roughhousing in favor of more elaborate gags, insightful stories, and substantial characters, especially his Little Tramp. Arbuckle followed a similar path by working out his gags more carefully, but he eschewed the sentiment or pathos found in Chaplin Mutuals like *The Vagabond*. Arbuckle instead incorporated the somewhat headier surrealism, such as the dream sequence in *Good Night Nurse*, which helped to inspire Buster Keaton's later films. Keaton's post-1920 work is often argued as being technically and aesthetically on par with Chaplin's. The inaccessibility of much of Arbuckle's best work has disallowed such an assessment for Roscoe. Now we can comprehend how Arbuckle challenged the limitations of the knockabout farce and probed more deeply into a different presentation.

Good Night Nurse is not so much remarkable simply for incorporating a dream sequence, but it is the sequence that is, itself, remarkable. In Arbuckle's vision while resting in the arms of morpheus, he perceives himself as the hero and protector of the amorous, unstable Alice, but he realizes her feminine fickleness, coupled with her obvious instability, likely reaches outrageous levels. While he is willing to help her escape, his subconscious mind realizes she is likely better off under care. He believes that even with her histrionics, she would likely conclude the same.

When the dream evolves into Roscoe's joining the fat man race it allows his subconscious to combine his escape from the hospital with his ability to outdo other big men with athletic prowess. His dream perceives him as a hero, this time in an athletic contest.

Fatty does not perceive himself as captured until he is about to wake up, and the attempts of the doctors to awaken him from the operating table translate to their capturing him in the context of his dream.

Arbuckle's presentation of Fatty's dream is interesting in how it translates as coming from his subconscious desires. Being a hero, winning a race, and avoiding pursuit clash with the reality of Alice's instability and being captured upon winning the race. However as he is captured, he awakens from his dream. There was nowhere else for his subconscious to go.

Finally, *Good Night Nurse* paces itself perfectly. It starts out slowly, builds, and concludes with a wild ending that does not relegate itself to merely being a slapstick free-for-all.

While it is one of Arbuckle's best and most fulfilled comedies, *Good Night Nurse* received a negative review from August 1918 issue of *Motion Picture Magazine* and for all the wrong reasons:

> Fatty Arbuckle goes just a little bit too far in this, his latest mirth-producer. *Good Night Nurse* contains many of the elements from which we have long been trying to separate comedies. It borders over much on the vulgar. The parading of a man in a supposedly blood-spattered physicians apron is not at all our idea of a comedy situation.

Perhaps this sort of humor was considered vulgar in some quarters back in 1918, but today it offers an edginess that separates Arbuckle's comedies from that which was merely the standard. The idea of a doctor leaving an operating room with a severed leg and a saw may have been far over the top in 1918, but nearly ninety years later is shows Arbuckle's penchant for experimenting with the sort of comic edginess that Keaton especially endorsed. While noted for frenetic slapstick that sometimes seems to go in several directions at once, Arbuckle had a great deal of artistic discipline when it came to taking these chances, and did so sparingly.

Good Night Nurse was, therefore, the subject of mixed reviews during its time. *Variety* reacted positively, stating:

> At the hospital, a great many familiar bits of slapstick comedy are perpetrated, many of them along new and original lines, but all of them can be classified as surefire laughs.

The New York Times, however, claimed: "Its fun is neither as clever nor as continuous as that of other Arbuckle farces."

This writer has a bit of trouble understanding the contention of the *Times* reviewer in that when compared to the other comedies Arbuckle had been producing, *Good Night Nurse* follows a consistent evolution of Roscoe's filmmaking style. More cohesive, funnier, and better paced than many of the comedies of this period, *Good Night Nurse* has the added element of the dream sequence which is both clever and inspired.

Fortunately, many period critics were quite positive in their reaction to *Good Night Nurse*, *The New York Morning Telegraph* reported:

> *Good Night Nurse* is one of the best comedies in which Mr. Arbuckle has been seen in some time. The production deserves the warmest praise from start to finish.

The *San Francisco Bulletin* raved:

> There is no more popular comedian in the movies today than Fatty Arbuckle. His new comedy vehicle, *Good Night Nurse*, is diametrically opposite from anything he has yet done, and to say that it is one wherein the comedy element reigns would be almost as unnecessary as shipping coal to Newcastle.

Louis Reeves Harrison in *The Moving Picture World* stated:

> There are plenty of laughs all through *Good Night Nurse*, not so much at the farcical incidents as at Arbuckle's characterization. Really an acrobat of great natural strength, in spite of his rotundity, a born comedian as well, the mere contrast of his physique with the role of a sanitarium patient evokes laughter and his antics do the rest.
>
> The story is naturally funny, one of the few of its kind, and it will prove a welcome relief to those which labor hard without a spark of real humor in them. A winner.

Keaton fans may be less interested in that Buster does not have as much to do here as he had in *Moonshine* or *The Bell Boy*, but his doctor with the blood-spattered smock makes a discernible impact. His performance, while limited in footage, is still wonderful, especially his reaction to the flirtations of Fatty in drag. Alice Lake's wild performance as the asylum patient is perhaps her best thus far, giving her ample opportunity to cut loose in a most uninhibited manner. Alice Lake was not afraid to cut loose, and is too often limited by the confines of her roles as the heroine or the ingenue. Here she is another one of the funny people, and her natural comic gifts are wonderfully on display. Alice is rarely given this much of an opportunity to exhibit her own comic prowess, and she rises to the occasion here. She is quite irresistible.

All of the disparate elements of *Good Night Nurse*, from slapstick to parody to dream-induced surrealism, manage to play with an even tempo throughout, gradually building and concluding satisfactorily. Its ideas are amusing and, to some extent, profound. Its performances are first rate on each level. Its structure is steady and sound.

Good Night Nurse is one of many comedies set in a hospital. Even a much later film such as Paddy Chayefsky's wry and challenging *The Hospital* (Arthur Hiller, 1971) can consider this Arbuckle film something of an influence. Presenting patients with improper care, doctors with blood splattered smocks, and the general pandemonium that belies its advertising, the sanitarium in *Good Night Nurse* was satirizing the very essence of health care that the Oscar winning script for the 1971 film visited from an equally challenging perspective. While the later film has a far more serious message, there are surface elements that can be found in *Good Night Nurse* (e.g. the crazy patient played by Diana Rigg in that 1971 feature is not far from Alice Lake's portrayal in this 1918 silent two reeler).

Good Night Nurse is such an exceptional two reel comedy on so many levels. It has structure, imagination, it takes chances, and allows for Roscoe to portray Fatty as a wealthy married man rather than a boyish bucolic innocent. Perhaps what is overall most impressive about *Good Night Nurse* is how it clearly displays the level to which Roscoe Arbuckle has evolved as a comedian and filmmaker. It remains one of the finest two reelers in the entire Comique series.

13

The Cook

Directed by Roscoe "Fatty" Arbuckle
Written by Roscoe "Fatty" Arbuckle
Produced by Joseph M. Schenck
Cinematography by George Peters
Film Editing by Herbert Warren

Cast
Roscoe "Fatty" Arbuckle
Buster Keaton
Al St. John
Alice Lake

Filmed at the Comique Film Corporation studios, Alamitos and Sixth streets in Long Beach, California
Released by the Comique Film Corporation for Paramount Pictures on September 15, 1918
Distributed by Paramount Pictures, Famous Players-Lasky.
Running Time: Two Reels
Black and White—Silent

    Arbuckle enjoyed doing food preparation routines, and included them in several of his films, as far back as his Keystone work. Flipping knives in the air which land point down on the counter, tossing food into the air and catching it in a pan behind his back, dexterously adding necessary ingredients and then tossing the entire dish to a nearby waiter, all of these were stock bits that Roscoe enjoyed doing, and were always amusing and impressive. It seemed only natural that he would make a two reeler with a title like *The Cook*.

That is how Roscoe worked. He would create a title, a character, a premise, or a setting, and from that point derive gags and situations. He had taught Buster Keaton a great deal about camera setups, editing, and performing gags for the camera. Buster himself observed more about the technical aspects of filmmaking. So Keaton's comments and suggestions during the course of the filming assisted Arbuckle's vision greatly, especially by the time they made *The Cook*.

Also by this time, Roscoe Arbuckle's popularity was enormous. While Charlie Chaplin was popular beyond standard measure, Arbuckle's films came in at a close second.

For years when examining Chaplin's tremendous impact on cinema, we are reminded how his popularity was at such a level that all theater owners had to put on their marquees was a picture of Chaplin and the announcement, "He's here today." Such a thing had not been said about Arbuckle. However note the copy on this Paramount-issued full-page trade ad from 1918:

Hey Fatty!
Are you human? Folks are beginning to believe you're not.
They don't believe any *human* being could turn out, month after month, such uproarious laughs as you do.
And every bundle bigger and better.
Is there no bottom to your laugh mine?
How do you do it? Are you a wizard? Or are you just a genius?
Whatever it is, keep at it. You have the public with you so strong that every time a theater advertises "Fatty's here today" the whole town is there too.

It was a case of truth in advertising. The only difference between the Arbuckle and Chaplin films is that Chaplin's were embraced by the intelligentsia quite early, even when they were still using the same slapstick that was proclaimed as vulgar when presented in the Arbuckle films. There was a discernible element of cleverness even in the crudest of Chaplin's Keystone productions that set him apart and promised greater things as time went on.

But critics occasionally tended to overlook the real cleverness that appeared in every Arbuckle comedy. His continuing to use knockabout slapstick was an effort to stay true to his audience, Roscoe having stated that he was interested in appealing to "the masses and the

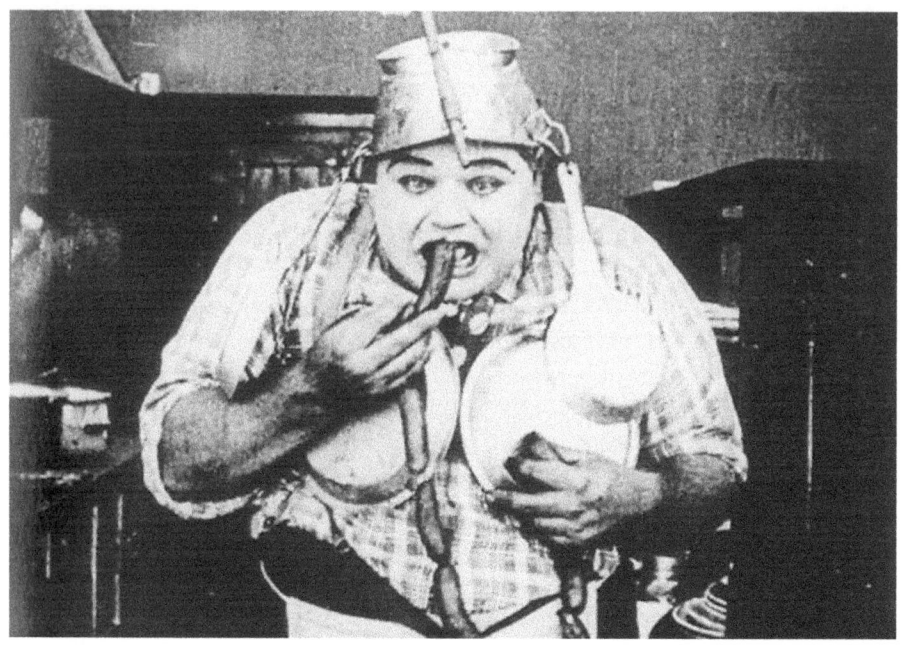

Arbuckle in the title role of *The Cook* (courtesy Milestone Film and Video).

classes." Arbuckle was secure in his success, and had a real affection for his fans. He did not want to let them down.

However his mind was very active, and he couldn't ignore his more innovative ideas. While maintaining his knockabout slapstick roots over most of his productions, Arbuckle was not above experimenting with more challenging ideas. *Fatty and Mabel Adrift* and *He Did and He Didn't* during his most productive period at Keystone were harbingers for such daring Comique productions as *Moonshine* and *Good Night Nurse*.

Arbuckle's popularity was so strong at the time of *The Cook* that a decision was made to capitalize on this popularity by rereleasing several of his older Keystone films with new titles. Many of these were distributed through W.H. Productions, and lasted well into the 1920s. Apparently when Mack Sennett formed the Triangle corporation in 1915, the films he had already produced were part of the package. Triangle president Harry Aitken sold these negatives to W. H. Productions, a company that had been re-releasing old William S. Hart films.

This has led some to believe W.H. stands for William Hart, but Hart had no part of this company. W.H. Productions would retitle the older Keystones and issue the films as new. Some Keystones were released under so many different titles, it can be quite daunting for a researcher to document them.

This practice of releasing older films was, at this time, out of the ordinary, and theater owners soon had customers with long memories complaining about having seen these retitled films years before. This practice was being done with Chaplin's earlier films as well, including those he made at Keystone and the subsequent two reelers Charlie produced for Essanay. The latter studio, in fact, took some unreleased discarded Chaplin footage from their vault, shot a few new scenes with actors currently on their lot, and released what they advertised as a new Chaplin film, *Triple Trouble*, in 1918, a full three years after Charlie had left the studio (he had already made his twelve classic films for Mutual and was now producing through First National Pictures). Chaplin eventually included a signed authentication in the ads for every new film he released, and it was presented in newspaper ads for his latest films.

With Arbuckle, it was the Keystones that were made available. The procedure was to retitle the one and two year old films so that exhibitors with long memories for titles would be fooled into booking the shorts as new releases. Since Keystone had both Chaplin and Arbuckle on the lot at one time, films of either actor were re-released. In 1918 Arbuckle's 1914 comedy *The Knockout* in which Chaplin did a small cameo was re-released to theaters. Retitled *The Pugilist*, the re-release ads gave Chaplin and Arbuckle billing above the title, with Chaplin's name listed first, and with larger print, despite his appearance being nothing more than a cameo that occurred towards the end of the movie.

This caused both Paramount and Arbuckle to balk. Publicity from Paramount featured a letter to exhibitors and theater owners written and signed by Roscoe Arbuckle which stated:

Dear Mr. Exhibitor,

The Cook is my latest comedy. It is a travesty on life at the beach and in a beach cafe. I am supported by my usual excellent cast, and Luke the funny dog you will remember in my earlier Paramount releases. I am giving you my best efforts. So take this tip. If you book my comedies released by Paramount for return dates you will undoubtedly do more business than by playing cheap reissues of worn out comedies featuring my name.

Be far-sighted! All comedies made by myself before my contract with Paramount are two years old. They are out of date and not qualified to amuse modern theatergoers because of this fact.

Your patrons are wise. You will find that they will much prefer a return date of one of my [Paramount releases] than a reissue of an ancient comedy camouflaged by a new title.

Think it over! My tip means better business.

Be just to your patrons and yourself. Book only Arbuckle-Paramount comedies.

It is perhaps a bit presumptuous on the part of the author to claim that Arbuckle may have been embarrassed by his Keystone films in that his current releases for Paramount offered more refinement and greater structure as well as so many extraordinary ideas from a technological perspective, partly as a result of Keaton's creative contribution. It could simply be a case of Paramount not wanting their contracted star to compete with his older product, realizing the Arbuckle name would draw patrons, and cruder comedy might indicate that Arbuckle had not advanced as an actor or filmmaker, thus causing box office receipts to falter. In any case, the publicity warning exhibitors against booking older (and maybe less expensive) Arbuckle comedies did not stop the distributors engaged in this practice, who had the legal right to re-release their own films as often as they chose, with whatever billing or new titles. At one point the Federal Trade Commission inquired as to this practice, but W.H. Productions argued that since they had replaced all the main titles and intertitles on these films, they were now new releases. The result was that W.H. Productions had to thereafter display the original Keystone title along with their new retitle.

The Cook is one of the better Arbuckle comedies, and one of the most typical. As with *Good Night Nurse*, *The Cook* derives its humor from its setting. The setting, a restaurant, is a very familiar one for Arbuckle, harking back to another of his finest Keystones, *The Waiter's Ball*. And in essaying the title role, Arbuckle allows himself to engage in his penchant for the food preparation bits of business that are always welcome and delightful.

The Cook begins at the Bull Pup Cafe where Fatty is the chef and

13. The Cook

Buster is the waiter. Along with meals, the establishment provides a floor show featuring an exotic dancer. Tough guy Al St. John enters and starts annoying cashier Alice Lake in his inimitable fashion. Both Buster and Fatty come to her defense, assisted by Luke the dog, who puts the bite on Al quite literally.

Arbuckle's graceful, amusing performance in *The Cook* is one of his best from the Comique series. Using his Sennett-produced short *The Waiter's Ball* as an obvious inspiration, Roscoe once again puts his Fatty character through a series of food preparation bits. Fatty playfully flips pancakes and catches them behind his back, tosses the knife in the air allowing it to twirl rapidly and land point down onto the wooden counter, uses a large cleaver to slice small pieces of meat, and makes pancakes by placing dough onto a chair, a plate over the dough, and pressing down on the plate with his foot.

When waiter Buster comes to pick up an order, Fatty fills a plate and tosses it to Buster, who catches it in his palm, sometimes behind his back, without spilling the contents. This routine was also used in *The Waiter's Ball* with Al St. John in the Keaton role. In either case, what Arbuckle did was film the waiter throwing the contents and run it backwards so it appeared he was catching bowls of soup and glasses of milk as they were heaved across the kitchen by the cook.

During a scene where the workers are on break having lunch, there is a spaghetti eating sequence that allows us the comparison-contrast between Arbuckle and Keaton using their body and objects as improvisational tools. Fatty playfully winds the noodles around his forefinger and daintily places his finger in his mouth. Buster stuffs a large forkful of spaghetti into his mouth and cuts the protruding ends with a scissors. At one point Buster stuffs the noodles into a teacup and mimics a haughty tea-drinking socialite. Fatty winds the spaghetti with an eggbeater, and plays with the knife and fork as knitting needles while the spaghetti represents yarn. When a long string of spaghetti stretches to either side of the long table, Buster and Fatty fold their cloth napkins over it to simulate sheets on a clothesline.

Perhaps the most delightfully uninhibited sequence in *The Cook* features Buster joining an exotic dancer during a floor show, matching her steps with slapstick abandon. Buster gets carried away with his mimicry and dances into the kitchen where Fatty gets caught up in the action while still cooking. Not limiting himself to the dance, Fatty has pots, pans, and utensils hanging about his person to mimic the dancer's exotic attire, including a straining bowl for a hat, pie tins for breastplates, and a dustpan dangling from his belt.

Al St. John enters, billed as "the toughest guy in the world," and immediately chooses hapless waitress Alice Lake, forcing her to dance with him. Keaton tries to intervene by breaking a bottle over Al's head, but the bully is unfazed and merely takes a bite from the broken bottle and chews on the glass. Al is finally defeated when Buster lets Luke the dog loose. The canine makes a beeline for Al and chases him from the restaurant.

The film shifts gears during the last half of the second reel. Fatty has a day off, which he chooses to spend fishing. At a nearby amusement park, Alice is being pursued again by Al, who is himself pursued by Luke. The existing footage does not include the conclusion, so the restoration released on DVD by Image Entertainment from Milestone Film and Video presents a title card taken from the original press kit which reads:

> While the pest waiter is rescuing his girl with the aid of the cook, the courageous Luke dives into the ocean after the tough guy, chasing him so far out into the ocean that he can't swim back to shore. It is fitting that after all this action, everything ends happily.

The Cook, like many of the Arbuckle films of this period, was lost until the end of the twentieth century when a print was discovered and restored by Milestone Film and Video, and released to VHS and DVD. According to Milestone Film and Video:

> *The Cook* was discovered in 1998 among a cache of unidentified nitrate prints at the Norsk Filminstitut. Then in 2002, film archivist John Gartenberg informed Milestone that the Nederlands Filmmuseum staff had identified additional footage.

Milestone Film and Video combined the discovered footage into a restoration that approximated the original U.S. release. The restoration was superb, and in the DVD's special features Milestone offers the footage from the Nederlands Filmmuseum and that which came from the Norsk Filminstitut. It is fascinating to see what one print included and the other did not. The Netherlands print is far more fragmented, and the Norwegian one more complete. But the scene where Fatty puts the straining bowl on his head while mimicking the exotic dancer is missing from the Norsk print and is included in the one from the Netherlands. The rest of the dance is missing from the

Netherlands print, and does appear in the Norsk one. Between the two prints from the two institutions, a reasonably complete two reeler was restored with its original tints. It is this sort of tireless preservation of our cinematic heritage that allows us to appreciate an important film like *The Cook*. While *The Cook* is filled with many hilarious moments, at least one member of the Arbuckle unit was dissatisfied. In interviews, Alice Lake complained to *Photoplay* that she felt Roscoe was just fine in the film, but "I was terrible in it."

Alice is cast in another ingenue role with little to do. She has no opportunity to cut loose and be funny as she had in *Good Night Nurse*.

Other producers were watching and Alice was getting offers to work elsewhere. She began to seriously consider expanding her horizons.

The Cook is also notable in that it is Keaton's last screen appearance before entering the armed forces. Keaton had enlisted in the service some time ago when his future was not so solid as it turned out to be by the time he was shooting *The Cook*. He was called for duty, and during his hitch Arbuckle made several films without his support. Examined in the following chapter, the films Arbuckle made without Buster are something of a series unto themselves. Arbuckle was certainly capable of working without Keaton's support, as he had successfully relied on his own ideas for many years. But if one compares his Comique productions sans Keaton, it can be discerned that Keaton's influence had at least some impact on Arbuckle's work. From the existing examples, Arbuckle's comedy consistently maintained the same disparate elements that elevated them from standard slapstick romps. Part of this is simply due to Arbuckle's growth as a comedian and filmmaker. However Buster Keaton's idea to incorporate a deeper, more intelligent sense to the comedy can especially be found in the brilliant two reeler *Love* and is evident in the existing information we have on *The Sheriff*.

Casting was less consistent by this time. Al St. John was still available for supporting roles, and funny though he is, he could not provide the sort of creative inspiration Arbuckle received from Keaton. Alice Lake was still in the unit, but was in only some of the next few films, concentrating more on offers she was receiving to star in prestigious features at major studios.

This point in Arbuckle's career could be considered another transition. For the past two years he had produced eleven successful two reel comedies, each one significant in and of itself. His comedy had developed considerably, and while some of the material he had done at Keystone was modified and refined, much of it was jettisoned for newer, more progressive ideas. Exhibiting a real growth as a comedian and filmmaker (Keaton would later indicate that Arbuckle was considered one of the finest comedy directors of his time), Arbuckle chose to maintain his approach while Keaton was away.

While working in these eleven films Keaton began making something of a name for himself. The Arbuckle two reelers were so popular, it would be impossible for Keaton to not be noticed by audiences and critics. Other studios were noticing as well, and when word got out that Buster was about to do a stretch in the armed forces, many studio executives checked off on their calendars as to when this member of the Roscoe Arbuckle stock company would complete his service and be available for offers.

The bigger studios were noticing Alice Lake as well, and offers were sent to her inquiring as to her interest in doing drama and sophisticated comedy rather than the slapstick in which she had been engaged for the past several years. Alice admitted that while she loved Roscoe and the company, she was beginning to tire of doing slapstick comedy. She considered some of the offers from Metro and Fox.

With Buster entering the army and Alice Lake looking to move on, Roscoe had to find a way to fill the void left by their absence. He couldn't simply hire an actor, although those were plentiful. Arbuckle needed someone who could handle the demands of physical comedy, something that is not often considered as to its difficulty. Even as late as the 1990s, Jerry Lewis told this author in an interview:

> When I did the Martin Scorsese drama *King of Comedy* the critics all raved. Suddenly I am called a great actor! I had been acting for forty years by that time, and suddenly I am a great actor! But critics never noticed physical comedy. I never broke a sweat doing *King of Comedy* but I can show you scenes from *The Bellboy* where I had to shower and change after just rehearsing. You can't do what Chaplin did, or Laurel, or Keaton, or Arbuckle without being a great actor.

14

Roscoe Without Buster

This period in which Arbuckle made several films without Keaton is a particularly interesting one and a good checkpoint for assessment. Keaton began his stretch in the army after completing *The Cook* and would not return for eleven months. During the time he was overseas, Arbuckle's films were created without Keaton's notable suggestions and ideas. Arbuckle's own capabilities were the reason for the success of these two reelers, but Buster's influence over the past several films had a discernible impact.

These films can be considered a transition. Arbuckle's work up to this point had evolved, had included a variety of ideas, experiments, and styles, and achieved a distinguished level of success and popularity. Keaton's role had grown, and his input had been significant. With him gone, Arbuckle continued to be inspired by what he had gained from Keaton on previous productions, while at the same time he was forced to rely completely on his own substantial creativity.

When Buster Keaton went into the army and Alice Lake left for a job at Metro around the same time, Arbuckle had to somehow fill the void. Al St. John remained, and his part was sometimes bolstered in Buster's absence. Some new girls were tried, including Betty Compson and Winifred Westover, but Roscoe had already worked with a few different ladies in his Comique comedies. He needed someone consistent and dependable, as Alice Lake had been.

Arbuckle appeared to finally settle on Molly Malone by the time he made *The Bank Clerk*, which was released April 5, 1919. She remained active with the unit after Keaton returned, and appeared as the lead girl in all of the Comique shorts from *The Bank Clerk* to the very last Arbuckle-Keaton collaboration, *The Garage*, which was released in early 1920 just before Keaton took over the department upon Arbuckle's move to feature length productions.

Molly was actually several years older than Alice, already past 30 when she joined the Arbuckle company, and only a year younger than Roscoe. However she had a cute, youthful appearance with some superficial similarities to Alice Lake, and fit in competently.

This text primarily examines those films Arbuckle and Keaton made together in an effort to examine Roscoe at his best and Buster during the genesis of his film career. However since Keaton did return to the unit upon completing his stretch in the armed forces, and was still technically a part of the unit, the writer believes it is essential to give some attention to those films Arbuckle made during Keaton's absence.

What is interesting about the Arbuckle Comique productions sans Keaton is Roscoe's continuing to use more experimental ideas with satire and parody As stated at the outset of this chapter, Keaton was not around to offer ideas and suggestions, so we can be sure that such films as *Love*, *The Sheriff*, and *Camping Out* are of Arbuckle's creation. Arbuckle aficionados point to these films as proof that it was Arbuckle's vision and brilliance that was the real key to his Comique successes. However they also still realize that the evolution of Arbuckle's work here, and the clever ideas found in his films without Buster, were a result of his having been influenced by Keaton to try new and different things with screen comedy and not concentrate so completely on the wild knockabout slapstick for which he had become known.

It should be noted that not all of the Arbuckle Comiques without Keaton are available at the time of this writing. *Love* and *Camping Out* have been restored, but *The Sheriff*, *The Pullman Porter*, and *The Bank Clerk* remain lost. This is terribly frustrating for researchers attempting to assess Arbuckle's short comedies, in that another interesting period in the Comique series is not complete. Just as a clearer look at the entire series of Arbuckle-Keaton collaborations was necessary to fully appreciate its significance to film history, examining each film during this period without Keaton is essential to understanding the extent to which Arbuckle chose to utilize his creative

Arbuckle buys a tent from a one-legged salesman (Al St. John) in the recently restored *Camping Out* (courtesy Cole Johnson/SLAP-STICK archive).

prowess during the time Keaton was overseas. It is maybe even more frustrating than the spate of lost films made during Roscoe's strongest period at Keystone in 1916, the period that gave us *Fatty and Mabel Adrift*, *The Waiter's Ball* and *He Did and He Didn't*.

Arbuckle aficionados will cite the recent restoration of *Love* as a significant example of this being a particularly strong period during Roscoe's Comique tenure, despite the absence of Keaton. *Love* is an extremely funny, incredibly clever short that presents some of Arbuckle's best gags within the context of a very standard plot. It is certainly one of Arbuckle's finest films from any point in his career. It also has a visual brilliance that owed at least something to Arbuckle's having been influenced by Buster Keaton's own vision. Roscoe and Buster socialized off the set, playing practical jokes and enjoying an off screen friendship. But they also spent some time discussing comedy and filmmaking ideas. Buster learned a tremendous amount from Roscoe's experience, which he always acknowledged. Roscoe learned a great deal from Buster about cinema's possibilities. Even in Keaton's absence, a film like *Love* shows that Arbuckle continued to be willing to explore.

Of the missing films from this period, *The Sheriff* sounds the most intriguing. While it is frustrating that any of the films from this period in the Comique series are missing, it is especially disheartening that one that sounds so intriguing as *The Sheriff* is lost.

Judging by the reviews and press materials available, apparently Arbuckle builds upon the parody offered in *Moonshine* and does a more direct western satire than *Out West* had been, specifically targeting his friend Douglas Fairbanks, who was the top action star of the era.

The review of *The Sheriff* for the November 23, 1918, issue of *Motion Picture News* noticed the parody. They also noticed the lack of Arbuckle's characteristic knockabout slapstick:

> This picture proves that, no matter how old situations may be, if handled intelligently, taking into consideration the gradual although unconscious development of taste, they can always be depended upon to make an entertaining picture.
>
> *The Sheriff* is a far better attraction than anything contributed by Mr. Arbuckle on the Paramount program. For one thing, it is free from vulgarity and sloppiness. The classic kick shines with its absence. For another, comedy though it is, the situations have been developed logically, producing maximum fun out of minimum action. Every move in it counts.
>
> The hero of the story is a sheriff, who, having often seen Douglas Fairbanks in pictures saving the heroine at the risk of his life, aspires to emulate him. At his last opportunity comes when the village schoolma'am is abducted by "Bad Men."
>
> [Luke] the dog may be justly classed as a star in his own right. His entry into the lonely cabin by digging below the wall in order to save the heroine is a feat that will win sympathy and a good round of applause.

A review at the same time in *Moving Picture World* also made reference to another star who they believed was being parodied:

> Roscoe may not be as handsome as William S. Hart nor as lithe and svelte-like as Doug Fairbanks, but when it comes to doing stunts he is

more than willing to take chances with either or both of them. In his latest picture, *The Sheriff*, he shows that his confidence in himself is founded on something more substantial than conceit. Trick riding, steeple climbing, headlong dives out of windows, pistol play, hotfooting it down the pike, lovemaking—nothing is too swift or too daring for the heavyweight comedian.

The story, written by Roscoe, is a frank admission of the yearning ambition that has been eating at his heart in secret. He has longed to emulate the deeds of the two Apollos of the screen and fill a new movie hero. His love scenes with a Mexican belle are models of fervent passion, and it is not his fault if any of the spectators choose to laugh at him. Later on he transfers his affections to a pretty schoolma'am and rescues her from a band of bad men with all the dash and bravery of his rivals, if not with all their grace....

"A willing intelligent dog who answers to the name of Luke [does] his best to fill Buster Keaton's place.... Al St. John is as useful as ever.

The arguably more prestigious magazine *Motion Picture* and its critic Hazel Simpson Taylor appeared to be less impressed with *The Sheriff* and, for that matter, with Arbuckle:

Roscoe "Fatty" Arbuckle's latest farce.... While it has a number of interesting and ingenious incidents, it fails to hold together as a play and falls short in real humor. When the story (?) beings to lag, they resort to that reliable old never-fail expedient of pie throwing, and every few minutes we are given, without any apparent reason a change of scene with an entirely new set of characters. In other words, there is no semblance to a plot or story—merely a conglomeration of incidents weakly joined together, as all of Arbuckle's plays are, and it makes us wonder why he does not try one with a real story running through it. There are those who, doubtless, will get some hearty laughs out of this picture, but the majority will look on it as merely amusing, rather than uproariously funny. Certainly it is amusing and certainly it is ingenious in places, and even clever. The dog is easily the star in this play...."

Along with mentioning Luke, each review also mentions an African American child appearing in the short. The author has no verification, but this could be Ernest Morrison, Jr., whose father is listed in some sources as appearing with Arbuckle in *Out West* and who would also work with the likes of Paul Parrott and Harold Lloyd at the Hal Roach studios. As Sunshine Sammy, the Our Gang series would be built around him and run for decades, and he would also be a member of The East Side Kids. The African American man in

Out West is said in some reference sources to be Ernest Morrison, Sr., Sunshine Sammy's father, but even this is unconfirmed. There is no mention of *The Sheriff* in Sunshine Sammy's credits, nor is there any record of his having discussed it in later interviews (he does refer to generally some silent comedies in which he appeared, without specifying, so it remains a possibility). Since at the time of this writing there is no print of *The Sheriff* available for screening, it cannot be verified which youngster the reviews are referring to.

It is particularly unsettling how each of these reviews refers to the young actor with offensive descriptions of the times. *Motion Picture News* called him "the little colored boy." *Motion Picture World* stated, "A little darkey who supports the name of Snowball." *Motion Picture* referred to the young actor as "a little pickaninny."

It is interesting that *Motion Picture World* makes note of Buster Keaton's absence, indicating that the African American child actor and Luke the dog "do their best to fill" the void he has left. Commenting on the usefulness of Al St. John's support is also commendable.

It is also interesting that while two of the reviews are impressed with the parody and the paring down of old style slapstick, the more prestigious (and pretentious?) *Motion Picture* makes note of pie throwing and appears confused by Arbuckle's experimental methods, stating, "every few minutes we are given, without any apparent reason, a change of scene with an entirely new set of characters" and adding, "there is no semblance to a plot or story...."

Without having *The Sheriff* to assess, we can only assume that while Arbuckle's boorish knockabout was considered low comedy to highbrow critics, his clever ideas could conceivably confuse them as to their reason and execution (this passage in the review may very well be referring to a dream sequence in which Fatty imagines himself a hero like Fairbanks).

Critics whose tastes were open minded enough to appreciate the style of comedy Arbuckle was known for doing had a more positive outlook on *The Sheriff*. One even stated, "The most amazing thing ... was the downright frankness with which [Arbuckle] impersonated [Fairbanks]. It was the most apparent piece of imitation ever seen on stage or screen, and that is why it proves one of Arbuckle's greatest mirth provokers. He is a perfect artist in burlesque." But the best compliment Roscoe received was from his good friend Douglas Fairbanks, who proclaimed him to be better than the original.

It is also rather curious that one reviewer makes note of there being less knockabout slapstick in *The Sheriff*, while another believes there to be too much. The different perspectives of the reviewers cannot be determined, of course, without screening the elusive film.

Another Arbuckle film from this period, *Camping Out*, had been lost for decades until reel one was discovered as recently as the year 2002 by Elif Rongen-Kaynakci of the Nederlands Filmmuseum. Reel two was reportedly discovered by Cristina D'Osualdo from the Cineteca del Friuli in the Cineteca Nazionale vaults in Rome. The Nederlands Filmmuseum agreed to do the restoration, so the reel from Italy was sent to them. It arrived in January 2003.

According to Ms. Rongen-Kaynakci in an issue of *Slapstick* (no. 8, 2003): "The print reached us in January, 2003; I viewed it and saw that their one reel was not reel two, but an early abridged version of the film."

Ms. Rongen-Kaynakci further explained that just around the same time, the Nederlands Filmmuseum was going through the inventory of a huge nitrate donation. Among the cans, they found reel two of *Camping Out*.

> I watched and compared everything. Now, although our print seemed to be complete (it was 2 reels), it was astonishing to see that the Italian print had additional material, because some gags were shortened, etc. Also, the scenes were in different order.

According to film restorer Simona Monizza in a note sent to the author:

> The reconstruction of *Camping Out* is a good example of joint forces between the archives, involving in this case, the Nederlands Filmmuseum and the Cineteca di Roma. As nitrate holdings of this film were found in both archives, a comparison of the material was the first necessary step to further determine what kind of approach to take. Once the decision was taken to restore the film at the Nederlands Filmmuseum we asked the Cineteca di Roma to have access to their nitrate fragment which corresponded to the Italian version of the film. As it turned out during the comparison, the Dutch nitrate and the Italian one differed a lot in terms of length, image quality, and in some places also in editing. The Italian material showed a fragmentary nature and was probably abridged to one reel, while the Filmmuseum's nitrate corresponded more to the plot description as found in an old censorship card. Only at this point we decided to reconstruct the Dutch version as

it was the most complete of the two, retaining, therefore, the Dutch intertitles, and completing it with missing sections from the Italian material. In some places, where our nitrate was suffering from severe deterioration, we were able to substitute those damaged parts with sections from the Italian nitrate. The original nitrate tints were preserved using the Desmet Colour Duplication Process.

The importance of this period in Arbuckle's series of Comique two reelers continues to be made clearer with the discovery of more efforts from when Keaton was overseas in the army. While *Camping Out* currently stands out as an important recent discovery and restoration that is extremely significant in our understanding and appreciation of Arbuckle's work, it does not appear to have been well received upon its initial release.

Motion Picture was even less impressed with *Camping Out* than it had been with *The Sheriff*. In their April 1919 issue they stated:

> Roscoe Arbuckle's latest is no better nor worse than his previous releases and not much different in character. He is the same Fatty whatever he plays. It will amuse and entertain many thousands and disgust many of them. Not many will go to sleep when *Camping Out* is on, for it is a continuous performance of funny incidents, mostly of the slapstick order. Unfortunately, there is a sameness to all of his pictures, and he never misses a chance to get in a vulgar or suggestive touch. If it is not a surgeon who has just performed an operation appearing with his white clothes smeared with blood, or a man trying to get in a woman's bedroom or peeping into her bathhouse or too conspicuously displayed human forms divine, or mistaking rank cheese for his socks, and so on it is an exhibition of vomiting from seasickness as in *Camping Out*. It is quite possible and probable that many people enjoy these and other similar vulgarities and I suppose the more refined patrons of the photodrama must endure them for the sake of the others. At any rate, no one will accuse Mr. Arbuckle of elevating the film art. Again, there is no accounting for taste. While I personally seldom get a laugh out of the Arbuckle comedies, and am always stirred hilariously by everything that Charlie Chaplin does, some people are affected quite the opposite, because I hear considerable laughter in every theater where Arbuckle is showing. While there are many clever and ingenious devices and incidents in all of the Arbuckle farces, I would say that while Chaplin is a genius, Arbuckle is merely a clown.

It is interesting that this critic used the review of *Camping Out* as an opportunity to dismiss Arbuckle's popular slapstick in favor of the more refined work of Chaplin, who had completed his Mutual series and was now at First National and appearing in films like *A Dog's Life* and *Shoulder Arms*, both of which remain among the finest silent comedies of their time. However to dismiss Arbuckle's more accessible audience-pleasing slapstick is to exert at least some level of snobbery, especially when the review says less about *Camping Out* than it does about the reviewer's disdain for Arbuckle. Details in the review offer gags the reviewer found unsatisfactory in other Arbuckle films (references to gags from *Coney Island*, *Good Night Nurse*, and *Oh Doctor!* are used to present what the critic considers Arbuckle's base vulgarity). The reviewer does admit to the positive audience reaction by stating, "I hear considerable laughter in every theater where Arbuckle is showing," but does not appear to realize that such a response would indicate that the reviewer who fails to find amusement is the one with the problem.

In fairness to the critic for *Motion Picture*, the more open minded reviewer for *The Moving Picture World* wasn't terribly impressed with *Camping Out* either, stating in their April 1919 issue:

> It is the story of a man who runs away from his wife's bad cooking to camp out on Catalina Island and do his own. Probably the most amusing part is devoted to Arbuckle's culinary exploits, getting a wooden-legged man to punch the holes in doughnuts. For the most part it is the same old slapstick of throwing messy things at one person, only to have them hit another, and the like. Arbuckle is an acrobat and a fine actor, but he seems to overlook the best part of his own interesting personality, that which always sets an audience laughing, the pure humor of his mental revelations. Then again, he gives himself very little true opportunity in such patchwork of incident as *Camping Out*, merely a lot of incongruous movements sewed together without general design. Like most director-actors, he cannot get the effect of what he is doing before the camera, and loses accordingly.
>
> This is not to say that *Camping Out* is not amusing, but it ranks far below other vehicles for Fatty's laughable psychology. He is largely in evidence every moment, and therefore not sufficiently in contrast with other characters to enforce the fun in his own. He does not need this prominence—it would be accorded him without solicitation on is part, and he is so rarely good in comedy of human nature that he ought to give more time to the quality of his medium and less to directing the presentation. He will get more than one laugh in *Camping Out*, but not near so many as he received in farces more naturally funny.

Of course these period reviews are interesting as historical checkpoints, but are not indicative of audience response nor can they represent current assessments of the same film. A noteworthy example is The Marx Brothers' 1933 feature *Duck Soup*, which is considered today to be their best film, but was dismissed at the time of its initial release as too frenetic. Audiences responded poorly, and reviewers had strong misgivings. After withstanding the test of time, *Duck Soup* has emerged as one of the most superb political satires in American cinema. The comedy team of Stan Laurel and Oliver Hardy was adored by moviegoers, but critics were often unimpressed, even with films that are today considered among their greatest. *Camping Out*, therefore, cannot be accurately judged by its period reviews, despite their offering an interesting perspective.

Because it has withstood the test of time as an important film from an area of Arbuckle's Comique period that benefits from deeper exploration, *Camping Out* is quite an important discovery today. The careful restoration by the Nederlands Filmmuseum not only presents to us an Arbuckle Comique from the period where Keaton was overseas, it allows us to see a movie that some reviewers, at the time, felt was flawed. This is an extremely important restoration for comedy film scholarship. It should also be noted that Alice Lake is listed as appearing in *Camping Out*, which means she did not leave the unit until at least a few films after Buster had gone overseas.

Film historian and preservationist Paul E. Gierucki was instrumental in the restoration of *Love*, for his Laughsmith DVD release of an Arbuckle anthology, *The Forgotten Films of Roscoe "Fatty" Arbuckle*. The film was restored from the only surviving elements, which were foreign release versions provided by The Danish Film Institute and La Cineteca Del Friuli. Each of these prints complemented each other, the same situation as had happened with the restoration of *The Cook* released on DVD by Milestone Film and Video through Image Entertainment. *The Cook* featured two versions found, one fragmented and one nearly complete, in the Netherlands and Norway. The missing footage in one was found in the other, although the final few moments remained missing. The restoration of *Love* appears to have been similar.

Paul Gierucki explained in his notes for the DVD release:

> Each of the two surviving elements contained the exact fragments that were missing from the other.... I truly believe that this reconstruction is as close to what Arbuckle had originally intended as we will ever

be able to get—that is, until someone locates a vintage American release print or negative.

Not only was the pictorial quality exceptional, but *Love* emerged as one of Arbuckle's most fascinating, funniest films. While its plotline involving Fatty and Al fighting over a rural girl is awfully standard, the short is filled with some of the comedian's funniest gags.

The New York Times review upon the original release of *Love* on March 2, 1919, agrees with this assessment, stating: "The comedy at the Strand, and also the Rialto, is *Love* with Fatty Arbuckle and his company of broad comedians. It is funny, uproariously funny in places."

The most fascinating thing about *Love* is how it continues to explore the amazing possibilities offered by the film medium, something that seemed to pique Keaton's interest perhaps even more so than it did Arbuckle's. A film like *Love* shows how far Roscoe had come from his Keystone roots as both a comedian and a filmmaker. Part of it has something to do with Keaton being so great an inspiration. Much of it had to do with Arbuckle's own comic prowess and cleverness as a filmmaker.

During this period, Arbuckle also appeared in at least two fundraisers, which were completed just after *The Sheriff* and just prior to World War I's armistice. According to Robert Young, Jr., in *Roscoe "Fatty" Arbuckle: A Bio-Bibliography* (Greenwood Press 1994):

> Arbuckle joined a phalanx of his contemporaries in appearing in these two short films aimed at encouraging the purchase of United States and Canadian war bonds. These were produced by Famous Players-Lasky Corporation, and released in November. Appearing in them as well as Arbuckle were Douglas Fairbanks, Mary Pickford, Wallace Reid, Lillian Gish, George M. Cohan, Mabel Normand, Alice Brady, Sessue Hayakawa, and William S. Hart.

The October 5, 1918, issue of *Moving Picture World* offered the following synopsis for the one reeler *Fatty Arbuckle in a Liberty Loan Appeal*:

> Fatty calls at the palace in Berlin and refused to be "raused" by the guards. Entering he confronts the Kaiser and the "Clown Quince," asks about their treatment of Belgium, and shows them "scraps of paper" from America (Liberty Bonds) which completely cow them. They attempt to escape, but are barred by the Italian, English, French,

and American armies. Fatty introduces "the boys you send were afraid to fight" rising from the midst of the scraps of paper (Fourth Liberty Loan Bonds) which make a snowstorm. The huns plead for mercy.

If more films from this period were available for screening, we would have a clearer and more complete understanding as to this being a good stopping point to assess Arbuckle's Comique output. With Buster's exit after *The Cook* and his return for *Back Stage*, this spate of films made while he was overseas serving his country are especially intriguing in the context of the Comique series. From the more raucous, yet wildly funny and comically inventive early Comique productions like *The Butcher Boy* and *The Round Up*, Arbuckle took advantage of the complete creative control this series afforded and experimented with visual ideas that specifically related to cinema. Accounts always cite Arbuckle as being more interested in raucous gags and wild slapstick, with the headier cinematic touches mere seasoning. Keaton felt that deeper exploration into the purely cinematic possibilities was a more interesting focus. During this transition period when Buster was away, we see how Arbuckle was inspired by Keaton to look beyond gags, but this is not to state that Arbuckle did not have ideas in this area himself. Buster's inspiration was likely from the perspective of giving Roscoe permission to tap into that area of his own creativity. Arbuckle had an interest in the bizarre, the surreal, even the macabre aspects of comedy. Keaton, the cinema newcomer, was eager to try offbeat ideas. Arbuckle, the veteran, was more careful not to possibly alienate his established audience. Keaton's daring and eagerness was enough to inspire Roscoe to try some ideas that could be considered offbeat.

Both Arbuckle and Keaton had an interest in cinematic opportunities, with Buster being far more technological (it is interesting that these ideas were said to culminate with Keaton's later starring feature *Sherlock, Jr.* which Roscoe was initially slated to direct). At this point in the Comique series, Buster had comfortably established himself as a budding comedian and filmmaker with aspirations that surpassed those of Al St. John. In his absence while overseas, Arbuckle exercised his creative control to not only engage in the familiar, popular slapstick, but to also delve into creative areas that he previously had held in check until Keaton's ideas helped to inspire and facilitate Roscoe's own.

Camping Out appears to be a more standard slapstick, *The Sheriff* seems to offer the same sort of parody as the offbeat Keaton-inspired *Moonshine*, and *Love* features some of Arbuckle's most ingenious presentations of comedy and uses of the film medium. This eleven month period without Keaton is essential in the filmography of Roscoe Arbuckle as a comedian and filmmaker, showing how he had evolved from his Keystone-to-Comique transition, how he felt more and more comfortable with experimentation, and how Keaton's ideas served as an inspiration, enhancing Roscoe's own creative vision in areas outside of general slapstick.

As the teens rolled towards the twenties, there were many very funny people making movies, but there were only two geniuses starring in them: Charlie Chaplin and Roscoe Arbuckle. Both were masters of comedy and of cinema. Both had evolved from Keystone knockabout into filmmakers of substance and insight. Both enjoyed full creative control over their work. Each would soon graduate to feature length pictures by the decade's end.

However despite his skill as a director, Arbuckle did not have the same artful presentation as did Chaplin. And while Arbuckle's parodies certainly rivaled Chaplin's *Burlesque on Carmen* (if we judge it by the recently restored two-reel version as per Chaplin's intention, and not the padded four reeler that was constructed by Essanay without his approval, after he had left the studio), and his Fatty character was arguably as beloved as the Little Tramp, Roscoe still appeared to have some concern about straying too far from his Keystone roots. Uninhibited knockabout slapstick violence was still very much Arbuckle's stock in trade, and there were many critics and moviegoers who, perhaps snobbishly, felt such unmotivated slapstick to be beneath them. Arbuckle likely had been paying attention to Chaplin's films, just as he had been paying attention to Keaton's suggestions. These inspirations permeated Arbuckle's own inimitable style to the point where he had reached a real peak and was ready to venture further. Soon the studio heads would agree.

A very popular star throughout the teens, 1919 was a banner year for Arbuckle, as we will observe with his final three short comedies and subsequent move to feature pictures. Thus, the eleven month period without Keaton is a good checkpoint in assessing Arbuckle's work as a comedian and filmmaker.

Along with being very important to Arbuckle, 1919 was also

a very important year for Keaton whose eleven month stretch in the army ended with him being swamped with high paying offers from a variety of major studios. Loyal to a fault, Buster returned to the Arbuckle unit at his same salary. It was a decision he did not regret.

15

Back Stage

Directed by Roscoe "Fatty" Arbuckle
Written by Roscoe "Fatty" Arbuckle and Jean Havez
Produced by Joseph M. Schenck
Cinematography by Elgin Lessley
Film Editing by Herbert Warren

Cast
Roscoe "Fatty" Arbuckle
Buster Keaton
Molly Malone
John Coogan
Al St. John

Filmed at the Comique Film Corporation studios, 1723 Allesandro Street in Edendale, California
Released by the Comique Film Corporation for Paramount Pictures on September 7, 1919
Distributed by Paramount Pictures, Famous Players-Lasky.
Running Time: Two Reels
Black and White—Silent

Back Stage marks Buster Keaton's return to the Arbuckle fold after eleven months overseas in the armed forces. As discussed in the previous chapter, Arbuckle naturally continued his series in Keaton's absence, but unfortunately many of the films from this immediate period are lost. Those that do survive, especially the remarkable *Love,* present us with an Arbuckle Comique sans Keaton that contains a number of wonderful comic ideas.

Keaton's contribution in the Arbuckle films up to and including *The Cook* did not go unnoticed by other studios. Upon returning from overseas, lucrative offers came from other production companies, proving that people in important positions were taking notice of Keaton's work in support of Arbuckle.

Jack Warner of Warner Brothers studios and William Fox of Fox Studios each offered Keaton a contract to do his own films at $1000 per week. He was promised by each studio the same type of creative control as Arbuckle had with Paramount. He would be given his own unit, be allowed to write, direct, and star in the films with final say over the finished product, and could choose his own supporting players.

The concept of his own Buster Keaton comedy series was quite daunting. And the offers were very attractive. One would imagine Keaton would at least consider these offers, but Keaton turned them both down. There was no consideration on his part at all, not for the extra money or the increased control. Arbuckle gave him his start, so he was headed directly back to the Comique unit for $250 per week. Loyalty meant a great deal to Buster, who believed he owed Roscoe everything as far as any film success was concerned. He did not believe himself quite ready to be moving on.

Back Stage is another Arbuckle comedy that makes use of its setting and stems from a premise set within those parameters. The theater, more specifically the stage, where Arbuckle, Keaton, and most of their support had started, seemed like a most appropriate setting for a two reel comedy. The possibilities of stages and studios as a backdrop for slapstick had some comic tradition. Chaplin himself used the theater setting for his 1914 Keystone comedy *The Property Man* and revisited it with his 1916 Mutual production *Behind the Screen*. As late as 1963, Jerry Lewis used the various trappings of a studio as a setting for slapstick ideas in *The Errand Boy*.

Acting that is about acting allows performers to stretch, to become more outrageous, to reach beyond boundaries. A good actor can play a bad actor, just as a comedian can make himself funny and endearing simply by being unable to cope in an imperfect world. Most of *Back Stage* takes advantage of the slapstick possibilities inherent in being a stagehand, dealing with props, sets, tools, etc. The film's con-

15. Back Stage

clusion, other than its slapstick finale, allows for Fatty and company to put on an impromptu stage show for a full audience, where each of them takes advantage of displaying amusing histrionics without the necessity for subtlety or any abbreviation.

Back Stage opens with Fatty as the stage carpenter at an opera house located in a small country town. Buster is his assistant. They are preparing for the performance of an acting troupe that includes a swishy eccentric dancer (John Coogan, a newcomer to the series), and pretty Molly Malone, a backstage assistant with a desire to perform.

While eavesdropping on a rehearsal, Fatty becomes annoyed with the way the head of the troupe, a strong man, is treating Molly. He bullies her about, forcing the long suffering performer's assistant to wait on him, which includes carrying over his 300 pound weights. Fatty and Buster get even by wiring up electricity to the strong man's barbell, offering him quite a shocking experience. Unhappy with the conditions of the theater, and their treatment by Fatty and Buster, the acting troupe quits.

Stuck for a show, Fatty, Buster, and a grateful Molly decide to put something together themselves. Showtime arrives and the house is packed with an eager audience. Fatty plays a Roman gladiator with Buster in drag as his queen. Molly plays a vamp who tempts Fatty. The audience applauds happily, but the strong man enters the front row of the balcony and starts a fight. When he pulls out a pistol and shoots Molly on stage, a frightened audience flees, so Buster swings up to the balcony with an onstage trapeze, wraps his legs around the bully, and brings him back to the stage area where he, Roscoe and Al subdue him.

Roscoe is then seen visiting Molly who is convalescing in a hospital bed. He pulls out an apple, supposedly a gift for her, but eats it himself as the film fades out.

The above is the actual plot and story of *Back Stage* based on the author's personal screenings of the two reeler. Oddly, a typed description of *Back Stage* at the Library of Congress tells the plot of this film somewhat differently. It indicates Al St. John plays the head of the acting troupe (he does not), states that the troupe sits in the front row during Fatty, Buster, and Molly's performance and pelts them with eggs and vegetables, which also doesn't happen, and that Fatty hurls Al over the balcony rail, which is also false. This may have been based on a rough draft of Jean Havez's story, but it would not likely be just an error. No such scenes exist in the film, and it is impossible to mistake the burly strong man for the skinny, lanky St. John. Of course this writeup also referred to Molly Malone as "Millie."

Short on knockabout and long on the more imaginative and skillful visual gags with which Roscoe had been experimenting since his days at Keystone, *Back Stage* is filled with interesting concepts.

As Fatty is pasting up a poster advertising the night's show, he is continually thwarted by a curious lad who keeps standing in his way. To alleviate the problem he pastes the child up on the wall while he prepares the poster. When he opens a sliding door, enough of the poster is obstructed so that it appears to state: Miss Skinny Will Undress Here. A passerby sees this ad and hurries to purchase a ticket for the night's performance.

John Coogan does his eccentric rubber-legged dance during a rehearsal. This was a bit for which Coogan became known on the vaudeville circuit, and his limber gyrations are impressive and amusing. However Arbuckle knew better than to merely spotlight Coogan's act. It had to be punctuated with something of his own. So, Arbuckle features Coogan's dance bit, and then presents himself, as Fatty, enthralled with the act. When Fatty becomes so caught up he tries to mimic the dancer's movements, his own outrageous gyrations, especially by comparison, are quite amusing. Roscoe often performed dance routines of this sort in his films, realizing a man of his bulk being so limber and dancing with such abandon would be an amusing visual experience for the moviegoers. Here his dancing is punctuated by presenting the Coogan act first, so that we have a comparison-contrast which serves to make Fatty's dancing that much funnier. At the same time, Coogan's vaudeville dance act is preserved on film, and not overshadowed by Fatty's punctuating it with his own bit of terpsichore.

Diminutive Molly's strength is established by showing her assisting the strong man with his heavy weights. After Buster and Fatty have subdued the strong man by wiring electric shock devices to his weights, a large barbell ends up on poor Buster's neck. Fatty works hard to extricate his friend from underneath the weight, pulling on his legs and twisting his head, but is not successful. Molly comes along and easily lifts the weight from the trapped Buster, then carries it away with one hand, as Fatty looks on incredulously.

15. Back Stage

The stage show that Fatty, Buster, and Molly put together features a lot of campy fun. While some of it directly parodies specific sequences from other notable shows, it is essentially a basic attempt at melodrama that comes off funny due to the cast's over-the-top histrionics.

Molly more or less plays it straight as the stage ingenue, but the highlight features Buster in drag dancing regally and provocatively as unlikely gladiator Fatty's queen, making good use of each actor's skills for physical comedy without relying on pure knockabout slapstick. This sequence is said to have been lifted almost verbatim from an act Buster did to entertain the troops during his army stretch.

In a more modern sequence, stage hand Al hangs in the rafters above Buster and Fatty on stage, dropping confetti from a large sack to simulate snow. The effect is successful until Al loses his balance and huge mounds of confetti crash onto the two actors and fill the stage.

The film's slapstick conclusion is typical, with a melee where right triumphs. However despite the ordinariness of its execution, this sort of slapstick finale drew laughs, cheers, and applause in movie houses across the country.

There has been a great deal of discussion in this text regarding Arbuckle's massive popularity with moviegoers. Arbuckle's success by the time of *Back Stage* was to the point where this two reel comedy played alone at some theaters, and not merely accompanying a feature length film. Even in those cases where there was an accompanying feature, *Back Stage* received top billing in advertisements. Ads for *Back Stage* in many newspapers across the country were large and inviting, with big print and a cartoon of Arbuckle, as if the film were a feature length production. No other cast members were listed. Only one other comedian of this era could headline his own movie showing with a two reel short subject, and that would, of course, be Charlie Chaplin.

As he defied the level of popularity usually afforded comedians limited to short films, Arbuckle also defied the stereotype as per an article in the *New York Sun*. Its reporter, Mary B. Mullett, observed during an interview session with Roscoe:

"After [Arbuckle] sat down he achieved the apparently impossible by crossing one leg over the other knee. And every time he got up and sat down he did it again. Each time I saw the performance beginning I secretly bet with myself that he couldn't make it but I always lost.

It was an acrobatic triumph. But it was also a sidelight on his character. For if there is one thing Roscoe Arbuckle has made up his mind about it is that he won't be the ordinary fat man. He won't sit like a fat man. He won't dress like a fat man.

When he is out of the movies he looks like a modern *Beau Brummel* under a magnifying glass. He has fifteen pairs of shoes. But he sighed again as he declared he works so hard he never has time to wear them.

His clothes are always immaculate. It sounds as if he gave a lot of thought to his personal appearance. And he does. But it is for just one reason.

There's nothing in the world so repulsive," he said, "as a fat man who isn't well dressed."

An article on Arbuckle in the *Literary Digest* stated:

A popular saying has it that nobody loves a fat man, but an older adage declares there is an exception to every rule. In this case, Roscoe Arbuckle is the exception. His elephantine form and jolly grin appear on the billboards at every movie between New York and Frisco.

While it is decidedly more typical than such innovative efforts as *Moonshine* or *Good Night Nurse*, *Back Stage* is a very funny two reeler with some especially fine moments. While Keaton and Arbuckle are somewhat of a team as the two stagehands, they are not working at the same co-starring level as they had in *The Bell Boy* or *Moonshine*. Keaton is the supporting player, although he does enjoy a good share of the footage, especially during the impromptu show that he, Fatty, and Molly perform. Despite his being away from films for nearly a year, Keaton is still able to take advantage of the freedom Arbuckle has allowed him the same way Roscoe enjoyed the advantages of complete creative control. Keaton could not realize he was only another year away from taking over the unit completely, as Roscoe made the prestigious move to Paramount produced feature length pictures that allowed him to be more an actor than a comedian, tapping into areas this series didn't explore.

While there have been many examples of Keaton's unique talents in the Arbuckle comedies, *Back Stage* offers some solid examples of just what Buster was capable of doing when left alone to spotlight, such as his appearing to walk down a flight of stairs only to reveal, after a prop door is removed, that he is bending his knees on a flat surface. These little bits of comic magic would appear frequently when Keaton began producing his own films a year later.

15. Back Stage

Fatty appears in a bit that Buster was to use at least twice more. When a prop wall tips over onto an unsuspecting Fatty, it lands with the open window going over him. This amazing sight gag can be found in Buster's first solo short *One Week* and his later feature *Steamboat Bill, Jr.* Since we have long attributed this gag to Buster, due to our familiarity with these two films before the accessibility of *Back Stage*, we find that it originates in an Arbuckle comedy, but is still generally considered to have been created by Buster.

Back Stage is also an excellent example of just why this series is so significant in relation to the development of either Keaton or Arbuckle's work. We not only get yet another a good look at early Buster Keaton left to his own ideas, *Back Stage* also offers yet another example of Arbuckle's generosity in allowing the spotlight to shine on someone up and coming in films. Buster would likely not have had this sort of opportunity even if he had opted for a bigger paycheck to star in his own series for one of the bigger studios that had beckoned him upon his release from the army.

Arbuckle's unit worked as an island unto itself, not having to worry about meddlesome producers. Soon Keaton would have that freedom, and it was a freedom he would eventually be forced to trade for the confines of a bigger studio. It would be a disastrous move, one that Buster would reject to no avail, and one that he, thankfully, had not made earlier. His sense of loyalty to Arbuckle paid off in that he might well have faded into unfair oblivion had he chosen to go with Fox or Warner Brothers. He may have made less money with Arbuckle, but a film like *Back Stage* shows that he made the right creative decision. Despite the gaggle of promises both Fox and Warner had made to him, the bigger studios would never be known for leaving a comedian alone. One can point to the films that Stan Laurel and Oliver Hardy made for Fox during the 1940s when their established comic style was unfortunately altered by meddlesome studio interference.

While Keaton is allowed many strong moments in *Back Stage*, Al St. John is given practically nothing to do. He is not a supporting player, but merely one of the nameless faces on the periphery. He has one particularly funny bit during the show when he is positioned above the stage dropping confetti to simulate snow. As described previously, the amount of confetti increases, filling the stage. Fatty is attempting to serenade Molly with his harmonica, but the confetti keeps getting in his mouth. Fatty then tosses aside the harmonica and pulls out a ukulele.

Al also shows up during the slapstick finale, but still remains on the periphery while Fatty, Buster, and the other supporting players become involved. But *Back Stage* gives him perhaps his smallest role, and one in which his acrobatics are not used at all, not even in the finale.

Buster was quite obviously the heir apparent. Even with his stint in the army, Roscoe apparently realized that it was Buster whose talent and insight was the most significant of his stock company. There was no pecking order that Buster was forced to stand behind. Keaton was returned to the forefront with ample footage.

Al St. John was a funny man, and his subsequent solo films that survive allow further evidence of his unique talents. But St. John did not have the creative prowess of Roscoe or Buster. He was a fine performer, not so much a creator. This was Al St. John's final appearance in the Roscoe Arbuckle comedies for Comique. He would later appear in films for Fox (who had wanted to sign Keaton) and Educational Pictures, augmenting his appearance that had been a part of his act since Keystone, and trying something different. He enjoyed commendable success.

But fate had something else in store for Keaton. In just two more films, Buster would be in charge. It would be his series, and he would be allowed the same absolute creative control that Arbuckle had been enjoying. He would take all that he had learned from Arbuckle, as well as the many more daring ideas for which an opportunity had heretofore not been presented, and create some of the most extraordinary comedy films to be produced during the first half of cinema's rich history. The Comique training ground continued to allow Buster Keaton to evolve.

16

The Hayseed

Directed by Roscoe "Fatty" Arbuckle
Written by Roscoe "Fatty" Arbuckle and Jean Havez
Produced by Joseph M. Schenck
Cinematography by Elgin Lessley
Film Editing by Herbert Warren

Cast

Roscoe "Fatty" Arbuckle
Buster Keaton
Molly Malone
John Coogan

Filmed at the Henry Lehrman Studio, formerly the Thomas H. Ince Studios, Washington Blvd., Culver City, California. Released by the Comique Film Corporation for Paramount Pictures on October 26, 1919.
Distributed by Paramount Pictures, Famous Players-Lasky.
Running Time: Two Reels
Black and White—Silent

    This text has made constant mention of Roscoe Arbuckle's evolution as a comedian and filmmaker over the course of his Comique two reelers. With *The Hayseed* coming towards the conclusion of his Comique tenure, we continue to clearly observe his development and his versatility.
    Roscoe Arbuckle's popularity was very strong in rural areas, and

putting Fatty in a rural setting as an affable bumpkin was as effective as casting him as a doctor, a harried husband, a cheerful alcoholic, or a bellboy with hair cutting skill.

Roscoe played the country bumpkin in many of his Keystone efforts, and he developed many of his screen character's consistencies within this guise. The bumpkin he played was essentially a boyish innocent, and it is this ingredient of the discernible human element in Roscoe Arbuckle's screen character that helped to make Fatty so endearing to moviegoers.

While Roscoe cast Fatty in a variety of roles during his Comique period, he tended to revisit the bumpkin character on occasion. *The Hayseed* is the best example from this period in his career of Roscoe using a rural setting. While it uses many elements that had become Arbuckle standards, the context in which they are used is somewhat different. Rather than lace the film with knockabout routines or conclude with a wild slapstick melee, Arbuckle chooses with *The Hayseed* to derive his humor from characters and situations completely. It is one of his most relaxed and most interesting Comique two reelers.

The Hayseed also digs up the oft-used conflict of Fatty and a rival pursuing the same girl. This time, however, it is not Al St. John playing his rival, as it had been so frequently in past films, all the way back to Keystone. Al had moved on, leaving the unit for his own series at Fox.

John Coogan, a limber performer who had been an eccentric dancer in vaudeville, and made a successful appearance in Arbuckle's previous two reeler, *Back Stage*, played Fatty's rival for the attentions of pretty Molly Malone in this rural comedy.

Curiously, there are many sources, including books, and online filmographies from the Internet that indicate Al St. John plays the role. This is an error, as Al is actually not in this two reeler at all. Perhaps there had been tentative plans for Al to play the role, but it is John Coogan as Fatty's rival for Molly's interest. It is worth noting that a 1921 two reeler that Al St. John made for Fox was called *The Hayseed*, but it has nothing to do with this film except for a coincidentally similar title.

In this film Fatty is a letter carrier who delivers the mail by traveling down the town's dirt roads in a horse drawn wagon, tossing the letters as they land perfectly in the mailboxes that are set in rows

16. The Hayseed

along the path. When he comes upon a larger envelope that will not fit in a mail slot, Fatty remedies the situation by ripping the item in pieces and pushing it through successfully.

Fatty is smitten with Molly, a girl on his route, but today delivers mail to her that appears to be a love letter. He nosily inquires, and she angrily tells him to allow her the privacy of opening the envelope and reading the letter herself.

Fatty and Molly's playful romance is presented as very sweet and childlike. His jealous nosiness results in a scolding. Their playfulness ends up with Fatty falling backwards in a tub of water, and soon incorporates a game of hide and seek where Fatty sends Luke to sniff out Molly's whereabouts. However the fun eventually has to end, as Fatty must return to his route.

Molly's mother entrusts Fatty with letter in an envelope that also contains three hundred dollars cash, which is to be used in paying off her mortgage. Immediately upon returning to the drug store, Fatty hands the letter to his boss and tells him to use caution because of the enclosed money. Jack, Fatty's rival for Molly's affections, overhears this and removes the money. Buster, a clerk in the store in which the post office is located, witnesses what has happened and confronts Jack, who beats him up.

Jack uses the money to buy Molly an expensive ring. Fatty buys Molly a cheap mail-order ring, but since it is bigger, she accepts it and refuses Jack's.

Molly's mother discovers her mortgage payment has never reached its destination. The town gossip points to Fatty, especially since he purchased what looks to be an expensive engagement ring. Fatty is confronted at a dance that everyone attends, and is shunned when suspected to be guilty of the theft. Buster explains, Jack is exposed, and Fatty gets the girl. The last time we see Jack he is being chased down the road by a vengeful Luke the dog, a fate that many of Fatty's rivals end up facing.

The exhibitor's press book for *The Hayseed* indicated:

> Fatty Arbuckle, the celebrated comedian in Paramount-Arbuckle comedies, has been seen in numerous diversified roles, but none of his creations excel in interest that of a letter carrier in a rural post office which he assumes in his latest comedy....
>
> Mr. Arbuckle has been provided with an excellent story in this mirth-provoking production, and it affords him opportunities not only

for the display of his talents as a comedian, but all-around acting as well.

There is a genuine sweetness to *The Hayseed* and Fatty comes off as perhaps more endearing than in any of Roscoe's other Comique productions. All of the gags place Fatty in a positive light. He is hard working, romantic, amusingly jealous, innocently playful, and trustworthy enough for Molly's mother to entrust him with a large sum of money. This allows further emphasis on the all important human element that we've often cited as a key ingredient in Arbuckle's (or Chaplin's) success. Fatty as the affable bumpkin allows for these positive qualities to manifest themselves through acts of honesty, affection, friendship, even heroism (although it can be argued that Buster is the real hero here, despite allowing Fatty to take the bows and ultimately get the girl). The moments where Fatty is suddenly accused of pilfering the mortgage money allow for a more amusing pathos than Chaplin might have used in the same situation. Fatty tries to explain but is given the cold shoulder. Finally he rushes open arms to his faithful dog Luke, but even the canine turns his back and scampers off.

It is interesting to compare and contrast the way John Coogan, as rival Jack, plays his role and the way it had been performed by the decidedly more bombastic Al St. John. St. John was the more seasoned film comedian, and his style is more familiar in the context of the Arbuckle two reelers. Thus, it is easy for us to accept St. John's method of presenting this characterization as being the better one. Coogan does not use his face for comedy, does not employ the blatant grimaces that Al uses to define his character. Where St. John is more blatant, Coogan is much more effete, more foppish, more of a dandy. Al's uninhibited chewing of the scenery presented his character as a very unappealing bully. He seems dangerous, almost scary, when in the company of the damsel with whom he and Fatty are both smitten. But the pretentious city bred type that Coogan plays is a good counterpoint to Fatty's affable bumpkin character in the context of a rural comedy. Again, the setting makes a difference as well as the presentation of the characters.

One amusing footnote regarding *The Hayseed* has to do with Charlie Chaplin and the plans he had for his first starring feature, *The Kid* (1920). Chaplin, of course, did costar in the first comedy feature in American film, Mack Sennett's *Tillie's Punctured Romance* (1914), but *The Kid* is the first feature length movie over which he would have full control.

For the title role, Chaplin was interested in acquiring the services of child performer Jackie Coogan, whom he had seen do an act on the vaudeville stage. Some minor investigation revealed a Jack Coogan to be under contract to Roscoe Arbuckle. Chaplin bristled upon hearing the news, but was friendly with Arbuckle, and had been since both were at Keystone some six years earlier. He contacted Roscoe at Comique and asked if he could visit him on the set. Arbuckle happily agreed, and Chaplin's visit to the set of *The Hayseed* was welcomed by Roscoe, his supporting players, and various Comique execs. Chaplin even agreed to appear in a couple of gag publicity photos. He also discovered, to his delight and relief, that it was not Jackie Coogan whom Arbuckle had under contract, but Jackie's father John (or Jack). He and Arbuckle got along quite well, but Chaplin still was concerned about the necessary negotiating that would occur if he wanted to use Jackie's services. Mr. Coogan was delighted that Chaplin wanted to use his son in a prestigious feature picture. Chaplin even allowed Coogan *père* a small role in *The Kid*.

There is a sad footnote to the Coogan story. In 1935, Coogan Sr. was killed in a car crash in which Jackie was a passenger along with young actor Trent "Junior" Durkin. Durkin and Jackie Coogan had appeared together in the original talking screen versions of *Tom Sawyer* and *Huckleberry Finn* (both 1931), while Durkin also enjoyed success in the juvenile delinquent prison drama *Hell's House* (1932). While Jackie survived the car crash, his father and Durkin were both killed. Some years later, Jackie's mother and stepfather squandered the sizable fortune that the elder Jack had saved for his son, and by the time Jackie was 21 years old, there was little more than a pittance for the grown man to claim. This resulted in the Coogan Law, which sets up a necessary trust fund of earnings percentages for all child actors. Jackie, of course, would go on to find success years later as an adult, becoming a household name playing Uncle Fester on the television series *The Addams Family* (1964–1966).

On the set of *The Hayseed*, Chaplin was also introduced to Buster Keaton, and was quite taken aback when in the course of friendly conversation he discovered Buster to be the child he had seen some years before in the Three Keatons vaudeville act. Keaton wanted to discuss filmmaking techniques, and was surprised to discover that Chaplin limited the conversation to pleasantries and said little about his work. Chaplin would figure prominently in Keaton's story some 33 years later when Buster's services would be requested for *Limelight* (1952).

The funniest sequences in *The Hayseed* involve bits of business that stem from Arbuckle's character. He uses a large drill to make extra holes in a slice of swiss cheese as per his customer's request. He measures Molly's ring finger by jamming it into a block of cheese and fitting it with a small pickle. He nervously consumes many onions prior to performing a song at a party, later finding that his breath precludes others from conversing with him. In the end, he tells Molly to also eat some onions so they can kiss. All of this is amusing enough, and still further examples of Arbuckle's employing the human element of his character to propel the comedy.

Buster Keaton is once again relegated to support in *The Hayseed* but it is in a pivotal role that makes a difference to the plot. Despite a few good pratfalls, there isn't a lot for Buster to do in this one. His reaction to being pummeled by an angry Jack is amusing, and he has a neat visual bit where he oils the legs of the horse that pulls Fatty's mail delivery wagon. He also gets to do a brief magic act during a party sequence, just as Coogan gets another opportunity to perform his eccentric dance specialty.

Period reviewers noticed a difference in *The Hayseed* from, say, *Out West*, another rural outdoor comedy. Most reviewers pointed out how Arbuckle had effectively refined his comic style and evolved completely from the more raucous knockabout that may have pleased audiences, but was condescended toward by many critics. Arbuckle always had a real concern for his audiences, and did not want to disappoint them. However he realized through years of experimentation that while his fans did enjoy the wild slapstick, they would also comfortably accept him in something a little more refined, even a bit quirky like the heavily satiric *Moonshine*. Keaton's ideas in this area inspired Arbuckle's own, and the two of them enjoyed the creative challenge of redefining what was considered the norm. When Arbuckle was willing to try an idea that Keaton felt would be fun to attempt, the result was often very inspired.

The Hayseed concerns itself with a very standard setup, one that Arbuckle had used quite often, and most recently in *Love*. Rivals vying for the attention of the same girl in a rural setting was hardly inno-

16. The Hayseed

vative. And casting Fatty as the boyish innocent and his rival as the villain was also standard practice for an Arbuckle two reeler. But wherein Roscoe had earlier settled for the knockabout slapstick for which he had become known, by the time of *Love* and *The Hayseed* he came up with hilarious, creative gags that allowed him to reveal deeper facets of his talent. The comedy does not come in short knockabout spurts. It is longer, more refined, and derives more completely from characters and situations.

Roscoe liked to present Fatty as the boyishly charming innocent whose childlike (not childish) qualities endeared him to his fans, especially children. This endearing character is what separated him from other Keystone comics, and allowed him to advance to a more prestigious studio and greater creative control. The oft-discussed human element set him apart from most of the comedians who still were relying on funny faces and mechanical gags, and was instrumental in the success of his two reelers and his opportunity to find his way into doing feature length pictures.

As *The Hayseed* unfolds, it maintains a quieter, more relaxed pace throughout. It never becomes truly frenetic, even during the fleeting dance bits at the party which include a few customary pratfalls. And the laughs that are obtained from gags concentrate on more the more intuitive nature of the comedy and less on the knockabout. Buster oiling a horse's leg joints, Fatty tossing mail into roadside mailboxes as he rides down the path and Fatty measuring Molly's ring finger by using a block of swiss cheese and a pickle, are among the highlights of *The Hayseed* and stem from character and situations, not isolated gags. Keaton may very well have been instrumental in helping Arbuckle to create some of these.

This pleasant pace works well for Arbuckle, and the gags seem well thought out and fit very comfortably. This more relaxed atmosphere, avoiding the frenetic pace of Arbuckle's more raucous comedies, allows for more in-depth acting on Roscoe's part as well. The character is not merely established as a bumpkin due to costume and setting, and then placed in a series of typically wild, knockabout slapstick gags. The bumpkin here is allowed to offer depth of character through his comedy, whether delivering mail, measuring for a ring, or trying in vain to explain that he is not, in fact, guilty of stealing mortgage money.

Arbuckle was soon to take the step that would allow him even greater prestige than he had been enjoying thus far. The roles he would be playing in feature films would call for him to concentrate completely on his acting skill. While Arbuckle was likely not aware that he'd soon be graduating to acting in more prestigious Paramount features, a film like *The Hayseed* prepared him for the task of concentrating on a character that was not specifically like the Fatty role he had played since joining the Keystone studios some six years before. *The Hayseed* is just one example of Roscoe Arbuckle shifting his focus from frenetic slapstick to comedy driven from character and situation, but it is perhaps the best constructed and most consistent example in that it eschews the old knockabout style almost completely. Even the fadeout of Fatty and Molly kissing is immediately preceded by the cuteness and warmth of Fatty shyly asking Molly to eat some onions so his breath will not be offensive to her.

The Hayseed turned out to be one of Arbuckle's most popular comedies, and not only in rural areas and small towns. The bigger cities also embraced Roscoe's bucolic comedy, respecting its more sophisticated presentation and more relaxed pace.

While much discussion has given attention to Arbuckle's cinematic conservatism, his interest in experimentation limited by his concern that being too offbeat would lose his established audience, *The Hayseed* allows us to point out his diversity. In this relaxed, more intuitive comedy, we see almost none of the Keystone-influenced slapstick.

But this did not signal an absolute change in style. Arbuckle had not effectively weeded out all slapstick knockabout gagging after years of evolving as a comedian and filmmaker. He simply made some choices with *The Hayseed* that resulted in a more relaxed comedy of situations that offered greater depth to the character he played. It was simply a decision by Arbuckle for *The Hayseed* to be a relaxed situation comedy with a rural setting, and he created clever gags that stemmed from this setting and these situations.

However for his very next film, Arbuckle went in the other direction and offered a comedy that was almost completely slapstick gags and did conclude with a wild melee. *The Garage* offered a setting that allowed for good, solid slapstick and that was how Arbuckle paced and filmed that particular two reeler. Arbuckle was now in the lofty position that allowed him to extend his range with each effort, but things were about to change. *The Garage* was to be Arbuckle's final

Comique two reeler before graduating to feature pictures. Perhaps because of his larger role, his greater contribution, or the fact that it was a portent to his taking control of the series with the very next film, *The Garage* has been singled out, more than once, as Buster Keaton's candidate for the best film of the Arbuckle Comique series.

17

The Garage

Directed by Roscoe "Fatty" Arbuckle
Written by Roscoe "Fatty" Arbuckle and Jean Havez
Produced by Joseph M. Schenck
Cinematography by Elgin Lessley
Film Editing by Herbert Warren

Cast
Roscoe "Fatty" Arbuckle
Buster Keaton
Harry McCoy
Daniel Crimmins

Filmed at the Henry Lehrman Studio, formerly the Thomas H. Ince Studios, Washington Blvd., Culver City, California.
Released by the Comique Film Corporation for Paramount Pictures on October 26, 1919.
Distributed by Paramount Pictures, Famous Players-Lasky.
Running Time: Two Reels
Black and White—Silent

Concluding his Comique series, Roscoe Arbuckle had run the gamut in comic styles, had evolved as a comedian and filmmaker, and had challenged the two reeler with a variety of interesting ideas and concepts, many of which were inspired by his collaboration with newcomer Buster Keaton.

As recently as *The Hayseed*, the film immediately previous to

17. The Garage

this, Arbuckle was critically applauded for offering less in the way of knockabout slapstick and concentrating more on thoughtful gags stemming from characters and situations. It is interesting, then, that for his final Comique two reeler, *The Garage*, Arbuckle chose to do another riotous gag-filled slapstick comedy.

There is no real plot to *The Garage*, just a series of sequences, some of which are quite brilliant. Assessing *The Garage* is difficult as it is such a completely visual comedy, with gags outnumbering situations. And, as with much good slapstick, the most creative gags do not translate well to the written word. But to assess a film like *The Garage* an attempt must be made to discuss its gag-filled structure.

The Garage opens with Fatty carefully washing and polishing a customer's car, delighted at the job he has done. Buster, nearby, loses control of an air hose, which sprays into the dirt, and splatters all over the freshly polished auto. Fatty's immediate response is an impulsive reaction: throwing a large wet rag at Buster, knocking him backwards. Buster responds by throwing mud towards Fatty, and dirtying the car even more. Fatty starts crying out of frustration, and heaves a full bucket of water at Buster, knocking him over again. Buster pushes a tire towards Fatty, who leaps over it, causing it to knock their boss into a vat of water.

This opening slapstick set piece sets the tone for the entire film. One bit of slapstick dovetails into the next, and the rigorous, rapidly paced, hilarious physical comedy that ensues causes *The Garage* to move along with a very steady, fast rhythm.

The man who owns the car comes to pick it up. Fatty asks Buster to stall him while he hastily cleans it back up. While Buster desperately tries to keep the customer's attention, Fatty puts the auto on a huge revolving island and sprays it down with a hose.

This piece presents Fatty and Buster as a quintessential screen team: one is helping the other in a scheme that allows them to right a wrong with nobody any the wiser. Buster's attempt to distract the customer are great. When casual conversation runs out, he begins dancing and doing pratfalls in an effort to amuse the confused patron. In an attempt to help, the boss stands on his head.

Jim, a nattily dressed dandy, comes to call on Molly, the tomboyish daughter of the boss. Her suitor is hiding flowers behind his back, while Fatty and Buster work with oil just behind him. The flowers get full of oil behind the dandy's back, which he does not realize as he presents them to Molly. She sticks her face in the flowers, taking a big whiff, and comes up with a face full of oil.

Standing too close to Fatty and Buster, Jim ultimately gets covered with oil. Fatty and Buster only make him dirtier in their attempts to wipe him off, smearing the oil all over his face and clothing. As a result, they decide to hose him down with gasoline, which washes away the oil, and then dry him off on the enormous rotating device used to dry freshly washed cars. As they hose him down, Fatty prepares to innocently light a cigarette while standing in a puddle of gasoline, and is stopped by Buster who jumps on his back and takes the cigarette. While Jim is being dried, he flies off the rotator and smacks into the boss. Fearing his wrath, the dandy hides in Fatty and Buster's bedroom in an attempt to see Molly and apologize for the grease-laden bouquet.

Jim springs a false fire alarm, which effectively gets Fatty, Buster, and their boss out of the garage in search of the fire (it appears the garage doubles as the headquarters of the town's volunteer fire department). When he gets locked in the garage, Jim tries to escape with a blowtorch, but soon the garage itself is on fire. Buster, Fatty, and their boss backtrack and attempt to put out the fire.

Fatty extends a long fire hose onto the street and connects it to a fire hydrant. A streetcar runs over the hose, causing it to leak. To fix the problem, Fatty runs out and sits on the leak, as water comes spewing out.

Jim is trapped in the burning building, so the firefighters stand below with a net. He rears back to jump, when the firemen discover Molly is trapped in the burning building as well. The firemen shift till they are below Molly's window with a net, just as Jim jumps from the window and lands on the ground. In a daze, he wanders off. Molly jumps to safety, bounces from the net, and lands atop a telephone wire. Just then, the lunch whistle blows and the firemen leave poor Molly stranded high above the street on a telephone wire. Fatty and Buster remain behind, climb the phone pole, and attempt to rescue Molly. As she makes her way down to the street, Buster and Fatty become entangled.

Throughout its fast pace *The Garage* has only the most basic situations, and concentrates completely on a series of hilarious gags. That the gags play off one another so effectively is a real testament to Arbuckle's growth as a director. While gag-ridden, *The Garage* still retains a linear pace. The gags are not freeform as they had been in many Keystone ventures. There is a significant structure and pacing, a discernible rhythm that is maintained. *The Garage* is the perfect example of a true laugh-out-loud comedy.

Along with Arbuckle, we see some of Buster's best Comique work here. And whether he is doing a backward pratfall upon being hit with a wet rag, or jumping on Fatty and stopping him from lighting a cigarette while they stand in puddles of gasoline, Keaton maintains his deadpan composure. While he had, up to now, experimented with a variety of facial expressions (smiling, laughing, weeping), Keaton realized that the more serious he looked, the more amusing the gag execution. He maintained the stone face persona for the remainder of his career. *The Garage* was not the first time he used it, but it appears to be where he finally settled on it.

While *The Garage* was well-received by audiences and most critics, there was at least one dissenter in Laurence Reid, one of those critics who appeared to condescend towards Arbuckle's brand of slapstick. In a review for *Motion Picture* in the late fall of 1919, he stated:

> Fatty Arbuckle's newest comedy, *The Garage*, doesn't carry the inspiration in its idea that was found in its immediate forerunner The Hayseed. Where Fatty caught genuine humanity even though it was burlesqued in the previous issue, this time he employs tried and true slapstick methods. And the picture follows too closely on the heels of the other to make its values appreciated, granting that it has any of these in the first place. Fatty belongs in subjects of rural life. He is supreme in delineating the country yokel and in his treatment of the character he has always approached the bulls eye of truth. The genuine clever comedy that which [sic] can exploit life with reasonable genuineness, colored of course with a vein of satire. That is where The Garage is lacking. True it generates a certain amount of humor. But that is to be expected with an Arbuckle piece.
>
> The point is, he is capable of offering us better achievements—achievements which his imitators cannot duplicate. Anyone who poses as a comedian on the screen could appear quite as acceptable as Fatty here. Still he acts the dunce enough to make himself original. You look upon him as the hostler of a garage—the man of all-work. The fun is derived from a pail of water, a hose, a flivver or two, and the mechanics that make these machines fall to pieces—and, of course, a slippery road. The hose is played upon Buster Keaton and likewise upon Fatty. It is slapstick any way you look at it. Playing at three New York theaters

simultaneously, we noticed that the piece roused the risibilities of the spectators to loud and emphatic appreciation. So it must be called a success. The humor is not spontaneous because it is conceived with labor—labor which does not spring forth from any inspiration. The laughter is gained through the employment of practical jokes and stunts, but it is not continuous laughter, at least not in the New York theaters. Some spectators exploded—some will always when a comedian finds his feet have left him.

The reviewer believing Roscoe should stick to rural themed comedies is surprising in that he had already played a number of city-bred family men even as far back as Keystone. And the idea that a gag-oriented two reeler like *The Garage* is a throwback to a lesser style than what Arbuckle had been doing is also incorrect. As stated previously in this chapter, *The Garage* is a very well structured comedy and its reliance on gags asks us to assess the film based on its propensity for presenting this type of slapstick. Critic Laurence Reid sees only, superficially, that *The Garage* is gag-oriented. He does not look at these gags within the context of their structure, and cavalierly dismisses the entire enterprise as not having the same finesse as *The Hayseed*, believing that rural audiences were all that Arbuckle could hope to please, and a bucolic character was his limitation as a performer. It is interesting that Reid indicates "explosions of merriment" from savvy New York audiences in the theaters where *The Garage* was playing in the big apple. These "explosions of merriment" from audiences is what mattered most to Arbuckle, as well as such positive reviews as:

"No picture bearing the Arbuckle brand has ever packed more laughs into two reels of film."—*Moving Picture World*

"There are really about a dozen good belly laughs in the picture. The tricks of a garage with a whirling turntable, the Human Roulette Wheel idea being used, and a breakaway Ford are the funniest things in the picture. A fast moving comedy that will be liked."—*Variety*

"Roused the spectators to loud and emphatic appreciation."—*Motion Picture News*

"More laughs than any other effort of his for weeks."—*Dramatic Mirror*

These review excerpts were used in the publicity ads for *The Garage* which Paramount advertised by stating, "Every New York daily spoke of *The Garage* as one of the funniest pictures ever filmed, when it played four Broadway theaters last week. Exhibitors who have played it are enthusiastic in their reports. And the public will laugh for weeks!"

Buster Keaton cited *The Garage* as his favorite among those films in which he collaborated with Arbuckle. Perhaps he was allowed a greater level of creative input, which would not be a surprise when one considers the inspired gags contained therein. Maybe he had a sentimental attachment to his final film with Arbuckle before he was given control of the series.

It was upon the completion of *The Garage* that Arbuckle was offered a contract with Paramount Pictures to star in his own feature length films. He would not be writing or directing, and would no longer be engaging in wild slapstick cutups. Arbuckle would now be an actor of light comedy, a level to which he had initially aspired to while still working on stage. He would accomplish this dream as a film actor, and his first movie would be the relatively straight western *The Round Up*.

Buster Keaton was put in charge of the Comique unit. He would now be in complete creative control of each film, as writer, director, and star. All of the inspiring ideas with which he had been brimming could finally be put on film. While Roscoe had been indulgent and encouraging, he was still the man in charge. There were still a lot of ideas that Buster had not had the opportunity to try. Now Buster would have the unit all to himself to experiment with his most creative comic ideas and how they could be enhanced with cinema's vast technological opportunities.

18

Arbuckle Thereafter

Shortly after filming *The Garage* Roscoe Arbuckle was promoted to starring in feature length movies for Paramount Pictures. It was a prestigious move that exemplified Arbuckle's major star status. Buster Keaton was signed as the star of the Comique films.

Keaton would now make the $1000 per week that both Jack Warner of Warner Brothers and William Fox of Fox Studios had offered him upon his completing a stretch in the army. He also would enjoy full creative control, 25 percent of the profits from a scheduled eight two reelers per year, and the creative surroundings of Chaplin's old studio on Lillian Way in Hollywood which Joseph Schenck had purchased for the unit. The films would be released through Metro. with no studio heads peeking in and hampering Buster's creativity with suggestions. It was the perfect setup, and the results would alter screen comedy significantly.

Roscoe Arbuckle would rise to the level of the highest paid actors in motion pictures. Along with making $3000 per week doing features, Roscoe would also be making another $1500 from his Comique interests, and 25 percent of Comique's profits.

Unlike Chaplin, however, Arbuckle's feature deal did not include the absolute creative control he had enjoyed with two reelers. Arbuckle was entering features as an actor who would be starring in classier, more sophisticated productions. He would not be making feature versions of his comedies.

Initially it may seem curious that Arbuckle would be graduating to a higher level of prestige in films and yet have somewhat less creative control over his product. But it would appear that even Arbuckle's most impressive two reelers such as *Moonshine and Good Night Nurse* would not translate to feature length, despite their brilliance as short subjects. The human element Arbuckle employed, which has been much discussed here as to its significance, could have allowed for greater substance in features along with the customary slapstick. Were audiences ready for a feature-length picture that featured the sort of satire that *Moonshine* used? Would a top flight studio like Paramount allow that sort of experimentation in their prestigious features?

It is perhaps a bit puzzling that the first feature chosen by Paramount Pictures head Adolph Zukor for Arbuckle was the straight western *The Round Up*. Arbuckle plays a generally straight role, and although his name is above the title, he does not play the lead role. Arbuckle was always very particular about not alienating his original fan base, and this was such a complete departure from the comedy for which he was known, it is a curious development.

But despite Arbuckle's going in a different direction, the prestige of features was a great one, as short films were generally dismissed by the industry. Ellwood Ullman, who scripted or co-scripted many short films, including several featuring The Three Stooges, stated that these efforts were always left off his résumé due to the industry's reaction to working in short subjects. He found it to be an amusing irony that he eventually was best remembered for having worked with the enduring Three Stooges.

The Round Up was released in October of 1920. *Variety* was a bit confused by Arbuckle's appearance in a rather straight feature, stating:

> It is evident that Fatty Arbuckle of the mammoth breeches and slapstick funnies has given away to Roscoe Arbuckle in a regular hero role, serious in personation with but a modicum of comedy for relief as behooves his corpulent build. The change has not been for the better.

Over time, critical reaction has changed little. Janiss Garza on the Internet's All Movie Guide writes:

> For some mysterious reason, producer Adolph Zukor decided to set the slapstick aside for Roscoe "Fatty" Arbuckle's first full-length feature. Instead he cast him in this Western comedy-drama with an emphasis on the drama. In addition, Arbuckle's role of sheriff "Slim" Hoover

was a secondary one in spite of his star billing.... Slim rounds up the U.S. Cavalry and captures the bad guys, ... [but] the final shot shows Arbuckle, alone, saying, "Nobody loves a fat man." Nobody loved this picture, and it was a disappointment to his fans.

However there were some reviews from 1920 that respected Roscoe's doing something new. *Photoplay* stated:

> I don't suppose anyone could possibly take Fatty seriously as a sheriff with notches on his gun, but it is something of a triumph for him that he keeps the faces of the audience straight while he is suggesting the possibility.

One interesting note of trivia: Buster Keaton did stunt work on *The Round Up*, simply as a lark, playing an Indian in one scene. He collected a fee of $7.50, which he framed and kept on the wall of his office as a memento.

While Arbuckle's slapstick fans were unhappy with *The Round Up*, Paramount Pictures head Adolph Zukor was pleased with its box office receipts. It may have been offbeat and a glorified supporting role, but The Round Up succeeded in establishing Roscoe Arbuckle as an actor in features.

Arbuckle's second feature, *The Life of the Party*, was another drama. However now that Roscoe had established himself in features that were nothing like his short comedies, critics and audiences knew what to expect, and *The Life of the Party* was well received. It became accepted that Fatty Arbuckle the slapstick comedian was now Roscoe Arbuckle the serious actor in prestigious feature length pictures. As one of the few surviving Arbuckle features *The Life of the Party* shows Roscoe toning down his mannerisms and enveloping a character with the sort of talent that is natural for comedians, but often overlooked. Even during cinema's earliest days, it was perceived that a comedian could not also be an actor (it is, arguably, the other way around). Only Chaplin seemed to have risen beyond that by the time Arbuckle did the same at this point in his career.

Once Arbuckle was established in features, Paramount put him to work in one project after another, in rapid succession. These were very lucrative both for the studio and for Roscoe, so the films were made in rapid succession.

Following *The Life of the Party*, Roscoe filmed *Brewster's Millions*, *The Dollar a Year Man*, and *The Traveling Salesman*, all of which were shot in 1920. *Gasoline Gus, Crazy to Marry, Leap Year,* and *Freight Prepaid* were all shot in 1921 and still more were planned. While many of these films no longer survive, reports from the era indicate that each released feature was better than the previous one.

Paramount president Jesse Lasky recalled in his 1957 memoirs:

> It would be hard to imagine more strenuous work than making those old-fashioned lightning-paced comedies. I don't know of another star who would have submitted to such extortionate demands on his energy. But Fatty Arbuckle wasn't one to grumble. There were no temperamental displays in his repertoire. He went through the triple assignment like a whirling dervish, in his top form. They were the funniest pictures he ever made.

Unfortunately, as indicated, few of Arbuckle's features survive, and those few that do are not immediately accessible to review. The most accessible one, *Leap Year,* gives us a good example of a successful Roscoe Arbuckle feature after his tenure in knockabout comedies had ended.

In *Leap Year,* Arbuckle plays Stanley, whose girlfriend, Phyllis, is the nurse for Stanley's gout ridden uncle. The uncle tells Phyllis that Stanley falls for every woman he meets, and must stay out of trouble. Stanley is committed to Phyllis, however, and feels that she is the one that will forever keep him uninterested in another.

On a trip to Catalina Island, Stanley is approached by several women, since he is wealthy and eligible. His response to these women is often misunderstood, because Stanley has a stuttering problem when he is nervous. When a woman with whom he is chatting misconstrues his conversation to mean a proposal, Stanley stutters too much to explain, and suddenly runs away with his golf clubs under one arm and his caddy under another.

This type of misunderstanding, and the stuttering result, continues to occur until there are three women who believe themselves to be Stanley's fiancée. Stanley tries to get out of this mess by pretending to be subject to fits, but this just brings out the Florence Nightingale instinct from each of the women. He tries to then pretend he has a disease that is highly contagious, which results in each of the women resolving to be his nurse. Phyllis, a real nurse and the real girlfriend, arrives just as this mess is happening.

While all is resolved in the end, *Leap Year* is a delightful feature that taps into less explored areas of Roscoe Arbuckle's talent. Roscoe would often put the Fatty character in embarrassing situations, and while Roscoe was no longer playing Fatty and did not direct this feature (it was directed by James Cruze), he was certainly adept at playing the role. Stanley is a good natured fellow, like Fatty, but unlike Fatty he is a man of means whose behavior can result in the sort of scandal he cannot afford. Stanley has the same boyish innocence as Fatty, but it is played without the wild, knockabout slapstick. By this time, however, Arbuckle had established himself in features with a new audience of eager moviegoers. This more mature, more subtle approach may not be as exciting in the same fashion as a slapstick two reeler, but it is certainly, in its quaintness, a very pleasant, enjoyable feature.

Lasky's contention that Arbuckle's last few pictures are the funniest he ever made can be taken into consideration. Leap Year is indeed a very funny movie, and perhaps had we not been so familiar with the Fatty of Keystone, we would not approach it with the preconceived idea of how the humor should be presented (in that this is the only feature many Arbuckle fans have seen and been able to assess). Examining the film with Roscoe Arbuckle as an actor in a lighter comedy, one can marvel at his performance with the same passion as any of his most creative Comique two reelers.

However despite the success and prestige of feature films, the Comiques remain Arbuckle's best work. While *Leap Year* is certainly an interesting film, and can be considered a great one, it does not tap into the extent of Roscoe Arbuckle's creative talents nearly as much as any of the Comique comedies had. As stated previously, Roscoe did not direct his features, nor did he write them. He did not have the same creative control as he'd enjoyed when making two reelers. Had he been able to continue with feature films, there may have been greater opportunities for Arbuckle to venture behind the camera.

While we have little by which to judge, Arbuckle's creativity manifested itself so completely and on so many levels in his Comique comedies, it seems likely that even particularly well received features like *Gasoline Gus* and *Crazy to Marry*, which *Variety* called "one of the funniest jazbo slapstick affairs ever conceived," would be at the same creative level.

But Arbuckle the actor had moved on, and was achieving the same sort of popularity with his feature pictures as he had enjoyed with his two reel comedies. The critics were taking notice as well.

Motion Picture World stated, when *Brewster's Millions* was released on January 28, 1921:

> Roscoe Arbuckle, erstwhile Fatty, now a full fledged comedian, while bound to please by sheer force of personality, works a little too hard in *Brewster's Millions* to be at his best. It is not at all necessary for him to interpolate any of the horseplay of the farce in order to win pure comedy. His expressive face is far more effective than his physical agility, and he need not fear to give larger development to other characterizations he plays, if only for the sake of variety.

While Roscoe had certainly worked hard to allow his character to evolve into a subtler approach, it appears by the review of Brewster's Millions that his overplayed comic expressions from Keystone were still in some evidence. These features certainly prove Arbuckle to be a fine actor, one with depth and versatility. But it can be argued that the Comique comedies showed that quite effectively already.

Leap Year was never released in the United States due to a scandal that upset Arbuckle's life and career in the fall of 1921. This scandal is, sadly, what Arbuckle is best known for today. Often if he is known at all, it is for having been accused of raping and murdering actress Virginia Rappe. It is perhaps not completely necessary to recount every lurid detail surrounding the case, but it is unfortunately essential to discuss some of the information and how it affected Arbuckle's later career.

Exhausted after filming several features, Roscoe believed himself well in need of a vacation after the completion of *Freight Prepaid*. He had completed seven feature films in eight months time and was eager to spend some time relaxing away from the studio. Buster Keaton, himself taking a break from filming, invited Roscoe to spend the weekend on his rented yacht and go to Catalina Island. Roscoe turned down the invitation as he already had made plans to go to San Francisco.

There was a party in Roscoe's room on Monday, September 5. One of the attendees was Virginia Rappe, an actress who had crossed paths with Roscoe at Keystone some years before. At some point during the party, Virginia was found on the bathroom floor. Roscoe went in and shut the door. A few minutes later, they ended up in the bedroom where Virginia fell asleep, Roscoe changed clothes, and went back out to join the party. Virginia's moans from the bedroom were audible, so Roscoe returned to the room to find Virginia lying on the floor in pain. She was taken back to her own room. After a few days, her condition not improving, Virginia was taken to Wakefield Sanitorium. She died on Friday, September 9. Joan Myers, who has researched the life and work of Virginia Rappe, told the author:

> Virginia died of peritonitis caused by a ruptured bladder. From what I can tell, Virginia was no unsullied rose, but she was also no worse than any other young woman who had to make her own way in the 20s. And she did better than a lot of those women, and she did it on her own without much help from anyone. Normally people refer to Virginia as a "starlet" (and we all know what that means), but in fact, she had a quite successful career as a model, and had begun a career as a clothing designer when she came to Hollywood.

Conflicting stories abound as to what had happened to Virginia Rappe at Arbuckle's party. Some believe that when he found her slumped on the bathroom floor, he took her to his bedroom to sleep, believing she was simply intoxicated. Others believe he raped her, and the force of his 300 pounds on her 100 pounds caused the injury that led to her death. Some say that Virginia was a woman of loose morals and she died of a botched abortion. There were people who believed Roscoe innocent, and those who thought him guilty.

Actress Gloria Swanson called him a "fat, vulgar, coarse man." Henry Lehrman, who was Virginia's fiancé, stated, "Arbuckle is the result of too much ignorance and too much money. There are some people who are a disgrace to the film business."

In her book *Love, Laughter and Tears*, Adele Rogers St. Johns recalled:

> Miss Rappe had been living only a few blocks from me in Hollywood. The day after Fatty had been indicted on the testimony of several girls and Virginia's own deathbed statements, the man who did my cleaning came and told me, "I did Virginia's cleaning. I see where one side says she was a sweet young girl and Mr. Arbuckle dragged her into the bedroom, the other witnesses say she began screaming and tearing off her clothes. Once I went in her house to hang up some clothing and the first thing I knew she's torn off her dress and was running outdoors yelling 'Save me, a man attacked me.' There I was standing in the kitchen with my hands still full of hangers with her clothes on them and she was running out hollering I tried to attack her. The neighbors told me whenever she got a few drinks she did that. I hated to lose a

good customer, but I thought it was too dangerous so I never went back."

This was also not the first time Arbuckle was in trouble. Even back when he was appearing in the Comique series, according to Gerald Mast in his book *A Short History of the Movies* (Bobbs-Merrill, 1971):

> In July, newspapers reported a mysterious Arbuckle party in Massachusetts that had taken place in 1917. The mysterious detail was that the District Attorney of a Massachusetts county received a $100,000 gift just after the party. The public wondered what the District Attorney had discovered that was worth such a sum to keep quiet.

Arbuckle was accused of murder, and even before the case went to trial, the newspapers, especially the Hearst press, printed damning accounts that shocked and stunned the public. No longer the boyish innocent of the movies in the eyes of the public, Roscoe Arbuckle was now the "coarse, vulgar man" whom Gloria Swanson described. He went from one of the most beloved actors in movies to one of the

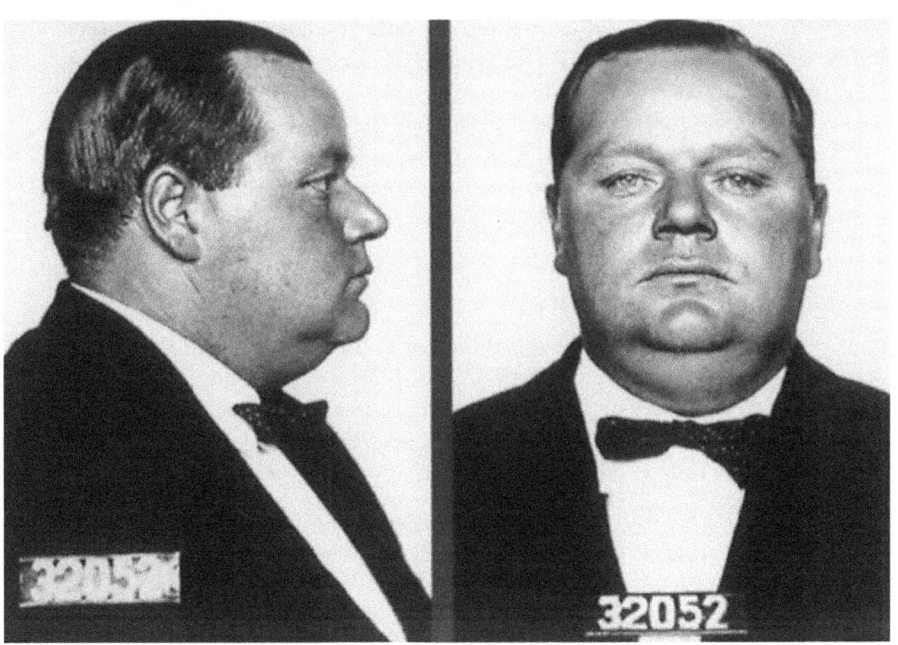

Roscoe Arbuckle's mug shot.

most hated men in America. His films were withdrawn from distribution (not everywhere, however—in many parts of Europe they continued to break box office records and were very well received).

Buster Keaton wanted to immediately run to his friend's support, but was barred by the studio from doing so, fearing negative publicity would hamper his success. Keaton was more about loyalty than success, believing he owed his career to Arbuckle, but the studio did not allow him to testify. Charlie Chaplin, in London at the time, dismissed the charges as being impossible for Roscoe to have done. Mack Sennett also proclaimed his support for Arbuckle in the nation's press.

The three trials were sensational, with Arbuckle eventually acquitted by a hung jury. The jury deliberated for only one minute, and spent another five preparing a statement that was read in court by the jury foreman:

> Acquittal is not enough for Roscoe Arbuckle. We feel that a great injustice has been done him. We feel also that it was only our plain duty to give him this exoneration. There was not the slightest proof adduced to connect him in any way with the commission of a crime. He was manly throughout the case and told a straightforward story on the witness stand, which we all believed. The happening at the hotel was an unfortunate affair for which Arbuckle, so the evidence shows, was in no way responsible.
>
> We wish him success and hope that the American people will take the judgment of fourteen men and women who have sat listening for thirty-one days to the evidence that Roscoe Arbuckle is entirely innocent and free from all blame.

Not everyone, however, agreed with the jury. Gloria Swanson stated in her autobiography:

> We knew Charlie [Chaplin] had girls, teenaged girls, all the time. But none of Charlie's girls ever died. Maybe three trials couldn't prove that Arbuckle was guilty, but nobody in town ever thought he was all that innocent. I know Arbuckle was acquitted, and I know that Al Capone's only crime was tax evasion.

Arbuckle didn't care about naysayers. He was found not guilty in a court of law. He wanted to return to work and put this sordid mess behind him.

But in the early 1920s, the American public was not as quick to forgive. The press indicted Arbuckle during the trial, and the verdict subsequently fell on deaf ears. It was generally determined that

Arbuckle's films would no longer be welcomed by the majority of moviegoers. Censorship czar Will Hays stated that Arbuckle deserved "a change to redeem himself," and authorized the release of Roscoe's withheld films. But if we look at the film *Leap Year*, with Arbuckle playing a stammering innocent pursued by women for his wealth, perhaps another perspective would have hampered the film as a result of the trial. Film and theater critic Walter Kerr agreed, pointing out the "back flips into boudoirs" that occurred during the sequences where the character was pretending to have fits.

Arbuckle took a trip to Europe to separate himself from the American moviegoers that disowned him. Europeans had no such reservations, and the trip was a huge success. He caught up with his friend and supporter Charlie Chaplin in London. In France he placed a wreath at the tomb of the unknown soldier.

There were a few successful stage bookings in America. In Milwaukee, Wisconsin, he was very well received, and in Chicago the front row was taken by gangster Al Capone, a longtime fan of Roscoe's who kept a framed picture of the comedian on the wall of his office. But often there were protesters, and frequently Arbuckle would be replaced on the bill when theater owners would cave under pressure from special interest groups. Roscoe continued to have the ability to spot new young talent. Bob Hope recalls Arbuckle championing his work during one of Hope's early vaudeville gigs.

But he could no longer appear in front of the movie cameras in his own country, nor could he enjoy domestic box office on his completed films. He received jobs directing films throughout the 1920s, under the pseudonym William Goodrich, featuring such performers as Lupino Lane, Poodles Hanneford, Johnny Arthur, and nephew Al St. John, who had been enjoying starring series for Fox and Educational Pictures since leaving Comique. Some of these films were credited to St. John as writer-director, but it was really Roscoe at the helm.

Some of the elusive Arbuckle-directed shorts were restored for inclusion on the Laughsmith DVD collection *The Forgotten Films of Roscoe "Fatty" Arbuckle*.

Keaton had Roscoe directing his feature *Sherlock, Jr.* (1924), until creative differences caused him to realize that it was not the best arena for Roscoe's talents. Keaton persuaded William Randolph Hearst to hire Arbuckle to direct Marion Davies in *The Red Mill*. Hearst agreed, which is ironic in that it was the Hearst press that was most instrumental in indicting Arbuckle before his trial had concluded. Hearst once stated that the Arbuckle scandal sold more papers than the sinking of the *Lusitania*. *The Red Mill* was made through Hearst's Cosmopolitan Pictures and distributed through Metro-Goldwyn-Mayer. Arbuckle directed, but was watched closely by another director, King Vidor, at Hearst's insistence.

Roscoe did approach Hearst at one point and inquired as to why the newspaper magnate gave him a job "when you did everything you could to hurt me." Hearst responded that he didn't care about the past, he simply wanted to sell papers.

Roscoe was still directing under a pseudonym when the talking picture revolution hit Hollywood at Educational and RKO where he also contributed gags, without credit, to Bert Wheeler and Robert Woolsey's World War I comedy *Half Shot at Sunrise* (1930). The work was steady, and Roscoe kept busy. He was reasonably happy, but he missed acting. The saddest event of 1930 was the passing of his old Keystone pal Mabel Normand, herself a victim of scandal. Roscoe appeared as an honorary pallbearer at her funeral.

It was at RKO where Roscoe wrote and directed comedian Louis John Bartels in *That's My Line* (1931) in which Bartels plays a traveling salesman who is framed by a scheming woman into a seduction that results in his being pursued by men trying to kill him. Many felt, and still feel, its inspiration was Arbuckle's own story.

According to actress Louise Brooks, who appeared in one of the films Arbuckle directed at Educational Pictures, Roscoe was well received by the performers at this small studio, especially Lloyd Hamilton who was pleased with the fact that Arbuckle allowed him more creative input than other directors had. Roscoe was always open to suggestions when directing a film. But Roscoe was considered just another out-of-work actor on the lot; according to Ms. Brooks, "Nobody cared who he was or how important he had been."

Producer Hal Roach wanted to sign Arbuckle to a starring series and get him back on the screen. It would be a great arena for Arbuckle, as the Roach studios boasted such stars as Charley Chase, Our Gang, and the wonderful team of Stan Laurel and Oliver Hardy. But his plan was thwarted when Women's Clubs across the country made it known that their sentiments remained against his ever again appearing in a movie.

18. Arbuckle Thereafter

In an article in the March 1931 issue of *Photoplay* entitled "Just Let Me Work," Arbuckle stated,

> All I want to do is to be allowed to work in my field. I've no resentment against anybody for what has happened. My conscience is clear, my heart is clean. I refuse to worry. I feel that I have atoned for everything.

In the May 1931 issue of *Motion Picture Classic* an article entitled "Isn't Fatty Arbuckle punished enough?" alluded to the Roach idea of hiring Arbuckle, and printed this statement representing four Women's Clubs in America" That man must not be allowed to make pictures. His very presence on the screen would contaminate our children. Surely such a plan is unthinkable!"

The article went on to state:

> Isn't a decade a long sentence for any man to serve? Hasn't Fatty suffered enough? Is he to be forever denied a chance to stage a comeback?
>
> It is all up to his public....

In September of 1931, *Motion Picture Magazine* ran a feature entitled "Doesn't Fatty Arbuckle Deserve a Break?" which also supported Roscoe's return to the screen.

James Cruze, who had helmed most of Arbuckle's Paramount features, told the press he would direct him for nothing. Charlie Chaplin, Buster Keaton, and Laurel and Hardy also made public statements supporting his return to the screen.

It was Jack Warner of Warner Brothers who took a chance on Arbuckle returning to films. Warner decided to try Roscoe in a two reel comedy for at the studio's Vitaphone unit in Brooklyn. If the film was a success, more would be made.

In the book *Clown Prince of Hollywood: The Antic Life and Times of Jack L. Warner*, author Bob Thomas quotes Warner as stating:

> Roscoe Arbuckle was a good friend of mine and the funniest man in pictures. He got a bum deal in San Francisco. I was the first guy to hire him as an actor when nobody else would.

Warner hired Arbuckle in February 1932 to appear in a sound two reel comedy for Vitaphone.

Shooting began on the short *Hey, Pop* on August 25, 1932. Upon completion, the film was screened in test engagements. In its October 11, 1932, issue, the critic for *Film Daily* stated: "Fatty had the customers fairly rolling in their seats, so it looks as if the rotund comic has scored his comeback decisively."

Before the ink was dry on this review, and after an eleven year absence from the screen, having been directing movies under a pseudonym, Arbuckle signed a contract with East Coast Warner-Vitaphone studio manager Sam Sax to make a series of two-reel sound comedies under his own name.

Vitaphone immediately had Arbuckle filming his second, and best, short for the unit, *Buzzin' Around*, for which he hired Al St. John to co-star. While the Warner shorts rarely concentrated on slapstick as the main focus of its comedies, preferring instead a more situational approach with lots of dialog, *Buzzin' Around* featured almost no dialog at all. And both Al and Roscoe reminded moviegoers how much they enjoyed their old fashioned knockabout. Although nearly fifteen years older than when they last appeared together in the Comique silent short *Back Stage*, both Roscoe and Al were still quite capable of slapstick performance. *Film Daily* called it "a swell action comedy" reviewing it in its issue of February 23, 1933, further stating:

> Compared to the general run of gabby comedies, this two-reeler ought to gladden exhibitors hearts, because it looks surefire for pretty nearly every type of audience everywhere.... Several original and highly amusing comedy bits are spotted in the story, and Arbuckle's performance resembles his old form.

During the filming of his fourth comedy, *Tomalio*, Arbuckle was featured running a foot race. The energy required for such a scene would have been much easier to handle in the Keystone days, but now Arbuckle found his energy spent far more rapidly. Arbuckle was breathing heavily and complained of chest pains, but refused medical attention. While filming *In the Dough*, the sixth and last short for which he'd been signed, with Shemp Howard and Lionel Stander, Arbuckle again was experiencing difficulty breathing and asked director Ray McCarey for a break in filming to catch his breath. After taking a leisurely walk around the studio, he returned to the set and completed his final scenes. Then early the next day at 2:30 A.M. on

June 29, 1933, Arbuckle died in his sleep. In an interview with the author, the late Lionel Stander recalled:

> The shorts Roscoe made for Vitaphone were just a testing ground to see if the boycott against him would still stand. He was told that if the shorts were successful, he would be allowed to make feature films.
>
> Well they were successful, so the top brass at Warners told him he would make features after he finished *In The Dough* in which Shemp Howard and I played opposite him. Roscoe was a nice guy and easy to work with. He would come up with the littlest things that could make the whole scene. And not just for himself. He would help all of us out. I was hoping to work with him again once he started doing feature pictures. Jack Warner assured him he'd be a big star once again, and we were all happy for him. Unfortunately he died before anything could happen.

It is likely that had Arbuckle lived, he would indeed have succeeded in Warner-produced comedy features. Perhaps a film like *Earthworm Tractors*, which was filmed in 1936 with Joe E. Brown, would have been the type of vehicle in which Warners would have featured Roscoe Arbuckle. One can only speculate what turns Arbuckle's career would have made had he lived into his seventies, which would have taken him into the 1950s. Perhaps he would have found his way into independent production, maybe more directing, or even becoming involved in the sketch-oriented comedy-variety shows of early television, reenacting his vaudeville sketches for new generations. Alas, it is something we can only speculate about.

19

Keaton Thereafter

From his auspicious beginnings in Arbuckle two reelers, Buster Keaton became fascinated by every level of the cinematic process. Performing for the camera, and having his performance filmed so that he, himself, could assess it, were the initial attractions. Buster indeed carefully examined his performance from his first screen appearance. He was known to sit in theaters that were showing The Butcher Boy and pay careful attention to how he presented the gags on screen, how the audience responded, and even more technical aspects like editing and camera placement.

Arbuckle's approach was more visceral and less intuitive than Keaton's. But Roscoe accepted Buster's headier ideas and attempts to challenge cinema's technical capabilities, finding them to be encouraging and inspiring. Keaton stated in later years that he was directing every time Arbuckle performed a solo bit on camera, even as early as the burning bed sequence in *The Rough House*, which was Keaton's second screen appearance. When we consider Keaton's solo work, beginning after he took charge of the Comique unit, and compare it to the films he did with Arbuckle, we try to assume just what gags he likely contributed. This becomes a bit daunting in that we have had years to understand and embrace Keaton's brilliant solo films, but are just now able to assess most of those he made with Arbuckle as so many had been unavailable for decades.

There is documented evidence of Keaton challenging cinema's technology with specific gags like in *Moonshine* when he films several people getting out of one small car, masking one side of the lens and then the other so that he could have the entire car on camera. This sort of cinematic magic would become much more evident once Buster Keaton assumed full control of the unit.

It can be argued that Keaton's solo films are far superior to anything Arbuckle had done, but this does not dismiss the importance of Buster's training with Roscoe.

Because so many years passed with so few Arbuckle-Keaton collaborations available, Buster's acknowledgment of Arbuckle was often understood as loyalty more than any real sense of cinematic education that could have been accomplished. Keaton's fascinating, ambitious solo works far outshone most of Arbuckle's existing Keystones, and a real sense of Arbuckle's talents became truly evident only by the end of the 20th century. Chaplin, Keaton, and Harold Lloyd were considered the true masters of screen comedy, while Harry Langdon was the likely candidate for the coveted fourth spot. It was the better availability of the Comique series, as well as the more layered later Keystones, that put Arbuckle up near the front rank.

Keaton learned a great deal while working with Arbuckle, and his ideas as to what a comedian could do with the film medium exhibited tremendous insight. However Keaton's contributions were also indulged only to a certain limit. Arbuckle was still the creative mind behind the Comique films in which he starred, and had final say. Buster enjoyed a substantial creative freedom with Roscoe, but when handed the company upon Arbuckle's graduation to feature films, he tapped into areas of experimentation that were not fully realized when working as Arbuckle's support.

Keaton's talents were immediately evident upon his first solo film, *One Week*. Buster is a newlywed who is given a prefab house as a gift. He must build the house according to the numbers on the various boxes. His romantic rival changes the numbers around so that the building of the house is difficult and the result is a disaster.

Immediately one can see comparisons to Arbuckle's comic structure. Buster already has the girl, and there is a romantic rival not unlike Al St. John who deviously arranges trouble for the newlyweds. The basic structure is really no different than *Fatty and Mabel Adrift*, but with another setting and a different story line.

Almost the entirety of the two reels involve Buster trying to build the house in this haphazard fashion. He leans out from ladders, goes through the roof while installing a pre-fab chimney, hangs from chandeliers, wrestles a piano into the living room, and, ultimately, completes his task. The house is in disarray, with unmatching roofs and shaky construction. When a rainstorm hits during a housewarming, the structure spins and propels on its axis, spitting the guests out the door.

One Week is filled with creative visual ideas as well as many wonderful gags and a fair amount of surprises. Even though it is Keaton's first solo effort, it remains among his best films.

Upon its release, *One Week* was given solid copy in most newspaper ads as "30 minutes of hilarious comedy" with Buster Keaton's name prominently displayed above the title as a star. *Motion Picture World* called it the comedy sensation of the year, indicating "His brand new gags will set moviegoers laughing. . . ."

Oddly enough, Buster was next put into a light comedy feature for Metro entitled The Saphead. It was not at all characteristic of Keaton's style. He did not write or direct, but merely starred as an actor.

According to Hal Erickson of the *All Movie Guide*:

> *The Saphead* was based on the tried-and-true Winchell Smith stage comedy *The New Henrietta*, previously filmed in 1915 as *The Lamb*. Buster Keaton, at the time a popular 2-reel comedy attraction, makes his feature-film debut in the role of the addle pated son of Wall Street lion William H. Crane.
>
> Surprisingly, *The Saphead* is almost bereft of slapstick, until Keaton forces the issue in a riotous stock-exchange climax.

While Arbuckle's uncharacteristic first feature was received with some confusion, Keaton was a less notable name at this point, and audiences did not have as specific of expectations for knockabout slapstick. *The Saphead* was well received.

The New York Times stated:

> With Mr. Keaton at its center of gravity, The Saphead becomes one of the gayest comedies of the season—for this Keaton gravity is a bubbling source of merriment.

Life magazine writer Robert Sherwood went so far as to state that had Chaplin's *The Kid* not been released first, *The Saphead* could very well have allowed Keaton to eclipse Chaplin as the leading comic of the motion picture screen.

Buster returned to making his own inimitable two reel comedies, writing and directing as well as starring in such films as *The Haunted House*, which was filled with clever variations on the title theme and never once plummeted to the level of merely predictable; *Cops*, a bonafide classic in which Buster uses one situation to build upon another in a most brilliant manner, until the entire police force is in pursuit of him; and *The Playhouse* where Keaton has fun experimenting with the motion picture medium at a higher level than ever before, including a remarkable (for its time) special effect in which the entire audience of a stage show is made up of separate shots of Buster.

One of the two reelers that is frequently pointed out as a sensation at the time of its initial release is *The Boat*. This one features a gag where Buster launches his newly built vessel onto the waters for the first time, only to have it slowly sink out of sight. There are write ups indicating that this sequence resulted in record breaking periods of audience laughter wherever it was shown.

During this incredibly creative and prolific period, Keaton was told of the accusations against Arbuckle in the death of Virginia Rappe. Keaton was passionately defensive, indicating that Roscoe couldn't swat a fly, much less kill a human being. He wanted to rush to his friend's defense, but his studio kept him from doing so, fearing the possibility of resulting negative publicity. After Arbuckle's acquittal, Buster worked hard to find him work, even suggesting the pseudonym William Goodrich, which Arbuckle hid behind as a director for many years. Keaton felt he owed all of his current success to Arbuckle, who gave him his start in movies and was instrumental in the creative freedom Buster was enjoying in charge of his own unit. "Things will never be the same in Hollywood," Buster was said to have told his wife at the time. One of Buster's comedies was titled *The Balloonatic*, which was a nickname for Arbuckle.

With the success of his short films, Keaton was allowed to make his own features by 1923. His first, *The Three Ages*, is an ambitious piece that tells three separate stories from different eras, as with D.W. Griffith's masterpiece *Intolerance*. Keaton's ambition is perhaps a bit beyond his capacity with this first feature, but it remains a solid comedy with a lot of interesting ideas. How Keaton weaves the three separate stories into a unified whole is evidence of how he was influenced by the higher level of filmmaking as employed by Griffith during cinema's earliest days, and Keaton's own interest in experimenting with and exploring the possibilities of cinema.

Buster Keaton in *The Navigator*.

Some of Keaton's best features are among the finest motion pictures ever made by any filmmaker of any era. Efforts like *Our Hospitality* (1923), *The Navigator*, and *Seven Chances* (1925), have a significant number of amazing sequences, perhaps the most remarkable being Buster's fleeing down a hill from a series of different sized tumbling rocks in *Seven Chances*. Every conceivable level of Keaton's cinematic prowess was evident in his best work, including his contribution as a writer, director, and performer. It was now that Keaton's Great Stone Face persona manifested itself. His expressionless face around whatever tumult by which he was surrounded enhanced the humor of the action.

Even Keaton's lesser feature work—*Go West* (1925), *Battling Butler* (1926), and *College* (1927) are examples—still contained a significant amount of brilliant ideas. The comparatively less interesting Keaton films were uniformly more interesting than the best work of so many others. Out of these many contenders, perhaps the three greatest Buster Keaton features are *Sherlock, Jr.* (1924), *The General* (1926), and *Steamboat Bill, Jr.* (1927).

Sherlock, Jr. is a four-reeler that taps more deeply into Keaton's creativity with the cinematic medium than perhaps any of his other films. As a rejected romantic, Buster the movie projectionist dreams himself onto the screen, allowing for some of the most amazing effects-ridden sequences of the era. Even short bits like Buster jumping from one scene into another are still impressive over eighty years later.

Over the years there has been some discussion that Roscoe Arbuckle directed, or co-directed, *Sherlock, Jr.* Actually, Arbuckle was asked to direct, but his despondency over his failed career was too overwhelming, and his creative differences with Buster were at a level that never occurred during the filming of the Comique series. This time, Buster was boss, and perhaps Arbuckle attempted a certain level of creative control that was not his to have. Whatever the reason, Buster felt his friendship was too strong to let it be hindered by creative difficulties. Arbuckle was replaced by Keaton himself before any filming began.

Keaton's biographer, Rudi Blesh, said of *Sherlock, Jr.*:

> It is easy to miss much of what a picture like *Sherlock Jr.* has to offer. Its appearance of almost childlike naiveté lulls us like a Rousseau jungle painting. We may miss both art and artist in the fairy tale. The simplicity of its stories (for it has two) can conceal the complexity of its structure and divert us too from its piercing appraisal of life and its witty comment on the very medium itself—the motion picture. Its psychological implications may also elude us because they are clothed in everyday situations.
>
> Being more playful, *Sherlock Jr.* does not register with the unequivocal

impact of *Cops* and *The Boat*. It is, however, a more mature work of art than either earlier picture. Insofar as it represents Keaton's retreat from the increasing fragmentation of his personal life back to the safety of childhood and the theater, it is important autobiographically. It is necessary, however, again to point out the complexity of Buster Keaton both the artist and the man. Thus, here the retreat from the situation from which he is retreating. It is, in other words, a retreat into his art, the metamorphosis of an unbearable situation into creative symbols.

The General is not only Keaton's masterpiece, it can be considered one of the three or four greatest films ever made by anyone. One can lean perilously close to toppling into hyperbole when discussing such a film at length, and certainly *The General* is the most studied of Keaton's films.

Sustaining a story and characters within the framework of a serious film with comic touches that truly use cinema's magic as seasoning, *The General* is not filled with the succession of brilliant visual ideas as was *Sherlock, Jr.*, but is remarkable in its subtle approach and exceptional execution.

Daniel Moews in his book *Keaton Close Up: The Silent Features* writes,

> In a film like *The General*, ... the movements of the locomotive are as often humanized by the presence of the hero—their regularity dramatically varied as they lead him to his triumphs and failures—as he is mechanized by his frequent imitations of them. Moreover, in the customary offhand manner of Keaton's visual fantasy, which comically conflates disparate things, the engine and the engineer are now and even then more curiously merged, the film casually accepting and casually presenting them as exactly alike, even though they are allowed to retain their distinctively mechanical or human identities. Finally, too, contrasts are as abundant as similarities, and one of the affinities of the machine to the man is that of the perfect foil. The mindless regularity of the locomotive is frequently used to counterpoint the individuality and ingenuity of intelligently human hero, who often must dexterously manipulate this regularity for his own irregular ends.

While Keaton's relation to machines and use of objects is one of the main points of his comedy, there still remains a very distinct human element to his character. While the Great Stone Face was essentially expressionless (the blatant expressions Keaton offered in an Arbuckle film like *Oh Doctor* were never used again), his use of pure body movement to convey emotion is clear.

In Robert Youngson's compilation of MGM films, *Big Parade of Comedy*, a running Keaton is pointed out by the narration as having a completely still head and shoulders, but with wild movement from his arms and legs. His leaps and flips exhibit the same athleticism that can be found in the Comiques, but where the previous films employed this ability for knockabout slapstick, the more graceful later product used them to enhance the sequence, to make it more exciting through the character's movement.

Steamboat Bill, Jr. is an exceptional Keaton feature, chiefly for the concluding sequence in which a cyclone overtakes the town, and the film deals with Buster's attempt to battle and survive the overpowering elements. As the wind blows fiercely, entire buildings topple, and Keaton runs about attempting to avoid flying debris, at one point trying to run against the wind's current, and, ultimately, maintaining a precise and consistent rhythm that never fails to leave the viewer awestruck. In these days of heavy computerized graphic images used as special effects to the point of leaving no real depth or humanity to so many movies, *Steamboat Bill Jr.* shows Keaton responding to cinema's capabilities with extraordinary thought and skill.

It is here where Keaton once again resurrected the bit where a building wall falls and the open window area lands perfectly on the bystander. It had been used by Arbuckle in *Back Stage*, by Keaton in his first solo two reeler, *One Week*, and now, and most dangerously, during the cyclonic climax of *Steamboat Bill, Jr.*

As described by Keaton biographer Rudi Blesh:

> If ever a sight spelled death, this is it. He stands there motionless, preoccupied, not aware that a building is falling on him. Now it is inches from his head. Now he is completely out of sight and surely crushed. And then, as the great timber rectangle smashes into the street, there he stands, characteristically unmoved. The open center second-story window has passed—narrowly, exactly around him.

Keaton told Blesh:

> The clearance of that window was exactly three inches over my head and past each shoulder. And the front of the building weighed two tons. It had to be built heavy and rigid in order not to bend or twist in that wind.

Oddly enough, while Keaton's silent features are today considered among the most brilliant contributions in all of world cinema, at the time of their release they enjoyed only moderate popularity. *The General*, perhaps his masterpiece, received rather tepid reviews. Its brilliant cinematic innovations were lost on a moviegoing public that simply perceived the film as a comedy with fewer gags.

Keaton's features, which he had been fully supervising, were being released through the newly formed independent company United Artists, which had been formed by Douglas Fairbanks, Charlie Chaplin, and Mary Pickford. Shortly after the filming of Steamboat Bill, Jr., Keaton was informed that his unit was being shut down, and he was now going to Metro-Goldwyn-Mayer.

Joseph Schenck tried painting an appealing picture of the move. A bigger studio, more money, greater opportunities.

Keaton was welcomed with open arms at MGM, and his first two silents, *The Cameraman* (1928) and *Spite Marriage* (1929), were quite worthwhile. Then, after the talking picture revolution, when films were hastily being rewritten to be filmed as talkies, Keaton's work suffered. It wasn't because of talking pictures, which is often what is blamed, but instead it was MGM's penchant for placing him in the most inappropriate vehicles.

Many accounts would have us believe that once talking pictures took over, Buster Keaton's career was effectively over. He would keep working, but never again would he make another film like *Sherlock, Jr.* (or, for that matter, *Moonshine*). Keaton still had a natural ability for comedy and could still be funny even under the most trying circumstances. Not all of his work in talkies was bad, but it did not match the level of his silent pictures. Keaton loved advancing technology and wanted to experiment with talkies the way he had with the primitive filmmaking process back in the teens. But he no longer had the creative freedom to do so, nor was there an open minded mentor like Roscoe Arbuckle encouraging his ideas.

MGM certainly had no idea what to do with Buster Keaton in talking pictures. For his first talkie, Buster was cast as support for Robert Montgomery and Anita Page in the extravagant MGM musical *Free and Easy*. The film, as with many talking pictures during their infancy, was a success. Keaton went to Thalberg and asked for the freedom to do his own pictures. He wanted to explore that new talking picture technology just as he discovered new ways to create comedy for the camera some 13 years earlier with Arbuckle at Comique.

His first starring talkie, *Doughboys*, has not held up well. While Keaton is cited as having supervisory control, the film is, at best, mildly amusing. It was a success, but the new talking picture revolution also caused an increase at the bigger studios in a snobbery against silent era slapstick. Thalberg next cast Buster in the wholly inappropriate drawing room comedy *Parlor, Bedroom and Bath* (1931). After that, Buster did the equally inappropriate *Sidewalks of New York* (1931). Keaton recalled the latter as "such a complete stinker, such an unbelievable bomb" and considered it his worst picture. While nowhere at the level of *The General*, these films have been victimized by terrible reputations that have carried over the years. The Keaton MGM talkies are actually not complete failures. Their chief problem is that they are pictures in which Keaton appears, not Keaton pictures. The idea that a cinematic genius is relegated to playing a role in a somewhat inappropriate comedy is off-putting to anyone who is familiar with Keaton's best work.

For his next three MGM features, *Speak Easily* and *The Passionate Plumber* (both 1932), and *What! No Beer?* (1933), Keaton was teamed with the bombastic Jimmy Durante, whose overbearing personality sucked the air out of every scene. Durante was wonderfully talented, and his exuberance could be contagious, but Buster, paired next to him, came off as quaint at best, dull at worst. Despondent over his situation, Keaton slowly descended into alcoholism.

Buster left the confines of the big studio to appear in low budget two reelers at Educational Pictures. Cheaply made, the series nevertheless offered several interesting efforts that brought Keaton back to his cinematic roots. *One Run Elmer*, *Allez Oop* (both 1935), and *Grand Slam Opera* (1936) are among his best work from this period. He was even reunited with old friend Al St. John in *Love Nest on Wheels* (1937).

Keaton did another spate of two reel comedies at Columbia Pictures, the studio responsible for the enduring slapstick of The Three Stooges. According to Ted Okuda and Edward Watz in their book *The Columbia Comedy Shorts* (McFarland, 1986), short subject producer Jules White recalled:

Buster was a very close friend of Clyde Bruckman, one of my writers.

Keaton reached the bottom of the barrel in *What! No Beer?* (MGM, 1933).

One day Bruckman came to me and said, 'Buster Keaton hasn't worked for a couple of years. He's not money hungry and you can make a good deal if you're interested in him.' If I was interested in him? I was thrilled at the prospect of having him work for us. Rather than call on him myself, I felt Buster would be more comfortable if Bruckman brought him in. So the two of them came to my office and before long, Keaton was signed to a contract.

According to Okuda and Watz:

A lot of effort went into the first one, *Pest from the West* (1939). Buster plays an idle millionaire in pursuit of a pretty young senorita (Lorna Gray) who is using him to make her employer (Gino Corrado) jealous. The film's funniest sequence has Buster mistakenly serenading Lorna beneath irascible Bud Jamison's window. As Buster strums his ukulele and croons "In a Little Spanish Town," Jamison punctuates each chorus by hurling crockery at the stoic Keaton's head. Buster plugs on with his tune, never missing a beat despite flying dishware.

Interestingly enough, this was a sequence that had also appeared in the Roscoe Arbuckle directed two-reeler for Educational *The Tamale Vendor* (1931) which starred Tom Patricola.

Keaton's costar in *Pest from the West* (1939), Lorna Gray, recalled:

> I was so new, and so unaware of Buster Keaton's stature. I was just a young girl when I worked with him, barely 21, and had only seen him in *The Cameraman*. I just loved that film, and thought it was pure genius. He was very quiet and serious on *Pest From The West*. I played a young Senorita and he got a kick out of my fractured Spanish accent. I only went as far as second year French, so the accent was improvised. Buster did his own stunts, which amazed me. He never got hurt. We did a crazy dance bit together and he showed me how I should do it. He was very pleased with my performance and complimented me. He was very kind, and it meant a lot coming from this veteran movie comedian. Off the set, we talked mostly about bridge, which we both enjoyed playing. I still believe Buster Keaton is as great a comedian as Chaplin.

While *Pest from the West* was directed by silent movie veteran Del Lord, many of Keaton's other Columbia two reelers were helmed by Jules White. White was co-director on the MGM feature *Sidewalks of New York* which Keaton abhorred, mainly because the directors "alternated telling me how to walk, how to talk, how to stand, and how to fall—where or when, how fast or slow, how loud or soft."

In an interview with the author, character actor Emil Sitka recalls Jules White as being the type of director who "acted out your part for you. It didn't matter how you prepared, he would have you do it his way. He would act it out, and expect you to copy him. I worked with him for years, and whenever I knew he was the director, I went in with no consideration as to how to play my scenes. I knew he would be pulling my strings like a puppet."

Sound man Edward Bernds, who later became a director himself, worked on several of the Keaton shorts directed by White, and was no fan of these methods. "Jules was an abortive ham," Bernds told Okuda and Watz. "Imagine telling Buster Keaton how to perform a comedy routine!"

In the book *Mr. Bernds Goes to Hollywood*, Edward Bernds did recall a particularly happy moment on the set of one of the Keaton films where Bernds was doing sound:

I approached Buster Keaton on the set, and told him that *The General* was the funniest picture I had ever seen. The Great Stone Face broke into a big smile and said, "Thank you.'"

According to Okuda and Watz:

> *Pardon My Berth Marks* (1940) is by far the best entry, a fast paced comedy directed by Jules White. As an aspiring reporter who boards a train and becomes involved with the wife of a mobster, Buster is in top form. For once, Keaton portrays a resourceful character able to think his way out of situations. It is the closes the series ever came to recapturing the youthful Keaton spirit.
>
> With *Mooching Through Georgia* (1939), the series hit rock bottom. It is a Civil War setting: An aging Confederate solider (Buster) relates in flashback, how he outwitted the Yankee Army, stealing their secret war plans. Though comparisons to *The General* immediately spring to mind, Mooching Through Georgia comes nowhere near Keaton's 1926 masterpiece. Buster is paired with Monty Collins, and it sadly recalls the Keaton-Jimmy Durante teaming of a few years previous. Collins, a more bombastic comic, overshadows Keaton in several scenes; at times it isn't clear who's supposed to be the star of the picture.

Keaton spent two more years appearing in these louder, brasher Columbia two reel comedies before finally giving up after *She's Oil Mine* (1941), vowing not to make "one more crummy two reeler" for the company. While the blatant slapstick of his Columbia efforts was a bit brash for his style, there are some amusing moments throughout his Columbia Pictures tenure. Keaton may have felt he was not artistically challenged, but his natural ability is still quite evident. To dismiss them all does the better ones like *Pest from the West* and *Pardon My Berth Marks* a disservice.

Keaton had not completely left MGM during the period when he did two reel comedies for Educational Pictures or Columbia Pictures. He acted as a technical advisor on films featuring the newer styled comedians such as The Marx Brothers and Abbott and Costello. Groucho Marx was not accepting of Keaton's ideas, which he found inappropriate even for silent brother Harpo. Keaton recalled Abbott and Costello as simply coming to the studio, doing their work, and moving on. He was made to realize that comedians like Roscoe Arbuckle, who lived for creating comedy, were not a part of this new style.

Keaton did see potential in Red Skelton, and one can see obvious homages to Keaton gags in Skelton features like *I Dood It* (1943)

From left: Elise Ames, Matt McHugh, and Dorothy Appleby surround Keaton in His Ex Marks the Spot (Columbia, 1940).

and *A Southern Yankee* (1948). Skelton's 1950 feature *Watch the Birdie* was a remake of the 1928 Buster Keaton feature *The Cameraman*. Keaton asked MGM executives to allow him to form a comedy unit with Skelton where the two of them could create great comedies. But MGM refused.

For the remainder of his life, Keaton made cameo appearances in films and on television. Some were good (his *Twilight Zone* appearance in a largely silent episode), others were sad (his appearances in various TV commercials), and still others were embarrassing (his stint in the beach party pictures for American International where Buster fumbles about among a bunch of scrubbed twentysomethings pretending to be teenagers in shallow movies with titles like *Pajama Party* and *How to Stuff a Wild Bikini*).

Perhaps Keaton's most famous appearance during the fifties is opposite Charlie Chaplin in one scene from *Limelight* (1952). Many

Keaton supports Chaplin in the latter's *Limelight* (United Artists, 1952).

find Keaton to be even funnier than Chaplin in this sketch, which is all done in pantomime. Keaton reportedly arrived on the set wearing his trademark flat porkpie hat, and had to be gently told his business had already been worked out for him. Chaplin gave Keaton more freedom than he was known to give other performers. Chaplin allegedly had summoned Keaton personally upon bristling at an article describing The Great Stone Face as something of a forgotten man as far as film is concerned. Chaplin respected Keaton's talent, and Buster was grateful for the break.

As the fifties became the sixties, a reappraisal of silent comedy came in many disparate forms. Producer Robert Youngson offered compilations of silent comedy, with Keaton prominently featured in such anthologies as *When Comedy Was King* (1960), *Days of Thrills and Laughter* (1961), and *30 Years of Fun* (1963). Many of Keaton's best films were being restored and shown in art houses across the country and in Europe. As he came towards the end of his life, Buster Keaton started to enjoy a resurgence of interest in his work.

Keaton was a working actor, and the employment he enjoyed in TV commercials, on variety shows, and in industrial films allowed him to continue being creative. In late 2005, Laughsmith Entertainment produced the DVD package *Industrial Strength Keaton*, collecting some of the most interesting work Buster did during this period of his life. Several of his commercials for anything from Simon Pure Beer, to Alka-Seltzer, to Milky Way candy bars show interesting sparks of the Keaton of yore. The industrial films compiled on this two-DVD set offered more chances for Keaton to use his creative mind productively towards the end of his life.

In 1965, Buster Keaton made another two-reeler, in color, for the National Film Board in Canada. The film was entitled *The Railrodder* and the making of it was filmed as a documentary entitled *Buster Keaton Rides Again*. This documentary is a fascinating look at Keaton in old age, making another film, discussing his ideas, and recalling comedy's history. Buster Keaton died in February of 1966.

It is very commonly known that Buster Keaton is among the greatest comedy filmmakers in cinema's history. And while his greatest accomplishments may have occurred after appearing with Roscoe Arbuckle in the Comique two reelers, this apprenticeship is still significant as an important training ground for what eventually became some of the finest motion pictures of any era.

20

Al St. John and Alice Lake

When starring comedians have a stock company of supporting actors, it helps to understand the success of their work by examining the contributions of the support.

Al St. John's background with Keystone has already been discussed briefly in the text. St. John was a natural athlete with an interest in performing. Even as a young child, Al would skip school and practice stunts on a bicycle. His natural sense of balance and precise coordination allowed him to create and perform several breathtaking stunts, and the trial and error in perfecting these would toughen him up for the pratfalls he would engage in later.

St. John was Roscoe Arbuckle's nephew. Al's mother was Roscoe's sister. The text has already discussed St. John's auditioning for Sennett much to Arbuckle's chagrin, Roscoe having promised the boy's father that he would not pave the way for his entrance in the movies. Al's parents were vaudevillians, and like many stage performers of the era, had a condescending feeling towards the "flickers."

When Sennett hired St. John it was for three dollars a day. According to Karlton Lahue and Samuel Gill in their book *Clown Princes and Court Jesters*:

> During St. John's early years with Keystone, his foolhardy personality became a most valuable asset on the wild and wacky Keystone lot. Sharing the trick driving with Dave Lewis, Al doctored the cars to make them operate in exactly the way he wanted. Al's favorite stunt was removing the brakes from the right hand wheel and soaping the street, a practice permitting some hair raising spins for the driver and any rid-

ers courageous enough to hang on. Al was not only an excellent stunt driver but an excellent all-around athlete capable of performing extremely high dives and more difficult stunts required of the Keystone stars.

Sennett considered Al St. John a valuable man on the lot, and Al's father settled into the realization that his son had found steady employment, thus Arbuckle felt he was now allowed to encourage his nephew.

Soon Al St. John was appearing as support in many Keystone films, affecting a villainous rube character that was usually at odds with Fatty over the affections of Mabel Normand. Al's use of blatant facial expressions and wild pratfalls added a great deal of fun to these uninhibited Keystone romps, and his roles soon expanded. Al is the chief villain in two of Roscoe's best films of 1916, *Fatty and Mabel Adrift* and *The Waiter's Ball*. And while he is relegated to smaller support in the innovative *He Did and He Didn't*, he added a necessary bit of knockabout so this very unusual Keystone farce would have at least some slapstick authenticity.

When Arbuckle left Keystone for Comique, Al came along. He used essentially the same character at Comique as he'd used at Keystone, with little deviation. Perhaps the wily city-bred con man he played in *Oh Doctor* is the most offbeat role he would have at Comique.

While St. John was great within his own limits at Comique, Buster Keaton's joining the group with the first film, *The Butcher Boy*, appeared to alter any real advance Al could make. It wasn't resentment, but simply that Buster was able to offer support behind the camera that was beyond St. John's capacity. Al was allowed to do what he could with the resources he had, and, within those parameters, he excelled.

Al St. John went as far as he could with his Uncle Roscoe Arbuckle's films, then, after completing *Back Stage* ventured on to star in his own. During Keaton's absence from Comique, while he was overseas serving his country in the armed forces, Al was able to enjoy a bit more footage, especially in the magnificent *Love* (1919). When Buster returned with *Back Stage*, Al knew his uncle Roscoe had enough support. Al realized it was time to venture on.

Film historian Tommie Hicks Jr. told the author:

Al started working for Fox in 1920 and abandoned the "Psycho-Rube" character that made him famous at Keystone and affected an "Affable Boob" character. Only a handful of his Fox comedies still exist, and, by my count, nobody starred in more Fox comedies than Al.

St. John enjoyed reasonable success with his own starring films, many of which he wrote and directed himself. While none achieved the level of popularity of Keaton's efforts, or Arbuckle's, he had the ability to carry one and two reel comedies as the star, which is significant. Fox was pleased at acquiring St. John's services after they had been unsuccessful in hiring Buster Keaton. When St. John left the Arbuckle unit after being beckoned by William Fox, he was allowed a certain creative control over his own vehicles, something that any good comedian sought.

Al St. John was with Fox until 1924, when he left and did several films for Educational Pictures. According to Tommie Hicks Jr.: "Al's work in the Educational series is also unfortunately sparse. I think less than ten survive."

According to Karlton Lahue and Samuel Gill in their book Clown Princes and Court Jesters:

> When St. John joined Educational in 1924 to work in the Tuxedo and Mermaid Comedies, he abandoned the [rube] character he had worked so hard to perfect, becoming the clean-cut, wholesome young man who sported white shirts and bow ties, coats, even two-toned or white shoes with spats. He was still an energetic youth, but more level-headed than the playful spirit of his earlier character.

St. John is credited with directing a handful of his Educational Pictures films, as is Roscoe Arbuckle, under the pseudonym William Goodrich, due to Arbuckle's name being, by that time, a stigma in the industry.

The knockabout comedy style in which St. John had flourished was dying out by the 1920s, replaced by a more refined presentation. Characters were not twisting their facial features in a blatant manner to convey evil. Gags were worked out more carefully. Characters had more depth. And humor built more subtly from situations.

Once talking pictures replaced the cinema of silents, St. John found yet another niche. He appeared as the grizzled sidekick Fuzzy in several low budget westerns.

According to Hicks:

20. Al St. John and Alice Lake

Al St. John starred in two reelers for major studios for ten years, a success by most standards. The reason Al quit making two reelers was because he was making a hell of a lot more money in supporting parts (he did sporadically appear in talkie two reelers in the early thirties). Because of the survival rate of the Keystones, he has been mostly remembered by them.

There is another story which states that in later years, St. John admitted that a deal with William Fox went awry and he was persona non grata at the major studios. He remained with Educational Pictures into the dawn of the talking picture era, did small roles in a few features, and soon found himself gravitating towards the western movie genre.

It has been stated that St. John's western sidekick nickname came about when producers of a Fred Scott western at Spectrum studios were seeking the talents of Fuzzy Knight, another western supporting player. Knight was not available resulting in St. John being brought in. The script was never changed, and St. John was referred to in the film as Fuzzy. Sporting a grizzled beard, he began using the nickname of Fuzzy as well.

St. John was Fuzzy in three western series simultaneously, supporting such cowboy stars as Bob Steele and Don "Red" Barry. St. John is perhaps best remembered from this period in his career for appearing with Buster Crabbe as Billy "The Kid" Carson in a series at the low budget Producers Releasing Corporation. At least two of the films, *Fuzzy Settles Down* (1944) and *His Brother's Ghost* (1945) center around Al

A bearded Al St. John in one of his many westerns, with Myrna Dell.

completely. He even dusts off his trick bicycle bit for *The Drifter* (1944), proving that his prowess for breathtaking acrobatic stunt comedy had not declined with his advancing age.

Buster Crabbe remembered no fondness for this low budget series, but remembered St. John with affection and respect.

In a 1980 interview Buster Crabbe told the author:

> My only asset in those cheap westerns was working with Al St. John. Fuzzy was a lot older than he had been in all those silent pictures but could still do a fall or a physical bit of business that would make the whole scene. He was a lot of fun on the set, and always willing to offer advice. The directors would rely on his background when they would stage a fight scene. He was terrific with the actors. The younger folks loved hearing his tales about working in the silent pictures. There was more than one time when Al would talk about Fatty Arbuckle and would end up in tears. He would always compose himself and be ready to get back to work, but it was obvious that whole thing still affected him.

The Crabbe series ended in 1946 and St. John then began acting as sidekick to Lash LaRue in a series of Producers Releasing Corporation westerns that were later headed by low budget producer Ron Ormond. These lasted until 1952.

LaRue echoed Crabbe's sentiments about St. John, telling western film buff Paul Dellinger for his Old Corral web page:

> Fuzzy was a wonderful guy. I wish he were still here to see how long the films had lasted. He was the greatest ad lib artist in the world. He could stumble over a matchstick and spend fifteen exciting minutes looking for what he stumbled over.

After the LaRue series ended, St. John reportedly made some appearances in Wild West reviews, still trading on the stunt expertise he had mastered in silent comedies nearly fifty years before. Much of his earnings were donated to the Muscular Dystrophy Association, Al being among the many celebrities to contribute to this noble cause. Jerry Lewis, who had been holding fund raisers for muscular dystrophy since the early 1950s, has recalled that many performers were very helpful with their time and donations.

Al St. John died of a heart attack on January 21, 1963. His obituary in major newspapers like *The New York Times* was sparse, usually referring to him as a "western actor" as that is what he had been doing most recently. There was usually no reference to his long career in silent comedy.

Alice Lake is the other noted member of the Arbuckle company whom the author feels deserves some discussion in this text.

Like her friend and fellow supporting player Al St. John, Alice was brought over to Comique by Roscoe from Keystone. Also like St. John, Alice enjoyed greater stardom upon leaving the Arbuckle unit. However Alice's career was far more short lived than Al St. John's had been. Leaving Comique for Metro, she was immediately given the lead in the feature *Should a Woman Tell?* (1919). The Internet Movie Database indicates, according to actor and writer Jim Beaver, perhaps best known for playing Ellsworth on the HBO western series *Deadwood*, the plot for this feature went as such:

> A village girl, on a visit to the city of Boston, is taken advantage of by a man there, and returns to her home feeling sullied and ashamed. A young man who had once sought her hand returns from years away in Europe and reiterates his suit. She returns his love and agrees to marry him, but has difficulty telling him the truth about her misadventure. When she finally does, his response seems to doom the pair to tragedy.

Alice Lake had leading roles in many typical silent era melodramas like *Should a Woman Tell?* throughout the 1920s, each of them being quite popular. *Shore Acres, The Misfit Wife, Body and Soul, The Greater Gain,* and *Uncharted Seas* are among her feature film hits from this period. She also worked in features for producers David O. Selznick and Samuel Goldwyn.

Popular enough with audiences to net several profiles in fan magazines of the period, Alice never failed to look back fondly on her slapstick beginnings with kind words about Roscoe Arbuckle.

In the spring of 1924, Alice Lake married actor Robert Williams. They were separated by the following February under suspicious circumstances as indicated by the *New York Mirror* in an article headlined "Gay Life Parts Couple." It was implied that Alice Lake and actress Viola Dana had a lesbian relationship that was the cause for her separation from Robert Williams. Dana told the press that she knew nothing of her friend's marital problems, and denied being a home wrecker. The couple were divorced less than a year after they had been married. Robert Williams, who lived only until 1931, is best remem-

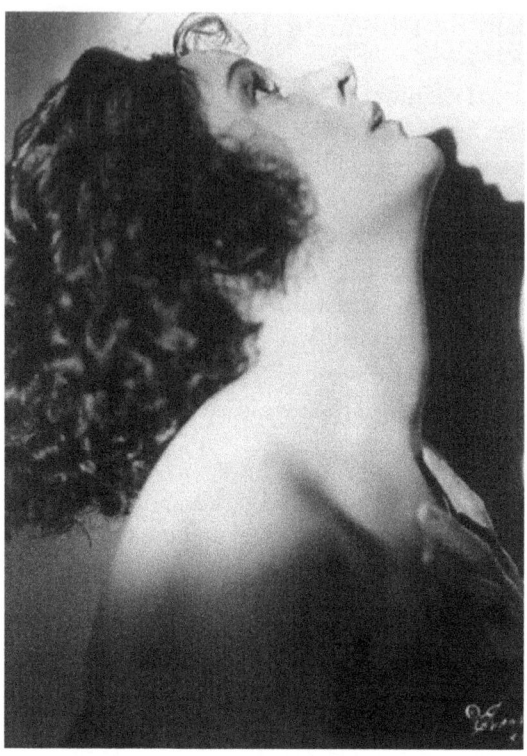

Alice Lake went on to star in dramatic features.

bered today for his wisecracking performance in Frank Capra's *Platinum Blonde* starring Jean Harlow and Loretta Young.

When talking pictures came along and the silent era ended, Alice Lake became one of the unfortunate stars who did not survive the transition. Her final lead performance was in the 1929 silent *Circumstantial Evidence*. Her first talkie, *Twin Beds*, also released in 1929, relegated her to a smaller supporting role. She was relegated even further to uncredited cameos by 1931, and was only doing mere bit parts by the middle of that decade. Her fleeting appearance in her last film, *Hollywood Boulevard* (1936), ended up on the cutting room floor. Alice Lake suffered a heart attack and died on November 15, 1967.

Afterword

In concluding this text, we not only can embrace a deeper appreciation of Roscoe Arbuckle's best work, and have a greater understanding of Buster Keaton's earliest cinematic development. Another factor is our continued understanding and respect for what the motion picture's past has to offer not only in the way of timeless entertainment, but the historical and cultural appreciation for cinema as art.

As time goes on and more impressive technological advancements continue to alter how we view motion pictures, the earlier films unfortunately fade deeper into history. Even with greater accessibility, early films are often considered archaic by the general moviegoing public. Unlike music or literature, the earliest cinema is often overshadowed by advancements in presentation that increase with each new era. A film is often cavalierly dismissed as "old" after only a couple of years. Unfortunately, this means that silent films are no longer even a novelty, but are virtually nonexistent in the eyes of current mainstream moviegoers. There is little sense of, or appreciation for, the cinema's rich history in much of the mainstream.

Fortunately, these advancements in technology have also offered us greater opportunities to preserve, restore, access and review earlier films despite their being relegated to a niche market. DVD producers like Kino, Milestone, Image, and Laughsmith are among those responsible for the greater availability of our cinematic heritage.

At the time of this writing, a revisionist look at Arbuckle's importance to the history of motion picture comedy has been underway for a few years. The release of nearly all of the Comique period two reelers was especially instrumental in reevaluating the significance of Arbuckle's contribution. While his Keystones offer many instances where he exhibited talents as a comedian and filmmaker that went beyond most of what was happening in cinema up to that time, his Comique two reelers offered much more.

According to Karlton Lahue and Samuel Gill in their book *Clown Princes and Court Jesters*:

> Arbuckle's Comique films continued the basic character he had evolved at Keystone, but were much slower in action and pacing. Characterization was more extensive, the plots were better defined, and Arbuckle showed much promise as an actor as well as a comic. His comedies were tremendously popular, as Paramount gleefully discovered.

When this account was written in 1970, not all of the Comique productions were available, so Lahue and Gill were limited in their understanding of the series. And still they accurately revealed the difference between this series and Arbuckle's Keystone work. They did not have the resources to note the evolution from later, more detailed Keystones like *Fatty and Mabel Adrift* or *He Did and He Didn't* to the first, more slapstick oriented Comiques like *The Butcher Boy* and *The Rough House*, on to the greater experimentation of *Moonshine* or *Good Night Nurse*. But the writers still understood the impact, the progression, and the significance of Arbuckle's work.

Buster Keaton's films have, at the time of this writing, been studied rather extensively for some forty years. There is a great deal of texture to his solo work, many of these films worthy of the deepest, most careful assessment as there are layers of intelligent ideas to peel back and examine. This is what initially made the Arbuckle Comique films so sought after. The earliest appearances of a comedian so honored as Buster Keaton are essential for any truly thorough examination of his work.

And to give further historical and cultural emphasis with our study of the Arbuckle films in which Keaton appeared, it seems evident that Keaton's often citing Roscoe as a major influence on his screen work was more than mere loyalty. The films in which Keaton and Arbuckle appear together show some of the innovations Arbuckle offered cinema as very direct influences on Keaton's work. At the same time, these films, when compared to Arbuckle's Keystone productions, display the influence Keaton's ideas had on Arbuckle's decisions. Had these films been available all along, we would have had a clearer understanding of both Arbuckle's and Keaton's total output. The sudden availability of the films allows us to revise or add greater clarity to our existing appreciation. It is also an interesting comparison-contrast as Arbuckle's approach was more intuitive while Keaton's was more conceptual. Both were interested in gags, but Arbuckle a bit more in episodes.

In the case of Buster Keaton, his reputation remains the same. His most important work has been available for some time, and we've already been able to establish him as one of the true geniuses of the American cinema. The availability of the Comique series allows us to see all of his earliest opportunities with the cinematic process, giving a clearer picture of the genesis of his development.

As these are perhaps Arbuckle's best and most important films, the impact on his current status is more significant. The Comique series shows him developing ideas he'd had at Keystone and exploring them further through the greater creative control he enjoyed in this series. While his development at Keystone had been clearly understood, having most of the Arbuckle two reelers from his Comique period emphasizes the cinematic evolution he'd already been showing at Keystone. When examined together, especially in chronological order, the Comique two reelers show a natural progression with different ideas and greater challenges. Some of this was due to Keaton's mind expanding suggestions as to how Arbuckle could experiment with the motion picture medium.

Audience reaction was important to Arbuckle. As much as he wanted to be creative, he also was concerned about alienating his fan base. It has been stated that Arbuckle was the first movie comedian to preview his films, using the reactions of these preview audiences to edit his films for greater impact. Keaton's suggestions were often incorporated, as we have discussed previously in this text, but, as has also been mentioned, Arbuckle could not always comfortably indulge the newcomer's ideas. While they blended perfectly onscreen and off, Arbuckle and Keaton did have one conflict—Arbuckle's idea that the average moviegoer had the mentality of a child, and Keaton's belief that there was a substantial percentage of the moviegoing audience that would be sophisticated enough to appreciate higher level comedy. Arbuckle used some, but not all, and it took Keaton's solo work to allow Buster the necessary creative control to truly indulge his own ideas more completely.

Despite this conservatism, Roscoe Arbuckle is certainly most worthy of being listed alongside the established greats of silent screen comedy, including Charlie Chaplin, Buster Keaton, and Harold Lloyd. An interesting bit of trivia is that each of these played support in Arbuckle comedies. Chaplin did a cameo in the Arbuckle Keystone *The Knockout* (1914), Keaton, of course, in several films, and Lloyd appears in the Keystone production *Miss Fatty's Seaside Lovers* (1915). He is also the first American comedy star to direct his own films (predating Charlie Chaplin by several months).

Because of his being best known for the scandal that ruined his career, and the poor survival rate of his work, it has taken until the 21st century for Roscoe Arbuckle to be respected in most circles among the truly important figures in silent screen comedy. It is a level he achieved during his career, and will likely maintain as more of his films, including his later directorial efforts, become available.

Buster Keaton is perhaps the greatest comedy filmmaker of them all. There are often arguments as to whether Keaton or Charlie Chaplin (or Harold Lloyd) is the most important comedian in films. Of course each of them is terribly significant in his own right, and for different reasons. Chaplin's establishing so much of what screen comedy is, has been, and may forseeably become so early in cinema's development makes him important almost beyond measure. However Buster Keaton's films extended further than many of his comic peers. They presented a vision for presenting the narrative, as well as gags, with visual ideas that truly used the motion picture medium. How the camera was placed to film the scene, how the resulting scene was edited, exactly which props were used, etc., were carefully considered for each scene. Along with Keaton's agility and acrobatics, a real sense of insightful, accurate filmmaking decisions permeates his work. Keaton learned a great deal about cinematography and editing from Arbuckle, but mostly his cinematic genius developed because Arbuckle left him alone to experiment and explore the technology on his own. Along with accepting and discussing some of Keaton's more intricate ideas as he learned the power of the cinematic process, Arbuckle indulged Buster's penchant to use the camera in ways other than merely shooting what was performed. Keaton's creating the effect of several people leaving a small car in Moonshine by masking one side of the lens and shooting the scene twice is a good example.

With the 20–20 hindsight that the existing Keaton solo films allow us, we already are aware of Buster's comic artistry as we assess the Comique two reelers. We can observe ideas that Keaton later expanded when in control of his own starring films. We can understand how this training ground was so important to his development as a comedian and filmmaker.

However with respect to Roscoe Arbuckle, the Comique two reelers prompt some questions, at least from this writer. Should Arbuckle have perhaps remained with the unit and not gone on to the prestige of features? Should Paramount have allowed Arbuckle's unit to try a feature length production rather than place him in offbeat stories the studio already owned?

Had Keaton and Arbuckle collaborated on a feature length picture it could have allowed for a fascinating result. But this speculation might have thwarted the eventuality of Keaton gaining control of the unit upon Arbuckle choosing to leave for feature productions of his own. Keaton's full control is too necessary for the development of screen comedy into a purely cinematic art form.

What the Comique two reelers best prove is how crucial cinema's history is to truly appreciate and understand its development, emphasizing the necessity for preservation and restoration. The availability of these short comedies is a huge piece of the puzzle in understanding the development of so great a film artist as Buster Keaton, and the clearer appreciation of Roscoe Arbuckle as a screen comedian who belongs comfortably in the front ranks.

Too often, stars whose careers concentrated on short films are not placed in as lofty position by historians as those who did feature pictures. Chaplin, Keaton, Harold Lloyd, and Harry Langdon all had strong feature film credits. Arbuckle's features were vehicles for him to star as an actor, and almost none are readily accessible. He is best known for starring in short films, these two reelers representing his best work. Thus, like comedian Charley Chase whose best work was also in short films, Arbuckle has been dismissed in the same fashion as the period review which indicated, "Chaplin is an artist, Arbuckle is merely a clown." Comedy film buffs frequently cite both Chase and Arbuckle with respect for each individual's significant output, but the general film critic appears to limit his or her appreciation (and experience) to those established high level artists like Chaplin, Keaton, and Lloyd who successfully supervised their own feature length pictures with work that has remained accessible for these many decades. The Comique two reelers are often referred to as an important training ground for the development of Buster Keaton, with little discussion about these being Arbuckle's films over which he enjoyed creative control. Again, Arbuckle is not lauded as the genius Keaton was. He is once again dismissed as "merely a clown."

Roscoe Arbuckle was not merely one of the divertingly amusing multitude who did pratfalls and made faces in countless knockabout slapstick efforts from an era too long ago to matter. He was, and still remains, one of the most daring, intelligent, skillful comedians and comedy directors of the silent era.

Buster Keaton's longtime status as a comedic genius and cinematic visionary received its genesis in a series of films for which he served as apprentice to Arbuckle, enjoying encouragement, support, and opportunities for advancement. And for the rest of his life, Buster reminded us of this.

The Comique two reelers featuring Roscoe Arbuckle with Buster Keaton are important films for each of these individuals and for all of the reasons stated herein. Along with being skillfully produced and timelessly amusing, these two reel comedies show experiments with challenging ideas, important insights into screen comedy presentation, a culminating look at one of cinema's greatest comedians, and the early development of one of the medium's most creative and intelligent individuals.

Selected Bibliography

Agee, James. *Agee on Film: Reviews and Comments.* Boston: Beacon Press, 1964. Includes a reprint of "Comedy's Greatest Era," *Life,* September 3, 1949. During the era of Bob Hope and Abbott and Costello, critic Agee longs for the simple days of slapstick comedy, remembering Charlie Chaplin, Buster Keaton, Harry Langdon, Harold Lloyd, Roscoe Arbuckle, Ben Turpin, and others.

Anger, Kenneth. *Hollywood Babylon.* New York: Dell, 1975. Anger's well known look at the seamy underbelly of Hollywood glamour includes a chapter about the Arbuckle scandal.

Bernds, Edward. *Mr. Bernds Goes to Hollywood* Metuchen, NJ: Scarecrow Press, 2000. Bernds recalls his career as a sound engineer, screenwriter, and director, with some comments on Buster Keaton's tenure at the Columbia Pictures short subjects department.

Blesh, Rudi. *Keaton.* New York: Macmillan, 1966. The first noteworthy biography of Keaton was written with his cooperation and released shortly after his death.

Bowles, Stephen E. *The Film Anthologies Index.* Metuchen, NJ: Scarecrow Press, 1994. Handy reference to a vast number of articles on various film topics and where they can be found in magazines, periodicals, and books.

Brownlow, Kevin. *Hollywood: The Pioneers.* New York: Alfred A. Knopf, 1979.

———. *The Parade's Gone By.* Berkeley: University of California Press, 1968. Affectionate, respectful look at silent cinema.

Dardis, Tom. *Keaton: The Man Who Wouldn't Lie Down.* New York: Charles Scribner's Sons, 1979. Another biography of Keaton that attempts to understand his lasting impact on cinema.

Doyle, Billy H. *The Ultimate Directory of Silent and Sound Era Performers.* Metuchen, NJ: Scarecrow Press, 1999. Helpful, accurate necrology offering birth and death dates for all sound era performers and silent era ones whose career extended into the sound era.

Durgnat, Raymond. *The Crazy Mirror: Hollywood Comedy and the American Image.* New York: Horizon Press, 1969. Intellectual study of screen humor attempts to understand the mechanics, creativity, and psychology of movie comedy.

Eames, John Douglas. *The Paramount Story.* New York: Crown, 1985. Oversized coffee table book listing all of the Paramount features. Not a great deal of information is given for each title, but it is a reasonably helpful reference for the elusive Arbuckle features made in 1920 and 1921.

Edmonds, Andy. *Frame Up! The Untold Story of Roscoe "Fatty" Arbuckle.* New York: William Morrow, 1991. Edmonds seems to truly appreciate her subject, as she attempts to back up claims that Arbuckle was completely innocent in the Virginia Rappe scandal using various testimonies and matters of evidence.

Edwards, Larry. *Buster: A Legend in Laughter.* Bradenton, FL: McGuinn and McGuire Publishing, 1995. Flattering biography and appreciation of Keaton's life and work.

Film Daily film reviews 1932–1933. Daily periodical, one of the few that extensively reviewed short subjects, helpful by offering reviews of the Arbuckle Vitaphone films.

Fowler, Gene. *Father Goose: The Story of Mack Sennett.* New York: Covici, Friede Publishers, 1934. Very early biography of the filmmaking pioneer, written with his cooperation, is rife with errors but still interesting in how it recalls the silent comedies of only ten to fifteen years earlier as if they were ancient history.

Fussell, Betty Harper. *Mabel.* New York: Ticknor & Fields, 1982. Thoroughgoing biography of Mabel Normand including her professional relationship with Roscoe Arbuckle and her support of him during his initial Keystone films.

Kanin, Garson. *Hollywood.* New York: Viking Press, 1967. Longtime screenwriter and director looks back at the film industry, including some comments on the Arbuckle scandal and its fallout.

Keaton, Buster, with Charles Samuels. *My Wonderful World of Slapstick.* New York: Doubleday, 1960. Keaton's autobiography offers several interesting firsthand insights. Some believe it is eclipsed by the Blesh biography (q.v.), but many of Keaton's detailed recollections about his earliest films remain useful and fascinating.

Kerr, Walter. *The Silent Clowns.* New York: Alfred A. Knopf, 1975. Very popular study of silent comedy by the astute theater critic. Impressive especially in that Kerr does not limit his text to the biggest stars. Interesting notes about Arbuckle and, especially, about Keaton.

Kline, Jim. *The Complete Films of Buster Keaton.* New York: Citadel Press, 1993. Film-by-film look at Keaton's work is a better resource for his solo efforts, as many of his collaborations with Arbuckle were still lost at the time of its writing.

Lahue, Karlton C., and Samuel Gill. *Clown Princes and Court Jesters.* South Brunswick, NJ: A.S. Barnes, 1970. Excellent collection of biographies on silent screen comedians, without including heavyweights Charlie Chaplin, Buster Keaton, and Harold Lloyd. The text instead concentrates on the lesser known Lloyd Hamilton, Billie Rhodes, Ford Sterling, Fred Mace, Snub Pollard, etc. Arbuckle, Mabel Normand, and Al St. John are among those profiled.

Lahue, Karlton C., and Terry Brewer. *Kops and Custards: The Legend of the Keystone Films.* Norman: University of Oklahoma Press, 1968. Interesting look at the Keystone productions, how the company grew, their methods of making films, and the significance of these films to early cinema.

Louvish, Simon. *Keystone: The Life and Clowns of Mack Sennett.* New York: Faber and Faber, 2003. Very good biography of the filmmaking pioneer, correcting errors found in other sources and examining details overlooked in books like *Father Goose* and *King of Comedy*. Louvish had access to the Mack Sennett Papers at the Academy of Motion Picture Arts and Sciences, something that previous writers like Walter Kerr and Kalton Lahue did not.

Maltin, Leonard. *The Great Movie Comedians.* New York: Crown, 1978. Maltin is among the pioneers in books on screen comedy. His book on the movie shorts offers the first filmography of the Keaton Columbias and discusses the Arbuckle talkies in a chapter on Warner Brothers. His book on the comedians includes chapters on both Arbuckle and Keaton.

_____. *The Great Movie Shorts*. New York: Crown, 1972.

Mast, Gerald. *The Comic Mind*. New York: Bobbs-Merrill, 1973. Another intellectual appreciation of humor in cinema, useful as a college text for film study programs specializing in comedy.

_____. *A Short History of the Movies*. New York: Bobbs-Merrill, 1971. Mast gives a learned overview of motion picture history, the book being especially valuable for details on some of the first moving pictures.

McCaffrey, Donald. *The Golden Age of Sound Comedy*. New York: A.S. Barnes, 1973. McCaffrey looks at sound comedy, offering the problem of Keaton's transition to talking pictures in comparison with his superior silent work.

Meade, Marion. *Buster Keaton: Cut to the Chase*. New York: HarperCollins Publishers, 1995. Another biographical appreciation of Buster Keaton.

Moews, Daniel. *Keaton: The Silent Features Up Close*. Berkeley: University of California Press, 1977. Careful analysis of Keaton's silent features.

Nash, Jay Robert, and Stanley Ralph Ross. *The Motion Picture Guide*. New York: Cinebooks, 1985. Reference guide to feature films produced in America.

Neibaur, James L. *Movie Comedians: The Complete Guide*. Jefferson, NC: McFarland, 1986.

The New York Times Film Reviews 1913–1921. Helpful look at what one of the nation's leading newspapers said about many of the films contained herein at the time of their initial release.

Oderman, Stuart. *Roscoe "Fatty" Arbuckle*. Jefferson, NC: McFarland, 1992. Biography of Arbuckle, much of its information garnered through the author's friendship with Roscoe's first wife, Minta Durfee.

Okuda, Ted, and Edward Watz. *The Columbia Comedy Shorts*. Jefferson, NC: McFarland, 1986. Outstanding, thorough look at the comedy short subjects produced by Columbia Pictures, including a useful chapter on Buster Keaton.

Rapf, Joanna, and Gary L. Green. *Buster Keaton. A Bio-Bibliography*. Westport, CT: Greenwood Press, 1995. Short biography, bibliography, filmography, videography. Part of a series of helpful reference books.

Robbins, Jhan. *Inka Dinka Doo: The Life of Jimmy Durante*. New York: Paragon House, 1991. Some discussion of the MGM features Durante made with Keaton.

Robinson, David. *Buster Keaton*. Bloomington: Indiana University Press, 1969. Robinson's biography of Keaton attempts to assess his significance more clearly as a filmmaker rather than merely detailing events in his life.

St. Johns, Adela Rogers. *Love, Laughter and Tears: My Hollywood Story*. Garden City, NY: Doubleday, 1978. Journalist's memories includes several interesting accounts of the Arbuckle scandal.

Sennett, Mack. *King of Comedy*. Garden City, NY: Doubleday, 1954. Sennett's autobiography repeats some of the same errors found in *Father Goose*, but still an interesting document of the pioneer filmmaker in old age.

Slide, Anthony. *The American Film Industry*. Westport, CT: Greenwood Press, 1986. Very helpful reference on virtually every aspect of the industry, neatly alphabetized, well indexed, and carefully annotated.

_____. *Nitrate Won't Wait*. Jefferson, NC: McFarland, 1992. Excellent documentation of film's fragility, its need for preservation, and those persons responsible for helping to find and restore lost cinematic treasures.

_____. *Selected Vaudeville Criticism*. Metuchen, NJ: Scarecrow Press, 1988. Interesting look at an era of show business eventually eclipsed by the movies, and where Arbuckle and Keaton both got their start.

Stahl, Jerry. *I, Fatty*. New York: Bloomsbury, 2005. Novelization of Arbuckle's life written in the first person.

Vazzana, Eugene. *The Silent Film Necrology*. Jefferson, NC: McFarland, 2001. Death information on silent screen performers citing reference sources.

Walker, Alexander. *The Shattered Silents: How the Talkies Came to Stay*. New York: William Morrow, 1979. The talking picture revolution and its impact on the industry.

Wead, George, and George Lellis. *The Film Career of Buster Keaton*. Pleasantville, NY: Redgrave Publishing, 1977. Another look at Keaton's screen work.

Yallop, David A. *The Day the Laughter Stopped: The True Story of Fatty Arbuckle*. New York: St. Martin's Press, 1976. First book length account of the Rappe scandal has been challenged by some, but still significant in helping to proclaim Arbuckle's innocence and mishandling by the industry.

Young, Robert A. *Roscoe "Fatty" Arbuckle: A Bio-Bibliography*. Westport, CT: Greenwood Press, 1994. Short biography, filmography, and bibliography on Arbuckle. Many of the films were still lost when this book was compiled.

Index

Abbott, Bud *see* Abbott and Costello
Abbott and Costello 77, 184
Abbott and Costello in the Foreign Legion 73
The Addams Family 147
Aitken, Harry 114
All Movie Guide 159, 174
Allen, Phyllis 36
Allez Oop 181
Alvarez, Bryan 42
Anger, Lou 17–18, 21, 74
Arthur, Johnny 67

Balboa Amusement Producing Company 83
The Balloonatic 7
The Bank Clerk 121
Bartels, Louis John 168
Battling Butler 177
The Beagles 73
Beaver, Jim 193
Behind the Screen 136
The Bellboy (1960) 120
Bergman, Henry 108
Bernds, Edward 183–184
Big Parade of Comedy 179
Birth of a Nation 48
Blesh, Rudi 177–178, 179
The Boat 175, 178
Body and Soul 193
Bordeaux, Joe 17, 29
Bournstein, L.J. 83
Brewer, Terry 16
Brewster's Millions 160, 163

Bright Lights 37
Brooks, Louise 168
Brooks, Mel 77, 80
Brown, Joe E. 77, 171
Bruckman, Clyde 181–182
Burlesque on Carmen 133
Buster Keaton Rides Again 187
Buzzin' Around 170

The Cameraman 180, 183, 185
Campbell, Eric 108
Camping Out 122, 127–130, 133
Candid Camera 37
Capone, Al 166, 167
Capra, Frank 194
Carey, Harry 97
Caricature 95
Chaplin, Charles 1, 9, 13, 18, 26, 40, 43, 66, 86, 88, 94, 108, 113, 120, 128–129, 133, 147–148, 166, 169, 173, 180, 185–186, 198
Chase, Charley 9
Chayefsky, Paddy 111
Cineteca Nazionale 127
Circumstantial Evidence 194
Clown Princes and Court Jesters 188, 189, 196
Cohan, George M. 131
College 177
The Columbia Comedy Shorts 20, 181–184
Columbia Pictures 181–184
Columbia University 22, 69
The Complete Films of Buster Keaton 84
Coogan, Jackie 147

Coogan, John 137, 138, 144–147
Cops 7, 175, 178
Corliss, Richard 9
Corrado, Gino 182
Costello, Lou *see* Abbott and Costello
The Count of Monte Cristo 98
Crabbe, Buster 191
Crazy to Marry 161, 162
Crosby, Bing 98
Cruze, James 162, 169

Dana, Viola 193
Davenport, Alice 36
Davies, Marion 167
Days of Thrills and Laughter 186
Deadwood 193
The Death of WCW 42
Dellinger, Paul 193
Desmet Colour Duplication Process 128
The Dollar a Year Man 160
Don, Davy 53
D'Osualdo, Cristina 127
Doughboys 181
Dramatic Mirror 156
Dream of a Rarebit Fiend 103
The Drifter 192
Duck Soup 93, 130
Durante, Jimmy 181
Durfee, Minta 28
Durkin, Trent "Junior" 147

Earthworm Tractors 171
Educational Pictures 58, 167, 168, 181, 183, 189
Erickson, Hal 174
The Errand Boy 136
Essanay Company 99, 115

Fairbanks, Douglas 77, 124, 126, 131, 180
Famous Players-Lasky 18, 53
Fatty and Mabel Adrift 14, 37, 49, 114, 123, 173, 196
Fatty Arbuckle in a Liberty Loan Appeal 131
Fatty at San Diego 35–36
Fatty's Tintype Tangle 35
Fickle Fatty's Fall 16
Fields, W.C. 28, 77
Film Daily 170
Film Threat 37, 51
First National Pictures 129
Fox, William 136, 158, 189
Fox productions 53, 58, 136, 141, 158, 167, 190

Free and Easy 180
Freight Prepaid 161
Fruits of Passion 53
Fuzzy Settles Down 191

Gartenberg, John 118
Garza, Janiss 159
Gasoline Gus 161, 162
The General 7, 177–178, 181
Gierucki, Paul 2, 130–131
Gill, Samuel 188, 189, 196
Gish, Lillian 131
Go West 177
The Gold Rush 40, 43
Goldwyn, Samuel 193
Goodrich, William (Arbuckle pseudonym) 167, 190
Grand Slam Opera 181
Grant, Ulysses S. 88
Graves, George W. 31
Gray, Lorna 182, 183
The Great Train Robbery 76
The Greater Gain 193
Grey, Zane 82
Griffith, D.W. 6, 48, 95, 97, 175
Griffith, Raymond 9

Half Shot at Sunrise 168
Hall, Phil 37, 51
Hamilton, Lloyd 168
Hanneford, Poodles 167
Hardy, Oliver 10, 86; *see also* Laurel and Hardy; Plump and Runt series
Harlow, Jean 194
Harrison, Louis Reeves 110
Hart, William S. 3, 77, 82, 114, 124, 131
The Haunted House 7, 175
Havez, Jean 138
Hays, Will 67
He Did and He Didn't 15, 37, 83, 93, 95, 99, 103, 114, 123, 189, 196
Hearst, William Randolph 167–168
Hell's House 147
Hey Pop 170
Hicks, Tommie, Jr. 58, 188–189
Hiller, Arthur 111
His Brother's Ghost 191
Hollywood Boulevard 194
Hop to It 86
Hope, Bob 77, 98, 167
Horkheimer Brothers 83
How to Stuff a Wild Bikini 185
Howard, Jerome (Curly) 10–11

Howard, Moe 10
Howard, Shemp 170–171
Huckleberry Finn 147

I Dood It 184
Image Entertainment 54, 100, 118, 130, 195
In the Dough 170–171
Industrial Strength Keaton 186–187
Intolerance 96, 175
It's a Gift 28

Jamison, Bud 182

Keaton Close Up: The Silent Features 178
Kerr, Walter 5
Keystone 11–19, 114–116, 120, 131, 136, 142, 162, 188, 189
The Kid 147, 174
King of Comedy 120
Kino on Video 100, 195
Kline, Jim 84
Knight, Fuzzy 191
The Knockout 66, 115, 198
Kops and Custards: The Legend of the Keystone Films 16

Lahue, Karlton C. 16, 188, 189, 196
Lake, Alice 16, 40–45, 48, 70–122, 130
The Lamb 174
Lane Lupino 67
Langdon, Harry 199
LaRue, Lash 193
Lasky, Jesse 161
Laughsmith 130–131, 186, 195
Laurel, Stan 120; see also Laurel and Hardy
Laurel and Hardy 77, 169
Leap Year 161–162, 163
Lewis, Dave 188
Lewis, Jerry 77, 120, 136
Life of the Party 160
Limelight 148, 185
Lincoln, Abraham 88
Literary Digest 140
Lloyd, Harold 3, 9, 93, 173, 198, 199
Loew's Victoria 60
Love 119, 122, 130–131, 133, 134, 148, 189
Love Nest on Wheels 181
Lubin productions 53
Luke the dog 29, 124

Mace, Fred 13

Malone, Molly 121–122, 137–139, 153–154
Mann, Alice 46–69
Marx Brothers 93, 184
Mast, Gerald 165
McKay, Winsor 103
McKim, Edward 53
Méliès, Georges 103
Metro-Goldwyn-Mayer (MGM) 180–181, 183
Milestone Film and Video 118–119, 130
Milne, Peter 83, 99–100
The Misfit Wife 193
Miss Fatty's Seaside Lovers 198
Mr. Bernds Goes To Hollywood 184
Mix, Tom 77
Moews, Daniel 178
Monizza, Simona 127–128
Montogmery, Robert 180
Mooching Through Georgia 184
Morrison, Ernest, Jr. (Sunshine Sammy) 80, 125–126
Morrison, Ernest, Sr. 80, 126
Motion Picture 125, 126, 155
Motion Picture Classic 169
Motion Picture Magazine 100, 109, 169
Motion Picture News 124, 126, 156
Motion Picture World 27, 71, 124, 126, 156, 163
Motography 18, 25, 31
The Moving Picture World 110, 129, 131–132
Mulford, Clarence 82
Mullet, Mary B. 33, 139–140
The Music Box 93
Muskateers of Pig Alley 97
Mutual Corporation 94, 108, 129
Myers, Joan 54, 164

Nardoni Filmovy Archiv 54
National Film Board in Canada 187
The Navigator 7, 176
Nederlands Filmmuseum 118–119, 127–128, 130
The New Henrietta 174
The New York Daily Mail 31
The New York Morning Telegraph 110
New York Sun 33, 44, 53, 84, 139–140
New York Times 100, 110, 131, 192
Nitrate Won't Wait 72
Normand, Mabel 12, 14–15, 83, 131
Norsk Filminstutut 118–119

Oderman, Stuart 74
Okuda, Ted 20, 181–184
One Run Elmer 181
One Week 7, 141, 173–174
The Other Man 37
Our Hospitality 176

Page, Anita 180
Pajama Party 185
Paramount Pictures 18, 53, 113, 116, 136, 145, 156, 158, 159, 161, 199
Pardon My Berth Marks 184
Patricola, Tom 183
Pearson, David 32
Perjury 53
Pest from the West 182, 184
Photoplay 45, 97, 118, 160, 169
    Pickford, Mary 131, 180
Platinum Blonde 194
The Playhouse 7, 175
Plump and Runt series 86
Porter, Edwin S. 76
Price, Kate 1
The Property Man 136
The Pugilist see *The Knockout*
The Pullman Porter 122

The Railrodder 187
Rappe, Virginia 54, 163–165
A Reckless Romeo 34–37
The Red Mill 167–168
Reid, Laurence 155–156
Reid, Wallace 131
Reynolds, R.D. 42
Rigg, Diana 111
The Rink 108
RKO Pictures 168
Road series 98
Roberts, Richard 54
Rogers, Will 77
Rohauer, Raymond 3, 30
Rongen-Kaynakci, Elif 127
Roscoe "Fatty" Arbuckle: A Bio-Bibliography 54, 87, 131
Roscoe "Fatty" Arbuckle: A Biography of the Silent Film Comedian (1887-1993) 74
The Round Up 157, 159–160

Safety Last 93
St. John, Adele Rogers 164–165
St. John, Al 5–6, 14, 16–17, 21–22, 24–71, 76–144, 167, 188–193
Schenck, Joseph 18–19, 21, 32, 158

Schubert, J.J. 22
Scorsese, Martin 120
Scott, Fred 191
Selznick, David O. 193
Sennett, Mack 1, 11, 12–13, 18, 62, 114, 166, 188
Seven Chances 176
The Sheriff 77, 119, 122, 124–127, 131, 133
Sherlock, Jr. 132, 177, 178
She's Oil Mine 184
Shore Acres 193
A Short History of the Movies 165
Should a Woman Tell? 193
Sidewalks of New York 181
Sitka, Emil 183
Skelton, Red 184–185
Slide, Anthony 72
Smith Center, Kansas 71
A Southern Yankee 185
Speak Easily 182
Spectrum Studios 191
Stander, Lionel 170–171
The Star Boarder 37
Steamboat Bill, Jr. 177, 179
Steele, Bob 191
Sterling, Ford 11, 18
Stevens, Josephine 3
Swanson, Gloria 164, 165, 166

Tale of a Black Eye 35
Talmadge, Natalie 83
The Tamale Vendor 183
Taylor, Hazel Simpson 125
Thalberg, Irving 180
That's My Line 168
Thirty Years of Fun 186
Thomas, Bob 169
The Three Ages 175
Three Stooges 10, 77, 159, 181
Tom Sawyer 147
The Tramp 99
The Traveling Salesman 160
Triangle corporation 53, 114
A Trip to the Moon 103
Triple Trouble 115
Turpin, Ben 13
Tuxedo Comedies 56
Twilight Zone 185
Twin Beds 194

Ullman, Ellwood 159

The Vagabond 108

Variety 110, 156, 162
Vidor, King 168
Views and Film Index 72
Vitaphone 169, 171

W.H. Productions 3, 114–116
The Waiter's Ball 16–17, 37, 47, 117, 123, 189
Walker, Brent 35
Warner, Jack 136, 158, 169, 272
Warner Brothers 136, 141, 158, 169
Watch the Birdie 185
The Water Lily 53
Watz, Ed 20

What! No Beer? 181
Wheeler, Bert 168
When Comedy Was King 14
White, Jules 20, 181–182
Wilhelm, Kaiser 88
Williams, Robert 193
Wister, Bob 82
Woolsey, Robert 168

Young, Loretta 194
Young, Robert, Jr. 54, 87, 131

Zukor, Adolph 159